ROUGH JUSTICE
Essays on Crime in English Literature

Throughout the history of English literature, issues of crime and justice have preoccupied writers of literature. In this collection thirteen literary scholars explore the subject of crime in a wide range of literary works.

The volume begins with an essay by Northrop Frye on crime and sin in the bible and concludes with one by Josef Škvorecký on detective stories. In between are essays by other noted contributors on crime in Chaucer's *Canterbury Tales*, Middleton's *A Fair Quarrel*, Fielding's *Jonathan Wild*, Scott's *The Heart of Midlothian*, Dickens' *Our Mutual Friend*, Faulkner's *Sanctuary*, Dreiser's *An American Tragedy*, Wright's *Native Son*, Wiebe's *The Scorched-Wood People*, as well as various works by Oscar Wilde and a number of Canadian playwrights.

Edited by a distinguished legal scholar, the collection offers insights into the history of criminal law and the criminal process, as well as wider questions of the meaning and forms of justice.

MARTIN L. FRIEDLAND is Professor of Law and University Professor at the University of Toronto. Among his earlier books are *Detention before Trial*, *Double Jeopardy*, *Access to the Law*, *The Trials of Israel Lipski*, and *The Case of Valentine Shortis: A True Story of Crime and Politics in Canada*.

ROUGH JUSTICE

Essays on Crime in
Literature

Edited by
M.L. Friedland

M.L. Friedland

UNIVERSITY OF TORONTO PRESS
Toronto Buffalo London

© University of Toronto Press 1991
Toronto Buffalo London
Printed in Canada

ISBN 0-8020-5906-6 (cloth)
ISBN 0-8020-6849-9 (paper)

Printed on acid-free paper

Canadian Cataloguing in Publication Data

Main entry under title:

Rough justice: essays on crime in literature

Based on presentations given by professors of
English literature from the University of Toronto
in a law school seminar at the University.
Includes bibliographical references.
ISBN 0-8020-5906-6 (bound) ISBN 0-8020-6849-9 (pbk.)

1. Crime in literature. 2. Justice in literature.
3. English literature – History and criticism.
4. American literature – History and criticism.
5. Canadian literature – History and criticism.
I. Friedland, M.L. (Martin Lawrence), 1932-

PN56.C7R68 1991   820.9'355   C91-093694-3

This book has been published with the help of the Faculty of Law, University
of Toronto, through its Law Foundation block grant and its Legal Theory
and Public Policy Programme, funded by the Connaught Fund of the University of Toronto. Publication has also been assisted by the Canada Council
and the Ontario Arts Council under their block grant programs.

To the memory of Northrop Frye

Contents

Acknowledgments

This project has been supported by the Faculty of Law at the University of Toronto through its Law Foundation block grant, as well as through its Legal Theory and Public Policy Programme, funded by the Connaught Fund of the University of Toronto. Dean Robert Prichard, now the President of the University of Toronto, and Professor T.H. Adamowski, the Chair of the Department of English, have over the past few years encouraged and supported this collaborative effort. I was also fortunate to have had the assistance of two excellent summer research assistants at different periods. Richard Owens, now a practising lawyer in Toronto, helped in the earlier stages to collect material. Douglas Harris, now entering his third year in the Faculty of Law, assisted in the later stages with the shaping of the introductory essay and with the preparation of the papers for publication. Kathy Tzimika provided first-class secretarial assistance. I am grateful to all of the above persons, as well as to the students who actively took part in the seminars at which the papers were presented.

Martin L. Friedland
Faculty of Law
University of Toronto

M. L. FRIEDLAND

Introduction

This collection of essays grew out of presentations given by professors of English literature from the University of Toronto in a law school seminar at the University. The series, to quote the Law School calendar, was designed to provide 'insights into aspects of crime, the criminal process, and the history of the criminal law by analysing the way perceptive writers have dealt with matters relating to crime.' By examining the criminal justice system as it is portrayed in the individual works (all, with the exception of the Bible, written in English), each study also considers the wider question of the meaning and forms of justice.

In a passage in Dickens' *Our Mutual Friend*, one of the novels discussed in this collection, a character, referring to a young man skilled in reading aloud popular accounts of crime in the newspapers, exclaims: 'And I do love a newspaper. You mightn't think it, but Sloppy is a beautiful reader of a newspaper. He do the Police in different voices.'[1] There are many 'different voices' in this collection. Each author represents crime, the criminal, and society in different ways: Chaucer's various pilgrims in the *Canterbury Tales*; Henry Fielding's cool irony in *Jonathan Wild*; the frank brutality of William Faulkner's *Sanctuary*; the avalanche of detail in Theodore Dreiser's *An American Tragedy*; and the almost surreal spareness of George Ryga's *Indian*. The lecturers themselves also speak in different voices, from Josef Škvorecký's confiding autobiographical account of his career in Czechoslovakia as a writer of subversive detective fiction to Northrop Frye's magisterial discussion of crime and sin in the Bible.

The collection does not consciously direct attention to the current battle being fought in the amorphous field of 'law and literature.'[2]

While it is clear that these studies are of 'law in literature' and not 'law as literature,' their purpose is not to concretize the emotional and social realities of our criminal law today. Rather, they indicate how often the criminal legal system serves as a metaphor for and a measure of the values of the societies the works evoke.[3] The emphasis is on the historical aspects of crime as reflected in literature, on the insights literature can provide into societal perceptions and representations of crime at the time. More important, these studies seek to examine the authors' own attitudes towards society and crime.

The Bible

To Northrop Frye, the Bible, while not itself a work of 'literature,' is a product of 'the power of the creative human imagination' which embodies the fundamental distinction between crime and sin: the difference between man's obligations within the social, secular order and man's obligations to God. Frye argues that the two are not unrelated: 'any legal code that goes back to a divine revelation has the conception "sin" as its major premise from which the conception of "crime" is derived.'

Frye describes Christianity as an originally revolutionary movement which, like most revolutionary movements, repudiated established authority, in that its private code (sin) represented a rejection of the public code (crime). The Christian 'revolution' separated sin and crime much more widely than did Judaism and, Frye argues, 'the consequences of doing so are still with us.' Crime and sin are not coextensive in the legal system today and attempts to resurrect such a relationship – for example, by the House of Lords in 1961 in *D.P.P.* v. *Shaw*[4] – have been strongly criticized by most observers.[5] Successful revolutions, Frye remarks, also frequently produce written constitutions which themselves are regarded as 'inspired' documents, restoring the lost unity of the secular law and an invisible, religious, morale.[6] While Frye specifically refers to the American Constitution as an example, Canada's own Charter of Rights and Freedoms[7] has come, in a short time, to assume the same symbolic, quasi-scriptural role in our legal system.

Frye reminds us that illegal or even criminal societies exist in which an even more substantial wedge is driven between crime and sin. Using the example of modern-day South Africa, Frye asks: What happens when secular and spiritual obligations conflict? Is it a crime to obey the law in a 'criminal' society? Frye concludes his examination by suggesting that 'a fuller perspective of the crime that traditionally derives from sin' would give us 'a saner and less anxious vision of the origins of human evil and of the methods of encountering it.'

Chaucer's *Canterbury Tales*

As Frye notes in his paper, the theoretical distinction between crime and sin in the Middle Ages was strong, but the practical division was less rigorous. Patricia Eberle explores the broad medieval conception of 'crime' which reflected the 'interpenetration of religious and legal thought' in the Middle Ages. As she shows, secular criminal concepts took on 'religious connotations,' while the Church began to define itself in 'increasingly legalistic terms' and broadened the jurisdiction of the ecclesiastical courts.

This integration of secular and religious legal structures, Eberle points out, was realized in what Harold Berman describes as the 'Papal Revolution' of 1075.[8] Pope Gregory VII and his supporters sought to centralize authority and impose 'right order' on society by establishing a legal hierarchy stretching from God, through the church, to secular government and ultimately into the home and the relationship between men and women. This 'revolution' was opposed by secular authorities who resisted the erosion of their power and subordination to the lowest church official. While violent confrontations were eventually quelled by a series of compromises, Eberle accepts Berman's argument that the ideal expressed by the Papal Revolution formed the basis of the Western legal tradition. She describes this model: 'For Berman, one of the most important effects of the Papal Revolution was in the ideal it attempted to express: the ideal of reforming the world by means of law, law re-organized and rewritten where and when necessary but based on a consistent and coherent ideal of justice and bearing within itself the principles of its own further growth.'

Eberle characterizes Chaucer as a literary law reformer and critic whose reaction to this model is expressed in the *Canterbury Tales*, written towards the end of the fourteenth century. Using the *Man of Law's Tale*, the *Wife of Bath's Tale* and the *Clerk's Tale* as examples, she maintains that Chaucer 'did not accept these ideals uncritically or believe they could be easily realized in practice.' Indeed, the tales suggest that 'Chaucer was seriously doubtful about the value and practical application of any systematic view of justice.'

Chaucer's portrait of the Sergeant of the Law – the first portrayal of a lawyer in English literature – perhaps reflects his reserve about the legal system and its practitioners. While the Sergeant is remarkably learned, knowing 'of every judgment, case and crime, / Ever recorded since King William's time,' he shares the characteristic of many other lawyers in this collection: 'Though there was nowhere one so busy as he, / He was less busy than he seemed to be.'[9] Chaucer knew the legal system well. He had been a legal practitioner and was a judge – and had the added experience of being personally charged with rape.[10]

Eberle calls our attention to the fact that the structure of the *Canterbury Tales*, in which the tales subvert each other and force the reader to attempt to reconcile their conflicting authority, mirrors a classic textbook of canon law and, appropriately, its humble descendant, the law student's casebook. The resulting plurality of views and profusion of crimes – murder (in many cases of blood relations), incest, bigamy, rape, treason, theft, assault, alchemy – suggest that 'if someone were looking for a text that reflected the thinking of ordinary medieval English citizens on crime and justice, it would be difficult to find a work better suited to this purpose than the *Canterbury Tales*.'

Middleton and Rowley's *A Fair Quarrel*

If the *Canterbury Tales* reveals Chaucer's response *to* the law, Brian Parker demonstrates that Middleton and Rowley's *A Fair Quarrel* was the literary response *of* the law to the growing problem of duelling in the early seventeenth century, a crisis caused by volatility in the class structure, the deadly introduction of the rapier, and an influx of continental fencing masters with elaborate, hair-splitting 'codes of honour.'

The play highlights the confusions that exist when there is 'a distinct gap between the legal code and what popular opinion or prejudice believe,' and Parker argues that the play is an unusual, perhaps unique literary work in that it was 'directly connected to major legislation at the very highest level' and may, indeed, have been secretly sponsored by the government. It bolstered anti-duelling legislation by King James I and his attorney-general, Francis Bacon, which provides one more example in the history of the criminal law of the state's continuing desire to centralize the administration of justice and monopolize violence, in this case by eliminating the practice of duelling to settle private disputes.[11]

This is literature as law reform in its purest incarnation. Yet Parker demonstrates that the play is not one-sided enough to be mere prop-aganda, but exploits distinctions between 'sin' and 'codes of honour' with an irony that ensures that 'instead of having a single, disapproving attitude drummed didactically home to them, the play's contemporary audience was cleverly drawn into the actuality of the dilemma by hav-ing to weigh a double response to the play.' The main plot shows duelling as less than honourable, and so undermines its very foun-dation. Similarly, the bawdy scenes provide an uncomplimentary dou-bling of the main action, rendering the hypocrisy and vocabulary of duelling ridiculous.

None the less, in a manner characteristic of the mixed genre of seventeenth-century tragicomedy, the audience maintains some sym-pathy with the characters in the central plot and their problem of having to decide between contradictory ideals of behaviour.

With its use of irony and mockery to subvert the bases of duelling, the role of *A Fair Quarrel* in challenging popular opinion is of more than historic interest. Given our efforts to change public attitudes in fields such as drunk driving, spousal assault, and rape,[12] Middleton and Rowley may have something to offer present-day policy makers.

Fielding's *Jonathan Wild*

John Baird characterizes Henry Fielding's *Jonathan Wild*, published in 1743, as a work 'directed at the corrupt legal system that a corrupt society deserves and gets.' Highlighting a gulf between the criminal law and the mores of Wild's society, Baird argues that Fielding used Wild as 'the supreme symbol of a society that has cut adrift from its moral moorings, a society which cannot tell the difference between right and wrong.' Such a society, 'like Wild, must sooner or later face the ultimately self-destructive consequences of its folly.'

Jonathan Wild's practice was itself a cruel parody of the state's crim-inal-law power, for he returned property stolen by his band of thieves to its rightful owners for a fee. Just as the character of Wild's enterprise parodies the criminal-law power of the state, so Newgate prison, 'the holy place, as it were, of criminal culture for more than a century,' in which the debtors form partisan attachments to the opposed bands of thieves who plunder them, represents democratic society. While *Jonathan Wild* is frequently read as a satirical attack on Sir Robert Walpole, Baird argues that it was written against *all* corrupt politicians and the societies which countenance them.

The correlation between the Wild of the book and the historical Wild raises the important question of the relationship between the fiction of a literary work and the reality of the author's subject.[13] Extending his analysis to Dickens' *Our Mutual Friend* and Scott's *The Heart of Midlothian*, Baird argues that 'fiction may extend history, supplement it, even humanize it, but it cannot change it.' This point is considered in many of the other studies, from the 'art' of Oscar Wilde's life, to the fictional adaptation of actual cases in *Native Son* and *An American Tragedy*, and to actual people like Louis Riel and Lizzie Borden. Does this grounding in reality give the fiction greater authority, or does it heighten our awareness of the author's own subjectivity and role in constructing history?[14] In *Jonathan Wild*, Baird asserts, 'Fielding deliberately violates not only history, but his reader's memories.'

None the less, a study of Wild's career gives insight into the problems the law has always faced in controlling the theft and receiving of stolen property,[15] and also the dangers inherent (now as then) in giving large rewards, either in money or immunity, to encourage prosecution.[16] As in *A Fair Quarrel*, one solution proposed is that the law should spread its net more widely (extending criminal sanctions to the seconds in a duel, making it an offence to receive stolen property, and seizing the proceeds of crime) in order to control all participants in criminal behaviour.

Scott's *The Heart of Midlothian*

While Jane Millgate asserts that 'legal right endings coincide with narrative right endings' in Walter Scott's fiction, the consequences of the division between crime and sin play a major role in *The Heart of Midlothian*. Madame Justice Bertha Wilson of the Supreme Court of Canada, in a recent lecture on Scottish literature, noted that *The Heart of Midlothian*, published in 1818, allowed Scott 'to treat the deep dilemma of justice and mercy; and the apparent conflict between the law of God and the law of man.'[17] At a crucial moment in her sister's trial, Jeanie Deans refuses to lie, even to save Effie from a wrongful conviction and hanging, saying 'I may not do evil, even that good may come out of it.'[18]

In that Jeanie is put in this situation by an unjust child-murder law, *The Heart of Midlothian* represents another literary law-reform text – although only in a retrospective sense, since the law in question had been repealed by Scott's day. Scott was deeply involved in the Scottish legal system in his position as one of the principal clerks to the Court of Sessions (the supreme civil court in Scotland). He was also keenly interested in the differences between English law and Scottish law at the time, and held firm views on the specific form which changes to the Scottish law should take: 'it is not enough that they [law reforms] have been found practically good in the country from which they are proposed to be transplanted [England] ... It is only in its natural soil, where it has long been planted, that the tree can be expected to flourish.'[19] Millgate supports Scott's view that effective law reform can only begin with an understanding of the law as 'the product of cultural and social circumstance,' an understanding which literature can, of course, articulate and highlight.

Even though Scott's depiction of actual criminal procedures is generally positive in the novel, he none the less challenges the moral supremacy of the criminal justice system with his depiction of Jeanie's successful efforts to transcend it on her sister's behalf. Millgate observes: 'the problem with the law seems to be that it is curiously beside the point ... While the law is presented as going perfectly through its motions, other processes and other systems of value simultaneously deny the validity of those motions ...' This is a strongly recurring theme throughout this collection: the institutional authority represented by the criminal law, as portrayed by the author, is unresponsive to the central issues raised by the work as a whole. In its place a kind of 'rough' justice often operates, so that 'right' resolutions are seen as being achieved outside of the legal system, and often in spite of that system. The Porteous riot and Jeanie's extra-legal machinations represent a rejection of the endings that the criminal law has prescribed in favour of endings that, while morally acceptable, undoubtedly subvert the authority of the criminal justice system.

Dickens' *Our Mutual Friend*

If we consider literature as an instrument of societal reform, John Robson convincingly shows that 'Dickens is probably the most obvious choice' for considering the role of the author as critic of the legal system. Charles Dickens' life, as Philip Collins observes, 'spanned a period of remarkable developments in the criminal law and its administration, in the scale and spirit of punishment, in police organisation and techniques, in the study of the causes of crime, and in attempts to remove or reduce these causes.'[20]

Even if James Fitzjames Stephen was correct in saying that Dickens' 'notions of the law ... are precisely those of an attorney's clerk'[21] – or, as he in fact was at one time, a court reporter – Dickens was none the less capable of giving us fascinating glimpses into criminal law and procedure and, perhaps more important, the criminal mind. The Inspector's observation 'that it was always more likely that a man had done a bad thing than that he hadn't'[22] is probably as representative of police attitudes today as it was then. And Dickens gives us a perceptive insight into the mind of a murderer when he states: 'If great criminals told the truth – which, being great criminals, they do not – they would very rarely tell of their struggles against the crime. Their struggles are towards it.'[23]

Despite Dickens' interest and activity in the area of social change, Robson notes, 'effective and prompt criminal and legal reform is for Dickens, as for most of us, equally urgent and impossible.' In *Our Mutual Friend*, the institutional criminal justice system is incapable of controlling the myriad criminal activities in the novel, so that many criminals escape its grasp. It is true, as Robson argues, 'looking only at the major crimes, at least rough justice is done' to Rogue Riderhood, Bradley Headstone, and George Radfoot, but, as in *Jonathan Wild*, society itself figures largely as a criminal element untouched even by rough justice, remaining 'unpunished and apparently unpunishable.' This is, of course, one of the recurrent themes of Dickens' later novels, and some of the more recent works discussed in this collection, like *Native Son, An American Tragedy, Blood Relations,* and *Indian*, take the charge to more radical extremes.

Chaucer's Sergeant of the Law is recalled, in both *The Heart of Midlothian* and *Our Mutual Friend*, by the characters of young, underemployed lawyers. Scott commented on the 'contents of a young advocate's pocket, which contains every thing but briefs and bank notes.'[24] In a similar vein, the young barrister in *Our Mutual Friend* confesses: 'I have been "called" seven years, and have had no business at all, and never shall have any. And if I had, I shouldn't know how to do it.'[25]

Oscar Wilde

Edward Chamberlin's study of Oscar Wilde portrays an author whose life itself was a kind of aesthetic creation. Indeed, Chamberlin remarks, the fact that his life and his art were difficult to separate 'always delighted Wilde – at least until his conviction.' In keeping with this close relationship, 'the public with whom Wilde's plays were such a success was also, with some exceptions, the public which relished his trial and disgrace,' even as we today are fascinated by Wilde's criminal history.

In his writings, as in his life, Wilde was concerned with style. Wilde often trivialized serious crime (in his *Phrases and Philosophies* he wrote: 'no crime is vulgar, but all vulgarity is crime'),[26] but he viewed certain other types of crime as political acts of the protesting imagination. While Chamberlin reminds us that Wilde was imprisoned not so much as a martyr to the 'Love that dare not speak its name'[27] as he was for his predilection for 'telegraph boys and grooms,' Wilde's view of crime motivated by oppression is true to the spirit of several of the later works in this collection: 'No: a poor man who is ungrateful, unthrifty, discontented and rebellious is probably a real personality, and has much in him. He is at any rate a healthy protest. As for the virtuous poor, one can pity them, of course, but one cannot possibly admire them. They have made private terms with the enemy, and sold their birthright for very bad pottage.'[28] Dreiser, Wiebe, Pollock, Ryga, and especially Wright all find 'real personality' in characters whose crimes are both a protest against and a product of an oppressive society.

After Wilde was imprisoned, however, he expressed a different view of crime. In a petition to the Home Secretary he stated that offences such as those for which he was convicted were 'diseases to be cured by a physician, rather than crimes to be punished by a judge.'[29] Whether or not Wilde believed this is another matter. The year of his sentence (1895) was in fact a turning point in penal philosophy. The Gladstone Commission was to recommend that England change from a deterrent-based penal system to rehabilitation.[30] As Wilde's biographer, Richard Ellmann has observed: 'Wilde's misfortune was to serve his sentence just before prison conditions were officially changed by the 1898 Prison Act.'[31] After a number of petitions, Wilde was eventually permitted to have a larger supply of books than prison rules allowed and he requested the prison governor to order the novels of Charles Dickens for the library: 'I feel sure that a complete set of [Dickens'] works would be as great a boon to many amongst the other prisoners as it certainly would be to myself.'[32] The governor approved a number of other books, but rejected works by Dickens. Perhaps he thought, as Robson has shown, that Dickens dealt too much with crime and criminals.

Faulkner's *Sanctuary*

Michael Millgate's study of William Faulkner's *Sanctuary*, written in 1931, explores a violent and compelling work. Faulkner described *Sanctuary*, in deliberately simplistic terms, as 'the most horrific tale I could imagine,'[33] but Millgate demonstrates that violence was 'a fundamental element in his overall conception of the world he wanted to portray.' The novel exposes the hypocrisy in lawyers and detectives who frequent a Memphis brothel, corruptly manipulate the legal process, and consort easily with the criminal element: as Millgate writes, 'the entire system of justice, of law and order, is inextricably implicated in the social and moral corruption that comprehensively riddles the novel's entire presented world.' Nor is such an analysis confined to this one novel. Millgate again points out that in Faulkner's work 'the arguments of lawyers and the decisions of judges rarely address the needs, the desires, or even the basic social and economic situations of those seeking justice at their hands.'

In *Sanctuary*, as in *Native Son* and *An American Tragedy*, the crimes for which characters are convicted are not necessarily those for which they are legally or morally guilty. The 'justice' in Popeye's execution for a murder he could not have committed, because he was murdering someone else at the time, borders (as does so much in Faulkner) on the grotesquely farcical. Lee Goodwin's situation is more problematic. Though he is wrongly convicted of murder and lynched for it (recalling the Porteous riot in *The Heart of Midlothian*), he would seem to have had the intention to rape Temple Drake, so that the reader is free to think that some kind of moral 'rough justice' was in fact done, despite the various travesties of legal procedure involved.

Dreiser's *An American Tragedy*

Barrie Hayne's study of *An American Tragedy* and Caesar Blake's analysis of *Native Son* explore the use of the naturalistic novel – a genre Frank Norris described as a 'drama of the people, working itself out in blood and ordure'[34] – to represent the experiences of the American poor and American blacks. Such experiences lead within the novels to an involvement in crime seen as inevitable because of the strongly deterministic world naturalism presents. In a deterministic philosophy, all people are the products of their environment, including heredity, and their actions can be traced to influences from within that environment. The free will/determinism debate was a prominent feature of penological discussion in the early twentieth century,[35] and Dreiser and Wright examine the difficult issue of criminal culpability and moral responsibility from within their deterministic visions of human activity. If the determinists are right, as Dreiser and Wright assert, the criminal is the true victim.

Theodore Dreiser's *An American Tragedy*[36] is, Hayne reminds us, the 'copy-book' example of the American naturalistic novel. In the naturalistic tradition, Clyde Griffiths has no defence in *An American Tragedy* because, in the deterministic world of the novel, society gives him none. In the end there is more rough justice (since Clyde did have the intent to murder Roberta, even if her death did not come about in the way he planned), so that, as Hayne points out, 'what is restored at the end of *An American Tragedy* looks much more like the continuation of chaos' than the triumph of law and justice.

As in *Native Son*, the murder scene is legally problematic.[37] Indeed, Dreiser's construction of the scene of Roberta's death forces a significant legal dilemma. The accused intends to drown a girl he has made pregnant. Before he can act on this intent (because of a 'sudden palsy of the will')[38] she accidentally falls out of the boat. Knowing she cannot swim, he does not rescue her. This scenario (which could form the basis of a law school examination question) raises the central issue of the relationship between legal and moral guilt – the difference between crime and sin.[39] But also compelling and relevant today is another tragic aspect of the story: the difficulty of getting an abortion at the time and its consequences for the lives of Clyde and Roberta.

Several of the works studied here shift dramatic attention away from its conventional place in the detective or murder mystery – the identification and apprehension of the criminal – to the events following a conviction. In *An American Tragedy* (as well as *The Heart of Midlothian*, *Native Son*, and *The Scorched-Wood People*) the story does not end with the verdict, but continues through the quest for a commutation – often a more dramatic process than the investigation and trial themselves.

Wright's *Native Son*

Native Son generated controversy not only among the reading public, but also within the ranks of literary critics responding to the book's naturalistic vision of American society and of the position of blacks within it. Caesar Blake argues that Wright 'regarded the determinants of human destiny or fate as heredity and environment against which a powerless individual human will could only struggle in futility.' As Dreiser did for Clyde Griffiths, Wright draws the picture of the life and background of Bigger Thomas – a poor black in Chicago in the 1930s – in order to establish the predetermining context of his actions. Indeed, Wright succeeds to such an extent that, despite the fact that he wanted to write a story which 'no one would weep over,'[40] the reader wants Bigger to escape the grasp of the law.

The defence that Bigger's lawyer Max presents is that which Wright himself asserts, portraying Bigger as a 'victim of murderous dehumanization and exploitation.' Indeed, Bigger's crimes come to define who he is in the society which created him. 'In all of his life,' Bigger Thomas believes, 'these two murders were the most meaningful things that had ever happened to him.'[41] The criminal justice system cannot do justice to Bigger because it is merely a part of the society which, having created Bigger, must destroy him. The best it can do, again, is rough justice: Bigger pleads guilty to a crime for which he was not legally guilty (having had no intent to kill or even harm Mary Dalton). Yet he was clearly guilty of another murder for which he was not charged, but which was used against him, in a shocking display, at his trial.

Native Son, like *An American Tragedy* and *Sanctuary*, shows politically ambitious district attorneys, inept lawyers, an aggressive press, and hostile public opinion as features of the American criminal justice system of the time. In none of the cases is there a change of venue or effective control of the press. In all cases there are either threatened or actual lynchings. And there is the ubiquitous handgun – the great 'equalizer' – in *Native Son* and *Sanctuary*.[42] In *Native Son*, Bigger thinks: 'He was going among white people, so he would take his knife and his gun; it would make him feel that he was the equal of them.'[43] Similarly, Popeye's ever-present pistol in *Sanctuary* compensates for his impotence. *Sanctuary*, *Native Son*, and *An American Tragedy* present together a damning depiction of American society and justice in the early decades of the twentieth century.

Wiebe's *The Scorched-Wood People*

Dennis Duffy brings home to Canadians the issue of the criminal within an uncomprehending society with his study of Rudy Wiebe's *The Scorched-Wood People*, based on the career of the Canadian nineteenth-century revolutionary, Louis Riel. Duffy argues that Wiebe's 1977 novel 'enables us better to understand crime than to establish blame for it' because of what he calls Wiebe's 'metafiction': a fictional work which is, in an important way, about fiction itself. Duffy's examination of *The Scorched-Wood People* develops his idea that 'recognizing the complexity of Wiebe's portrayal takes a first step toward grasping the importance of his treatment of Riel's crime.'

Just as conventional literary treatments have failed to capture Riel's essence, Duffy argues, so did Riel confound white criminal justice (including his own defence lawyers, who urged him to plead insanity to avoid the gallows), so that *The Scorched-Wood People*'s implicit message becomes 'the incompatibility of differing cultural discourses.' Whereas Wiebe constructs a portrait of Riel from the inside, incorporating his visions into the novel, other literary treatments and the criminal trial itself do not delve into the mind of the accused (even when he gives evidence) and rarely look into his past or his motives. Wiebe's emphasis on the visionary existence of Louis Riel contrasts sharply with the legal system's focus on the criminal event alone.

Duffy's discussion of 'metafiction' and Wiebe's fictional portrait of Riel can be usefully compared to John Baird's study of Fielding's use of history in *Jonathan Wild*. Both studies consider the uneasy and shifting distance between historical 'fact' and literary 'fiction' in works of this kind. To this end, Duffy acknowledges that subjectivity is, indeed, inevitable, and that 'the fact remains that we are looking at imaginative constructs, and so whatever actuality Wiebe's figure possesses may not be inherently greater than any accruing to other versions of Riel.'

Ryga's *Indian* and Pollock's *Blood Relations*

Ann Saddlemyer highlights the theatre's affinity to a criminal trial: 'Action ... Suspense ... Immediacy ... Persuasion ... Conflict ... Revelation ... Climax ... Resolution. These are the qualities of theatre, of story-telling, and, coincidentally, of the lawcourts.' As in criminal trials, theatre audiences are frequently forced to try to recreate the past, never sure what is truth and what is fiction. Reality, as we saw above, is always an uncertain reconstruction of the past.

Unlike, however, a criminal jury sitting in judgment to determine responsibility, the audiences of George Ryga's *Indian* and Sharon Pollock's *Blood Relations* are challenged 'to accept some responsibility in turn for the deeds enacted before them.' Society (through its surro-

gate, the audience) is put on trial for the crimes it has engendered.
But Saddlemyer cautions us that these plays do not allow any easy
responses, that they force 'the audience members to respond as individuals, unable to duck out of responsibility, while at the same time
refusing to let them wallow in that equally evasive response, the breast-
beating *mea culpa* of the educated white liberal prepared to condemn
faceless and nameless society and go home satisfied with a good job
well done.' These plays also challenge us to go back to Dickens, Wright,
Dreiser, Wiebe, and others to consider whether our responses have
in fact been evasive in pinning the blame on 'faceless and nameless
society' rather than questioning what undesirable aspects of society we
ourselves share in perpetuating.

There is no question but that white, patriarchal society is indicted
in the respective plays for its treatment of native people and women.
Ryga asks, 'can law and white man's justice apply to those for whom
it apparently does not exist?' while Pollock examines 'women imprisoned in a man-ordered universe.' Both Lizzie Borden and Ryga's Indian, according to Saddlemyer, 'feel they have nothing to lose, had
no rights to begin with, and attempt to gain them through their crimes.'
But the criminal law is incapable of adjusting its vision to respond
sensitively and constructively to such situations. The best that can be
done is, again, rough justice: Saddlemyer observes that social hypocrisy
led Lizzie to kill while moral hypocrisy acquitted her.[44]

The title of Pollock's play highlights a theme which many of the
works in this collection share: the murder of blood relations. Ryga's
Indian murders his brother, Lizzie Borden is acquitted of murdering
her stepmother and father, Effie is accused of murdering her child in
The Heart of Midlothian, and Walter leads Griselde to believe he has
murdered their children in the *Clerk's Tale*. This theme is, however,
more popular in literature than it is in criminal statistics.[45]

Detective Stories

Finally, Josef Škvorecký presents an autobiographical portrait of his
career as a writer of criminal fiction in a time and place where his
works were banned. We reach the point, then, where literature itself
becomes a fugitive criminal, the victim of what for Škvorecký was a
'criminal' society along the lines suggested by Frye. Such regimes suppress detective fiction; according to Škvorecký, they '*make* corpses, but
they don't *write* about them. If a writer does write about them, they

must be *heroic* corpses, not the bodies of wealthy old gentlemen found stabbed to death in libraries who deserved what they got anyway.' Just as Wilde's life and art were analogous, so did both Škvorecký's fiction and his political situation represent subversion.

Škvorecký gives us insights into the construction of the detective story, the most important rule being to work backwards: 'the final effect must be sought, established, and constructed before the fact.' This final effect is usually the restoration of order by the detective – whom P.D. James has described as 'an avenging deity'[46] – after the discovery of the criminal's identity. Moreover, the detective story, as Dorothy Sayers has observed, 'does not show us the inner workings of the murderer's mind – it must not; for the identity of the murderer is hidden until the end of the book.'[47] This is a focus opposite to that of some of the works studied, which give us an internal portrait of the pursued (Riel, Bigger Thomas, Clyde Griffiths) and the effect of his crime on his mental state before and after the criminal act.

Rough justice is, as we have seen, a strongly recurring theme in this collection. The criminal justice system, as portrayed by the various authors, is shown to be either corrupt and cynical, or at the very least insensitive and unresponsive to the real issues in the work. The agents of criminal justice – police, prosecutors, defence lawyers, judges – are repeatedly portrayed as ignorantly or wilfully blind to the truth, causing the reader to question the justice of their disposition.

But pulling repeatedly in the opposite direction is the reader's feeling that justice has in some sense been done in spite of the criminal justice system, even if by a wrongful conviction. Characters whose behaviour falls short of criminal culpability may none the less appear to the reader as deserving of some kind of punishment. Many of the works thus provide sufficient 'poetic' justice to satisfy society's desire for retribution, and the tension between these two visions of justice, the one legalistic and the other approximative, is what gives the works force and validity as examinations of the criminal justice system and its role in society.

Notes

M.L. Friedland was called to the Ontario Bar in 1960 and received his PHD from Cambridge University in 1967. His publications include *The Trials of*

Israel Lipski, which won the Crime Writers of Canada Award for non-fiction, and *The Case of Valentine Shortis*. He is currently working on a manuscript about a true crime that took place in turn-of-the-century New York City.

1 Charles Dickens *Our Mutual Friend* (Harmondsworth: Penguin 1971) 246. T.S. Eliot's first choice for the title of *The Waste Land*, John Robson points out in his essay, had been 'He do the Police in different voices.'
2 The present centre of this campaign is Richard Posner's *Law and Literature: A Misunderstood Relation* (Cambridge: Harvard University Press 1988) and reaction to it. As a small sample, see Robin West 'Law, Literature, and the Celebration of Authority' *Northwestern Law Review* 83 (1989) 977; Richard Weisberg 'Entering With a Vengeance: Posner on Law and Literature' *Stanford Law Review* 41 (1989) 1597; Joseph L. Brand 'How Can We Know the Dancer from the Dance?' *George Washington Law Review* 57 (1989) 1018; Judith S. Koffler 'Forged Alliance: Law and Literature' *Columbia Law Review* 89 (1989) 1374; Peter R. Teachout 'Lapse of Judgement' *California Law Review* 77 (1989) 1259; Robert Weisberg 'The Law-Literature Enterprise' *Yale Journal of Law and The Humanities* 1 (1988) 1; Stanley Fish 'Don't Know Much About the Middle Ages: Posner on Law and Literature' *Yale Law Journal* 97 (1988) 777, a response to Posner's 'Law and Literature: A Relation Reargued' *Virginia Law Review* 72 (1986) 1351. See generally, the *Cardozo Studies in Law and Literature* that started publication in 1988.
3 See Weisberg 'The Law-Literature Enterprise' 2.
4 [1962] AC 220
5 The leading critic was the Oxford philosopher-lawyer, H.L.A. Hart. The so-called Hart/Devlin debate, paralleling the Mill/Stephen debate in the nineteenth century, is too extensive to cite here. Lord Devlin's ideas are developed in his book *The Enforcement of Morals* (London: Oxford University Press 1965) and Hart's criticism can be found in his *Law, Liberty and Morality* (Stanford: Stanford University Press 1963) and *The Morality of the Criminal Law* (London: Oxford University Press 1965).
6 Max Lerner remarked that the Constitution and courts serve as secular versions of religious institutions: 'the very habits of mind begotten by an authoritarian Bible and a religion of submission to a higher power have been carried over to an authoritarian Constitution and a philosophy of submission to a "higher law;" and a country like America, in which its early tradition had prohibited a state church, ends by getting a state church after all, although in a secular form' ('Consti-

tution and Court as Symbols' *Yale Law Journal* 46 (1937) 1294–5). It would be interesting to study the extent to which the 'habits of mind' and 'religion' of Canadians are reflected in the Charter of Rights and Freedoms.

Sanford Levinson and Thomas Grey have developed this idea of the Constitution as secular scripture, comparing interpretivist theories to Catholic beliefs about divine revelation (that revelation consists of both the Bible and supplementary sources, like tradition) and non-interpretivist views to Protestant beliefs about revelation (that the Bible is the sole source of divine revelation); see Sanford Levinson '"The Constitution" in American Civil Religion' *Supreme Court Review* [1979] 123; Thomas C. Grey 'The Constitution as Scripture' *Stanford Law Review* 37 (1984) 1.

7 Constitution Act 1982 pt I

8 Harold J. Berman *Law and Revolution: The Formation of the Western Legal Tradition* (Cambridge: Harvard University Press 1983)

9 Geoffrey Chaucer *Canterbury Tales* trans Nevill Coghill (Harmondsworth: Penguin 1951) 28

10 See P.R. Watts 'The Strange Case of Geoffrey Chaucer and Cecilia Chaumpaigne' *Law Quarterly Review* 63 (1947) 491, and T.F.T. Plucknett. 'Chaucer's Escapade' *Law Quarterly Review* 64 (1948) 33.

11 But see Warren F. Schwartz, Keith Baxter, and David Ryan 'The Duel: Can These Gentlemen Be Acting Efficiently?' *Journal of Legal Studies* 13 (1984) 321.

12 See the comparison between controlling duelling and controlling rape in Susan Estrich 'Rape' *Yale Law Journal* 95 (1986) 1181.

13 The historical Wild, Baird notes, had the dubious distinction of being the only felon personally named in Blackstone's *Commentaries*. William Blackstone *Commentaries on the Laws of England* IV (Oxford: Clarendon Press 1769; photorepr 1966) 132, cited in Baird. For a discussion of the historical Wild, see Gerald Howson *Thief-Taker General: The Rise and Fall of Jonathan Wild* (London: Hutchinson 1970).

14 Three recent works in this field are David Cowart *History and the Contemporary Novel* (Carbondale: Southern Illinois University Press 1989), Barbara Foley *Telling The Truth: The Theory and Practice of Documentary Fiction* (Ithaca: Cornell University Press 1986), and Harry E. Shaw *The Forms of Historical Fiction: Sir Walter Scott and His Successors* (Ithaca: Cornell University Press 1983).

15 See the analysis by Jerome Hall in *Theft, Law and Society* 2nd ed (Indianapolis: Bobbs-Merrill 1935) 70ff.

16   In *Our Mutual Friend*, Mortimer Lightwood explains to Boffin that the offer of a large reward 'is a temptation to forced suspicion, forced construction of circumstances, strained accusation, a whole tool-box of edged tools' (Dickens *Our Mutual Friend* 137).

17   Bertha Wilson 'The Scottish Enlightenment' *Saskatchewan Law Review* 51 (1986–7) 262

18   Walter Scott *The Heart of Midlothian* (Oxford: World's Classics 1982) 156

19   *Edinburgh Annual Register, 1808* 345–53, cited in J. Millgate

20   Philip Collins *Dickens and Crime* 2nd ed (London: Macmillan 1965) 10. There is, unfortunately, nothing in *Our Mutual Friend* on prison conditions, which are discussed in several other books, including notes on a visit by Dickens to the new Kingston Penitentiary in 1842: see D. Curtis et al *Kingston Penitentiary: The First Hundred and Fifty Years, 1835–1985* (Ottawa: Supply and Services 1985) 38.

21   James Fitzjames Stephen 'The Licence of Modern Novelists' *Edinburgh Review* 56 (1857) 128, cited in Robson

22   Dickens *Our Mutual Friend* 206

23   Dickens *Our Mutual Friend* 609

24   Scott *The Heart of Midlothian* 24

25   Dickens *Our Mutual Friend* 61–2

26   'Phrases and Philosophies for the Use of the Young' in *Complete Works of Oscar Wilde* gen ed J.B. Foreman (London: Collins 1966) 1205

27   The title of a poem by Alfred Douglas published in the *Chameleon*, which figured in Wilde's 1895 trial for alleged homosexual offences with minors. See Richard Ellmann *Oscar Wilde* (London: Hamish Hamilton 1987) 435.

28   'The Soul of Man Under Socialism' in *Complete Works of Oscar Wilde* 1081

29   'To the Home Secretary, 2 July 1896' in *The Letters of Oscar Wilde* ed Rupert Hart-Davis (London: Rupert Hart-Davis 1962) 402

30   See *Report from the Departmental Committee on Prisons* 1895 C 7702, 8.

31   Ellmann *Oscar Wilde* 475

32   'To the Home Secretary, 2 July 1896' in *The Letters of Oscar Wilde* 405n

33   *Sanctuary* (New York: Modern Library 1932) vi

34   Frank Norris 'Zola as a Romantic Writer' in *Novels and Essays* (New York: Library of America 1986) 1108

35   See Report of the Canadian Sentencing Commission *Sentencing Reform: A Canadian Approach* (Ottawa, 1987) 36.

36 Dreiser's *An American Tragedy* (1925) and Wright's *Native Son* (1940),
   though separated in time by Faulkner's *Sanctuary* (1931), are dealt with
   together because of the naturalistic attributes they clearly share.

37 See generally, C.R.B. Dunlop 'Law and Justice in Dreiser's *An American
   Tragedy' University of British Columbia Law Review* 6 (1971) 379.

38 Theodore Dreiser *An American Tragedy* (New York: New American
   Library 1925) 492

39 The facts would probably not have brought about a conviction for
   homicide at the time, but would probably do so today. They would
   certainly do so if the Law Reform Commission of Canada's
   controversial section of its proposed new Criminal Code, imposing
   a duty to rescue, is enacted. Section 10(2) of the proposed Code
   provides:
   (a) General Rule. Everyone commits a crime who, perceiving another
       person in immediate danger of death or serious harm, does not
       take reasonable steps to assist him.
   (b) Exception. Clause 10(2)(a) does not apply where the person cannot
       take reasonable steps to assist without risk of death or serious harm
       to himself or another person or where he has some other valid
       reason for not doing so.
   See *Report 31: Recodifying Criminal Law* (Ottawa: Law Reform
   Commission of Canada 1987).

40 Richard Wright, 'How "Bigger" Was Born,' introduction to *Native Son*
   (New York: Harper & Row 1940) xxvii

41 Ibid 225

42 Dickens referred to the prevalence of guns ('murderous little
   persuaders') in his American-based novel *Martin Chuzzlewit*, following
   his visit to America in 1842. *Martin Chuzzlewit* (Oxford: World's Classics
   1984) 460

43 Wright *Native Son* 44

44 Saddlemyer, citing Ann Jones *Women Who Kill* (New York: Holt,
   Rinehart and Winston 1980) 209–37

45 See Martin Daly and Margo Wilson *Homicide* (New York: Aldine de
   Gruyter 1988).

46 Douglas Marshall 'Reigning Queen of Gore is Certainly no Bore' *The
   Toronto Star* 4 October 1986, G1. See also W.H. Auden 'The Guilty
   Vicarage' in *The Dyer's Hand and Other Essays* (New York: Random
   House 1948) 146.

47 Michiko Kakutani 'Mysteries Join the Mainstream' *New York Times Book
   Review* 15 January 1984, 1

Rough Justice:
Essays on Crime in
Literature

NORTHROP FRYE

Crime and Sin in the Bible

The legally trained reader knows much better than I do how difficult it is to define a crime, a misdemeanour, or any form of anti-social behaviour, apart from a violation of a specific law already in existence. Some legislation may be empirical or pragmatic in its basis, like traffic regulations, but there seems to be a powerful deductive force in law that impels us to look for principles and premises from which we derive our laws. A country with a written constitution, like the United States, has at least that means of providing principles, though the amount of amending and reinterpreting needed to keep it functioning so often reminds us of the well-known old knife with its new blade and new handle.

A written constitution is often the consequence of a successful revolution, and a country with a revolutionary tradition normally acquires a strongly deductive attitude to the social contract, or at least the more doctrinaire of its citizens do. Thus the American Revolution brought with it a popular involvement in the conception of what should be considered genuinely American behaviour and attitudes, a feature of American life that De Tocqueville discusses at length.[1] Similarly, Marxist revolutions may produce a climate of opinion in which undesirable behaviour can be characterized as remnants of bourgeois attitudes. Not all of these ethical trends are incorporated into actual law, but they can act as a powerful legal force none the less. The importance of this factor in law is that it seems to point further back than the major premises of a constitution, the rights of man, equality before the courts, and the like, to something more primitive embedded in human nature and destiny. Every constitution has to be thought of, in practice, as in some sense an inspired document. Defining the nature of its inspiration is another matter.

We may find it more relaxing to live in Canada, where nobody thinks about what a hundred per cent Canadian is, and where a committee on un-Canadian activities would be faced with a totally unintelligible agenda. But even a system of law based on precedent has problems with the pressures exerted by the majority on individuals and minorities. In Canada, before the Charter, our own 'inspired' document, we had a series of ad hoc agreements and compromises like the Quebec Act,[2] which made some effort, in fact a rather remarkable one for the eighteenth century, to keep the civic rights of both English- and French-speaking Canadians in mind. But the indigenous peoples, the Japanese Canadians during the Second World War, and other such groups, would tell a different story.

The theory of precedent, of course, as formulated by Burke and by what is called the Whig interpretation of history, is that it operates in a liberal direction, toward increasing freedom and equality. The barons who compelled King John to sign Magna Carta were, on this view, ultimately acting for the benefit of the common man. But this conception of precedent has had to be modified a good deal, the reason that concerns us just now being that it does not go back far enough. If we pursue the ancestry of precedent, we eventually move into a prehistoric period in which laws are rationalized by a myth-telling society that they have been revealed by the gods. Once revealed, they are then enforced by an ascendant class, in whose interest the laws are interpreted. No conception of precedent can wholly shake off the influence of these mythical and pre-legal origins. Let us listen to Blackstone, in the eighteenth century, commenting on the regulations about Sunday observance:

Profanation of the Lord's Day, vulgarly (but improperly) called *sabbath-breaking*, is a ninth offence against God and religion, punished by the municipal law of England. For, besides the notorious indecency and scandal of permitting any secular business to be publicly transacted on that day, in a country professing Christianity, and the corruption of morals which usually follows its profanation, 'the keeping one day in seven holy, as a time of relaxation and refreshment as well as for public worship, is of admirable service to a state, considered merely as a civil institution. It humanizes by the help of conversation and society the manners of the lower classes, which would otherwise degenerate into a sordid ferocity and savage selfishness of spirit: it enables the industrious workman to pursue his occupation in the ensuing week, with health and cheerfulness; it imprints on the minds of the people that sense of their duty to God, so necessary to make them good citizens, but which yet would be worn out and defaced by an unremitted continuance of labour, without any stated times of recalling them to the worship of their Maker.'[3]

The one secular principle involved here, that mandatory holidays create better working conditions, gets in by the back door. It is clear that the major premises from which Blackstone is deriving his argument are, first, the traditional rituals of Christianity, which go back to still earlier Jewish ones, and, second, the principle that the lower classes should be kept firmly in their lower place. Clearly, it would be profitable to look at some of the origins of these assumptions: in particular, the religious origin, which so often includes the myth already mentioned, that the original laws were handed down to a specific human society by divine beings.

The word 'crime' is social and secular in context: murder and theft are crimes because they are disturbances of the social order. The word 'sin' is religious in context, and has no meaning outside a religious framework. Sin is primarily man's effort to block or frustrate the will of God, and though, in a normal state of society, crimes are usually regarded also as sins, they are so only when and because God is assumed to disapprove of them. So any legal code that goes back to a divine revelation has the conception 'sin' as its major premise from which the conception of 'crime' is derived.

In primitive societies the conception of sin begins in such features as taboo, where, for example, certain things must not be touched, certain foods not eaten, certain ceremonies not witnessed by outsiders. There then develops the sense of certain ritual obligations owed to the gods, the neglect of which, even if unconscious, will bring disaster. In the Book of Exodus there is a list of prescriptions in chapter 31, described as 'the ten commandments,' which are concerned almost wholly with these ritual obligations, and consequently may be older than the better known Decalogue in Exodus 20 and Deuteronomy 5, which I shall return to in a moment. Central to these ritual obligations is the conception of sacrifice. At each of the three major festivals, sacrificial offerings are to be brought to God, 'and none shall appear before me empty.'[4] Similarly, the period from Friday to Saturday sunsets is to be withdrawn from social and utilitarian pursuits, including the making of money. Every first-born male animal, including the first-born son of human beings, belongs to God as a sacrifice, though the son is to be redeemed by a lamb instead, or may be devoted to God in a more sublimated sense, like the infant Samuel.

The conception of sacrifice also enters warfare, and the most ferocious penalties are connected with disregarding the claims of God in war. If the Israelites are to conquer Canaan, all the loot they acquire belongs to God, which in practice means the priesthood. Joshua takes the city of Jericho, then meets with a sharp repulse at the city of Ai. He learns that an Israelite named Achan has kept some of the loot from Jericho for himself, so not only is Achan stoned to death, but his entire family is wiped out and all his possessions confiscated.[5] Similarly, prisoners captured in battle are to be killed as sacrifices to God. When King Saul captures the Amalekite king Agag he spares his life, as we should think, out of ordinary human decency, but the prophet Samuel, after denouncing Saul for having committed an utterly unforgivable sin against God, falls on Agag and hews him in pieces, and from then on King Saul never has any luck again.[6]

No doubt in pre-Biblical times these sacrifices were thought of as actually feeding the gods, as they still seem to be in Homer.[7] We can also see clearly enough a pre-Biblical cult of human sacrifice, which the Mosaic code is designed both to abolish and to re-establish on a more rational moral basis. But the prophets are emphatic that God has no need of the smoke of sacrifice and the like, and the rationale for these ritual obligations has to be looked for elsewhere.

The Hebrew word *torah* means the whole body of instruction necessary for the people of Israel, including the laws and such ritual obligations. The New Testament writers relied mainly on the Septuagint (Greek) translation of the Old Testament, and as the Septuagint rendered *torah* as *nomos*, the King James and other translations speak simply of the 'law.' But if we look at the Book of Deuteronomy we see something far bigger than a legal code: it is a contract or treaty between God and Israel transmitted through Moses, and it gives us not merely a code but a theological and historical context for that code.

The details of this context are filled out in the other books of the Pentateuch. First comes the founding of the society of Israel on a revolutionary basis. Moses in Egypt is informed by the voice speaking from the burning bush that the God of Israel is about to give himself a name, enter history, and take a very partisan role in it, the role of delivering an enslaved people from the bondage of the Egyptian establishment.[8] The revolutionary origin gives, as remarked earlier, a strongly deductive cast to the structure of laws, and we are constantly being referred back to the original contract. For example, one of the most attractive features of the Deuteronomic code is its relatively humane attitude to slavery, and the Israelite community is frequently reminded of the central reason for adopting such an attitude: that they themselves were once slaves in Egypt.

Most of us, I assume, would share the assumptions about liberty and equality, which oppose slavery, as the basis of law that have been formulated at least since John Stuart Mill's time.[9] We take for granted the principle of the equality of all citizens before the law and the principle of the greatest amount of individual autonomy consistent with the well-being of others. To the extent that the laws are bent in the interests of a privileged or aggressive group; to the extent that citizens live under arbitrary regulations enforced by terror; to that extent we are living in an illegal society. If we regard our own society as at least workably legal, we also take largely for granted that the real basis for the effectiveness of law in such a society is an invisible morale. The law in itself is compelled to deal only with overt actions, so that from the law's point of view an honest man is any man not yet convicted of stealing. But no society could hold together with so loose a conception of morality: there has to be a sufficient number of self-respecting citizens who are honest because they like it better that way.

The Pentateuch in general, and the Book of Deuteronomy in particular, is an extraordinary tour de force of social thought in which certain obligations toward God are assumed to build up in each person this inner morale that, so to speak, insulates that person from becoming a disintegrating force in society. The *torah* is designed, among many other things, to provide a kind of vertical dimension to law. The relation of the individual Israelite to the God of Israel, built up by the habits of action and thought fostered by the laws of the Sabbath and the like, is the source of the inner moral energy that is needed to keep society together. Sin, thought of as primarily the neglect of ritual obligations, thus becomes the sources of crime, so that one can never eradicate crime from society by secular legislation alone.

If we look at the familiar structure of the Decalogue, the ten commandments as we know them, we can see an illustration of this conception of secular crime being derived from ritual neglect.[10] The first four commandments are concerned with the obligations of religion:

Israel must be faithful to its God, not make images of him or of other gods, take the name of God seriously, and rest on the Sabbath. The fifth commandment, to honor one's parents, makes a transition to the moral sphere, but is connected with the ritual group by the promise that observing it will be rewarded by God with long life. The four commandments, following the prohibitions against murder, adultery, theft, and slander, would, if they stood alone, be thought of as purely moral and secular. The final commandment against coveting brings us back to that inner state of mental integrity which is the real basis of all law.

This deductive construct, in which the commands of God, the neglect of which is sin, form the premises for social morality, or law in the context of 'law and order,' is not unmatched in the ancient world: the role of sacrifice and other ritual practices in Hinduism is very similar, and there are other religion-based legal codes, like that of Islam, that develop later partly under Biblical influence. Still it is a rare achievement: the legal code of Hammurabi in Babylon, for instance, impressive as it is, does not seem to have acquired anything like the same prestige among its people.[11] We note in passing that such codes enclose a specific society and mark it off from others. The Deuteronomic code implies that God is uniquely related to Israel, and that Israel's ritual obligations are not necessarily binding on other nations. But for most of its history Israel was not an independent nation, but a province subject to the authority of Egypt, Assyria, Babylonia, Persia, Greece, and Rome. These heathen nations were the source of the secular and moral law, not less so when they allowed the Israelites to keep their ritual obligations. So the question arises: what happens when sin and crime are violations of conflicting structures of authority?

We may take an example from perhaps the most haunting situation of the sort in human culture: the dilemma of Antigone in Sophocles.[12] Here Antigone is forbidden by Creon, the ruler of Thebes and the source of its secular law, to bury her brother's body, and yet not to bury it would be a sin against one of the most solemn of Greek ritual obligations. Antigone does not hesitate: it is the sin that it is important to avoid, not the crime. She suffers accordingly, but the disaster that befalls Creon vindicates her, in the eyes of the audience at least. Similar dilemmas rise to a climax in the persecution of the Jews under Antiochus of Syria, the persecution that provoked the Maccabean rebellion.[13]

When the Christian religion began, a century or so after the Maccabees, this problem of a possible clash between religious and secular authority was very much in the foreground. Paul strongly advises submission to the secular authority of the Roman empire, but what he says sounds a trifle hollow in view of the persecutions that started, almost immediately, affecting Christians and Jews alike. Apart from this, there was also the question: how far is the Old Testament code binding on Christians? In what sense are Christians to be regarded as a new Israel? In this controversy Paul emerged as the leader who proclaimed that Christianity was to be brought to the Gentiles outside Israel, and that the ritual obligations of Judaism, such as circumcision, were no longer binding on Christians. The effect of the Christian reformulation of law was to drive a much wider breach between the two conceptions of sin and crime, and the consequences of doing so are still with us.

In the teaching of Jesus, especially in the Sermon on the Mount in Matthew,[14] which includes commentaries on some of the ten commandments, the distinction between the inner integrity that resists sin and the overt action of a crime is pushed about as far as it will go. The overwhelming emphasis is on the inner state of mind. If A murders B, and C merely wishes with all his being that D were dead, A is legally a murderer and C is wholly innocent of murder. From the point of view of the Sermon on the Mount the chief difference between the A who murders and the C who feels murderous is that A has more guts. Again, Jesus interprets the prohibitions against murder and adultery and theft as positive enthusiasms for human life, for the respect and self-respect of women, for property. There is nothing here that cannot be paralleled in contemporary rabbinical teaching, perhaps, but some of the inferences drawn in the New Testament, more particularly by Paul, forecast another revolution.

Paul sees in the story of the fall of Adam in Genesis the existence in human life of what is called original sin. The beginning of sin for him is an inherent condition of the soul, which is there before any act is. Consequently ritual obligations, while they symbolize a desire to be rid of original sin, are still ineffective: it is the inner condition itself that has to be transformed. This transformation sets one free from the law, according to Galatians, which is perhaps the earliest of Paul's writings. But one is not set free from the law by breaking the law, only more tangled up with it than ever. Jesus said that he thought of his teaching as fulfilling the law, not abolishing it: that means that there is an aspect of the law, called by Paul the 'spiritual' aspect, which is re-established, and another aspect that disappears.

This means that, for example, justice is the internal condition of the just man, and the external antagonist of the criminal. But the just man, to maintain his justice, has to be far stricter with himself than any law could provide penalties for. Justice as conceived by the gospel cannot be legalized: if we tried to make the transformed inner state spoken of by Paul and Jesus into a new code of law, the most frightful and fantastic tyranny would result. One can have a law against rape, but Jesus' conception of adultery includes all the men who mentally rape every woman who catches their eye, and this kind of 'adultery' cannot become a basis for legislation. If it did, we should have the situation of black farce in Gilbert's *Mikado*:

> The youth who winked a roving eye,
> Or breathed a non-connubial sigh
> Was thereupon condemned to die ...[15]

This was the basis on which Milton argued for divorce in the seventeenth century.[16] Divorce is permitted in the Mosaic code, but is apparently prohibited by Jesus.[17] Milton claimed that Jesus was talking about marriage in the spiritual or gospel sense, as a life-long union that can be consummated, which means finished, only by the death of one of the partners. Its model is the relation of Adam and Eve before the Fall, for each of whom there was, quite literally, no one else. But it is clearly nonsense, Milton says, to pretend that every sexual union in society is a spiritual marriage of this kind.

Of course the fact that Milton had to make such an argument, and was bitterly denounced for doing so, indicates that the original distinction between sin and crime was very largely ignored in practice. It was there in theory: in the Middle Ages the deadly sins were divided into seven groups, pride, wrath, sloth, envy, avarice, gluttony, and lechery. Preachers tended to leave lechery to the end as the most interesting. All crime is the result of one or more of these sins, but not one of them in itself necessarily results in crime. Still, the bulk of canon law was incorporated into secular law, and deviations from it were treated as crimes, whether the crime was eating meat in Lent or holding heretical doctrines. A new set of ritual obligations was set up, and it is clear that there is no change of principle when the day of rest is altered to Sunday from Saturday or the rite of circumcision replaced by the rite of baptism. Then, of course, there have always been the moralists, who want to turn as much sin, or what they consider sin, into crime as possible, and pass laws accordingly. In the seventeenth century there were also extreme Nonconformists who held that nothing was either sinful or criminal unless it was explicitly said to be so in the Bible. The Bible obligingly came through with denunciations of everything they disapproved of anyway except polygamy, which it nowhere condemns; that one had to be chalked up to the law of nature, a frantically muddled area of thought which I shall have to glance at in a moment. During the Prohibition era, the drys, most of whom had strong Protestant commitments, ran into a similar difficulty with a Bible which, while it condemns drunkenness, never conceives of the possibility of a human life totally deprived of fermented beverages.

The original Christian distinction between sin and crime was a part of the revolutionary aspect of Christianity, and the progressive blurring of the distinction was the result of the revolutionary impulse being smothered under new forms of entrenched privilege. The significance of the revolution which appears at the beginning of so many legal codes, of Israel in Egypt, of the American, French, and Russian revolutions of our times, is that a revolution repudiates an existing structure of law and authority. Christianity holds that Jesus was without sin, yet he was put to death as a criminal. This means that crime represents a social judgment, but society is never wholly capable of making such a judgment. It has no standards, in itself, for distinguishing what is below the law from what is above it: it cannot tell a prophet from a blasphemer, a saint from a witch, a philosopher from a teacher of subversive doctrines. Hence the martyred careers of Jesus, Joan of Arc, and Socrates.

This issue can hardly be called obsolete today, when Nazi Germany and similar dictatorships have made us familiar with the conception of a criminal society. Many liberal-minded Canadians, highly respected people who never come within sight of arrest or imprisonment, would, if they were living in South Africa, find their consciences nagging them because they were *not* in jail. Anti-social behaviour may result from motives that are considered good in other societies, or by the same society in a different phase of its history. Whether the relativity of crime could also apply to sin or not is a more difficult question. I think of a sardonic story by Marcel Aymé, in which a simple and saintly man in a French provincial town wakes up one morning to discover that he has acquired a halo, clearly visible except when he wears a hat. His wife is furious: nobody in *her* family ever had haloes, and how was she to explain this to the neighbours or to the concierge? As he could not wear his hat all the time, he would have to choose between her and the halo. So he conscientiously sets out to commit all the seven deadly sins, loses his reputation, his friends and his job, and finally ends up as a pimp in a brothel. But his motive in doing all this was so fundamentally innocent that the halo stayed firmly in place.[18]

The story, farcical as it is, indicates a genuine dilemma about the criteria for sin and crime. In a normally functioning society a crime is a breach of the legal code. But a society may pass laws so grotesquely unjust that obeying the laws of such a society may be the real crime. This at least, I assume, was the principle the Nuremberg trials after the Second World War attempted to establish. What criteria come into focus then? Many of the liberal-minded people I just spoke of, who would be dissidents in a racist or dictatorial country, have strong religious commitments, and for them a criminal society derives its criminal nature from sin, from being under the judgment of God. But the experience of our century indicates that any religious ideology, Christian or Jewish or Islamic or Hindu or whatever, is a most insecure basis for a modern state. In fact, as in South Africa or Iran, a religious ideology is often a major contributing factor to an intolerable legal code.

Conceptions derived from natural law or the law of nations as the basis for a 'legal' society concern me here only insofar as they have been traditionally a part of the relation of crime to sin in the Bible. The notion of natural law is really not in the Bible: in the Bible the same God is in charge of both the moral and the natural orders, and nature is thought of as a fellow-creature of man, who, like man, has an order imposed on it by divine will. In the Biblical view there cannot be such a thing, strictly speaking, as a miracle, because God does as he likes in both human and physical worlds. Natural law grew out of the sort of questions asked by the pre-Socratic philosophers. What is the world made of? Is there a primary substance? What really are the stars? Are there such things as atoms? These are questions that move in the direction of science, and from them came the observation that some things in nature behaved regularly enough to be predictable. It was a considerable set-back to science that this emerging view of natural law should have been associated, by a violent and foolish pun, with law in its human and social context. Natural laws are not 'broken'; if we fall out of a tree we do not break the law of gravitation: we merely illustrate it. But the confusions engendered by the pun still persist, even when the conception of God is replaced by a mother-goddess figure of Nature. We have it still in Einstein's unwillingness to accept the element of chance in quantum mechanics, and in the frequent assertion that evolution did not arise by 'blind chance,' but chance operating within a framework of law. As long as law in nature means simply the human observation of the predictable element in it, this amounts to saying that things happened as they did because they happened as they did.

The law of nations, the *jus gentium* of Grotius[19] and others, which is often associated or identified with natural law, arose, according to Sir Henry Maine, in Roman efforts to define the legal status of non-Romans.[20] It is thus extra-Biblical in origin, but it became attached to the central myth of the Bible in a way that persisted down to at least the eighteenth century. According to this myth, which derives from Paul's emphasis on the fall of Adam and the original sin that resulted, there are two levels of nature. The upper or human level is the one God created with the garden of Eden and the original Adam and Eve. The lower or physical level is the one that Adam fell into, which all of us, being his descendants, are now born in. Man is not adjusted to this lower level of nature, as the animals and plants appear to be. Many things are 'natural' to man, such as wearing clothes, being conscious, and using reason, which are natural to nothing else in the environment. Edmund Burke was insisting as late as the French Revolution that 'art is man's nature,'[21] not something man has imposed on nature.

It follows that we cannot appeal to anything in physical nature to determine the answer to the question 'what is natural to man?' In Milton's *Comus* a chaste Lady is imprisoned by Comus, who tries to seduce her with arguments drawn from the animal world and its lack of self-consciousness about sexual intercourse. The Lady's answer is too virtuous to be altogether coherent, but the general line of her argument is that on the human level of nature it is her chastity that is natural, not promiscuity.[22] On the other hand, 'nature' is often invoked as a standard against which socially disapproved behaviour, such as homosexuality or incest, may be measured. The hero of the late Greek romance *Daphnis and Chloe* is tempted to a homosexual relationship, but refuses because, though a simple and untutored country boy, he has never seen such relationships among animals.[23] Being only the hero of a pastoral story, he does not do the research into animal behaviour that might have qualified his position. But we can already see what the general conclusion is. The humanly natural is what is natural on the human level of nature; that is, the form of human society sanctioned by custom and tradition and authority. What is natural to man, then, is a question with a completely circular answer: it is whatever constituted authority says is natural, and you will accept this or else.

Nothing in any of the traditional conceptions of natural law will help us to arrive at criteria by which to judge an unjust society. Let us go back to where we started, the Biblical view that crime is a by-product of sin, sin being rooted in one's obligations, ritual or moral, to God. These obligations, however universal the religion aims at being, are essentially tribal: they enclose the group of believers, even if they can be numbered in millions, and separate them from others with different obligations or with no traditions of any kind at all. Some of these excluding obligations are very potent: dietary laws, for instance, which separate different groups on the basis of what can become something like physical nausea. The nausea may work negatively also: a Moslem woman in Pakistan, for example, once remarked to me about Hindus: 'I hate those people; they don't eat beef.' An American senator of some years back similarly opposed any aid to the starving people of India on the ground that India had plenty of cows wandering around, which the Indians were too perverse to eat.

Those who know more law than I do will know better than I how such mutually exclusive bodies can be absorbed into a secular state. All I can contribute is the social vision I have picked up from the study of literature. The sense of obligations to God of course makes God objective to man, and his revelation of them equally so. It would not be difficult, however, to see behind every religion an expression of human concern, a word so broad that I hope it is self-explanatory. I think there are primary and secondary concerns. Primary concerns rest on platitudes so bald and obvious that one hesitates to list them: it is better to be fed than starving, better to be happy than miserable, better to be free than a slave, better to be healthy than sick. Secondary concerns arise through the consciousness of a social contract: loyalty to one's religion or country or community, commitment to faith, sacrifice of cherished elements in life for the sake of what is regarded as a higher cause. All through history primary concerns have had to give way to secondary ones. It is better to live than die; nevertheless we go to war. Freedom is better than bondage, but we accept an immense amount of exploitation, both of ourselves and of others. Perhaps, with our nuclear weapons and our pollution of air and water, we have reached the first stage in history in which primary concerns will have to become primary.

The reason why this interests me is that I think primary concern expresses itself in mythology, in the stories and rituals surrounding the food supply, the sexual relation, the work which is a socially creative act and not an alienated drudgery, the play which is the expression of energy and not a mere distraction. It is this mythology that develops into literature. Secondary concerns produce ideology, and the normal language of ideology is the dialectical language of argument and thesis, which is invariably aggressive, because every thesis contains its own opposite. I am not suggesting an original Golden Age of pure myth: every myth, in the most primitive society, also has an ideological social function. Every work of literature, therefore, which descends from mythology, is an ideological product, an expression of the culture of its age. But some literary works show the capacity to make contact with an audience far removed in space, time, and culture, and it is the task of the critic to reveal in such works the primary myth underlying the ideological surface. In an age of ideological deadlock like ours, with so many foolish and irresponsible people saying 'Let's go to war to smash somebody else's ideology,' I feel that this critical task has taken on a renewed social importance.

Not all mythology develops into literature. The Bible is a mythological sacred book, but not a work of literature, though it is full of literary qualities.[24] What keeps it from being literature is the objective nature assumed about its God and his revelation. This objectivity restricts its appeal, or much of it, to the special response of belief, which includes belonging to one definite community and not another. But we may also think of the Bible as coming to us through the power of the creative human imagination, which it clearly does whatever we believe about its ultimate source. In that context, we can perform the same critical operation we undergo with literary works, trying to isolate the original myth under all the accretions of ideology, which for the Bible extend over several millennia.

Central to that original and underlying myth within the Bible is the legal metaphor of the trial, with prosecutors, defendants, and, of course, a supreme judge. We find this most explicitly in the Book of Job, in some parables of Jesus, and in the Book of Revelation that concludes the New Testament, but it is there all through in some form. The role of accuser is typically that of the devil, the Satan or adversary of mankind; the role of the defendant is identified with that of Jesus in the New Testament, with that of the restorer of Israel in the Old. Accuser and defendant represent the aspects of our lives that relate to past and future: the accuser says 'This is what you have done,' the defendant says 'This is what you still may do.' In history, a revolution, which so often results in a new legal code, may sweep away the accumulated crime and sin of the past and usher in a new social order looking to the future. As time goes on, the future vision fades out and the record of the past resumes its continuity. I think it is possible to see, in the central myth of the Bible, a vision that rises above the progression from past to future into a higher form of the present, a vision of human creative power continually making the new by reshaping the old. On this level we pass beyond the specific religious revelation into a more comprehensive view of human destiny. In such a view there would be included, I should think, an understanding of what has been called sin that does not have the arbitrary quality of the objectified revelation. This would include a fuller perspective of the crime that traditionally derives from sin, giving us a saner and less anxious vision of the origins of human evil and of the methods of encountering it.

Notes

Northrop Frye was ordained in the United Church of Canada in 1936 and received his MA from Oxford University in 1940. His great number of publications include *Fearful Symmetry: A Study of William Blake; Anatomy of Criticism; The Secular Scripture; The Great Code;* and *Northrop Frye on Shakespeare*, which won the 1986 Governor-General's Award for non-fiction. He died as this book was in production.

1 Alexis De Tocqueville published his analysis of American society in 1835 and 1840. See his *Democracy in America* ed Phillips Bradley 2 vols (New York: Knopf 1945).
2 The Quebec Act (1774) re-established French civil law as the law of Quebec, counteracting a royal proclamation by King George III (1763) which had imposed English civil and criminal law on the colony. Quebec Act 1774 (UK) RSC 1985, appendix II no 2

3 William Blackstone *Commentaries on the Laws of England* 4 (Boston: Beacon Press 1962) 59

4 Exodus 34:20

5 Joshua 7:1–8:29

6 1 Samuel 15

7 See for example *The Odyssey* III, 51ff; VII, 201ff. See also Henri Hubert and Marcel Mauss *Sacrifice: Its Nature and Function* (Chicago: University of Chicago Press 1964) 37.

8 Exodus 2:23–4:17

9 See John Stuart Mill 'On Liberty' (1859) in *Collected Works of John Stuart Mill* vol 18 'Essays on Politics and Society' ed John M. Robson (Toronto: University of Toronto Press 1977) 213–310.

10 Exodus 20:1–17

11 Hammurabi was King of Babylon from 1792–1750 BC, and the code (a record of 282 of his decisions) represents the most complete extant account of Babylonian laws. Perhaps best known for its principle of restitution, the *lex talionis* (ie, an eye for an eye, a tooth for a tooth), its resemblance to the Mosaic code – see Stanley A. Cook *The Law of Moses and the Code of Hammurabi* (London: Adam and Charles Black 1903) – is apparent. The correspondence, once viewed as evidence of the dependency of the Mosaic code on that of Hammurabi, is now attributed to a common source.

12 Sophocles' tragedy dates back to 441 BC. A modern translation can be found in *Antigone* trans Richard E. Braun (London: Oxford University Press 1973).

13 1 Maccabees

14 Matthew 5:1–7:27

15 W.S. Gilbert and Arthur Sullivan *The Mikado, or The Town of Titipu* in *The Complete Plays of Gilbert and Sullivan* (New York: Modern Library 1936) 348

16 Milton's primary argument is found in 'The Doctrine and Discipline of Divorce' (first published in 1643). See *The Works of John Milton* 3, pt 2 (New York: Columbia University Press 1931).

17 The two key passages are Deuteronomy 24:1 (which describes a 'certificate of divorce' in the Mosaic code) and Matthew 5:32 (part of the Sermon on the Mount, in which Jesus explicitly contradicts the passage from Deuteronomy).

18 Marcel Aymé 'La Grâce' in *Le Vin de Paris* (Paris: Gallimard 1947) 79–96

19 Hugo Grotius' (1583–1645) most influential work on the law of nations was *De jure Belli ac Pacis* (1625). A translation is found in *The Rights of War and Peace* trans A.C. Campbell (New York: M. Walter Dunne 1901).

20 See chapter 3 of Maine's *Ancient Law* (London: Dent 1917) 26–42, in which Maine argues that the Romans sought to create a jurisdiction covering non-Romans which featured only the laws common to several legal systems or codes, and thus somehow 'natural' or given.

21 'An Appeal from the New to the Old Whigs' (1791) in *The Works of the Right Honourable Edmund Burke* 6 (London: Rivington 1826) 218

22 'A Mask Presented at Ludlow Castle, 1634' in *The Works of John Milton* 1, pt 1 (New York: Columbia University Press 1931) 85–123

23 For a modern translation, see Longus *Daphnis & Chloe*, trans George Thornely (London: Heinemann 1916).

24 See generally Northrop Frye *The Great Code: The Bible and Literature* (Toronto: Academic Press Canada 1982); *Words With Power: Being a Second Study of 'The Bible and Literature'* (Markham: Viking Press 1990).

PATRICIA J. EBERLE

Crime and Justice in the Middle Ages: Cases from the *Canterbury Tales* of Geoffrey Chaucer

One of the advantages of reading Chaucer's *Canterbury Tales* in the context of an examination of crime and justice in literature is that it calls attention to an important feature of the work which is seldom discussed in studies by Chaucer specialists: a very high proportion of the tales deal, in one way or another, with the subject of 'crime' as it was understood in England in the later Middle Ages.[1] A number of the crimes that occur in the *Canterbury Tales* are familiar to us today: treason, murder, and rape appear, together with various forms of theft and assault. In addition, Chaucer's tales also involve some medieval crimes that are less well-known: some, like alchemy, because they are no longer widely practised; others, like fornication, because they are no longer widely regarded as crimes. Since most of the written records dealing with crime and justice in the medieval period were the work of legal professionals of one kind or another, Chaucer's *Canterbury Tales* is especially valuable. If someone were looking for a text that reflected the thinking of ordinary medieval English citizens on crime and justice, it would be difficult to find a work better suited to this purpose than the *Canterbury Tales*.

It is worth noting at the outset that the difference between medieval and modern notions of 'crime' is not merely a matter of which offences are put into that category. The medieval concept of 'crime' itself, as a special category for certain kinds of violations of law, was very different from the modern one: as a semantic field, the medieval concept of crime was not only larger, but of a different shape and with fuzzier boundaries than its modern counterpart.

The different shape of the concept of crime in Chaucer's England arises from the fact that some of the theoretical distinctions with which we are now familiar were not then a part of legal practice or theory.[2] As is the case in many modern legal systems, the practical definition of crime was in large part a matter of procedure, but the boundaries of the medieval English field of crime took on a different shape depending upon which aspect of procedure one looked at. In addition, the classification by procedure was not always consistent. The most significant aspect of procedure was the distinction between the cases dealt with by the Court of Common Pleas, where most, but not all, cases heard were of the type that would now be treated as 'civil actions,' and the cases dealt with by the Crown, most, but not all, of which would now be treated as 'criminal actions.' There were still other courts, presided over by the justices of the peace, which heard both kinds of cases.[3] If, on the other hand, we look at another aspect of procedure, the nature of the penalty for a given violation of law, the whole field becomes still more unclear, because of the very widespread use of fines. In the words of the famous nineteenth-century historian of English criminal law, Sir James Fitzjames Stephen, 'Fines were paid on every imaginable occasion ... at every stage of every sort of legal proceeding, and for every description of official default, irregularity, or impropriety. In short, the practice of fining was so prevalent that if punishment is taken as the test of a criminal offence, and fines are regarded as a form of punishment, it is almost impossible to say where the criminal law in early times began or ended.'[4]

The conceptual field covered by the medieval concept of 'crime' in Chaucer's time becomes larger still when we realize that it included not only what modern legal historians would call 'crime' but also what the medieval church called 'sin.' One of the most important sources for the medieval church's concept of sin was the 'penitential,' a handbook of discipline for the use of monasteries; from the sixth century onwards, these penitentials, modelling their language on the language of secular law, called offences against the monastic rules 'crimes' or *crimina*,[5] and they included among these 'crimes' not only actions but words and even thoughts. In fact, the 'chief crimes' (*crimina capitalia*) in the penitentials were the habits of mind which eventually came to be called the Seven Deadly Sins: pride, envy, anger, sloth, avarice, gluttony, and lust.[6] The order of these seven sins varied somewhat from one penitential handbook to another; the order used here is taken from the handbook of sins Chaucer includes in the *Parson's Tale*, the last of the *Canterbury Tales*. This spiritual category of crime persisted throughout the Middle Ages, as the basis for examination in private confession, which was viewed by canon law as a sort of trial or judicial inquiry taking place 'in the internal law court' (*in foro interiori*).

The spiritual category of crimes also formed an important basis for those offences which were tried in the external law courts; that is, the ecclesiastical courts which were established in the late eleventh century. Ecclesiastical courts did not punish all sins as crimes, only those which represented a violation of a specific ecclesiastical law, following the important principle of the theologian Peter Lombard: 'There is no sin if there was no prohibition.' This principle set a limit to criminal jurisdiction as an important precedent for later ages, the principle of 'No crime, no punishment without a law (*Nullum crimen, nulla poena sine lege*).'[7] In practice, however, that principle of limit was all but lost to view for the average layman, who might be summoned to the ecclesiastical court to answer for any one of a bewildering variety of offences made criminal by an increasing number of ecclesiastical laws. In a passage from the opening of the *Friar's Tale*, Chaucer conveys his sense of the wide range of actions which the ecclesiastical courts punished as crimes, as he describes the practices of 'A fine archdeacon, one of high degree':

Who boldly did the execution due
On fornication and on witchcraft too,
Bawdry, adultery and defamation,
Breaches of will and contract, spoliation
Of church endowment, failure in the rents
And tithes and disregard of sacraments,
All these and many other kinds of crime
That need have no rehearsal at this time,
Usury, simony too. But he could boast
That lechery was what he punished most.
They had to sing for it if they were caught,
Like those who failed to pay the tithes they ought.[8]

Still more to be feared than either the internal lawcourt administered by the confessor or the external lawcourt administered by the archdeacon was the Last Judgment, over which God himself would preside as judge. In a passage on the Last Judgment in the *Parson's Tale* Chaucer describes it in traditional terms as a sort of supernatural court of law, similar to courts of law in this world, but lacking both their imperfections and their loopholes. In this court of law, Chaucer's Parson says, no 'essoyne' or 'excusacioun' will be of any use; he is using two terms from the legal language of fourteenth-century English courts to say that two common expedients to avoid standing trial – sending a legal substitute or obtaining a legal excuse – will not be allowed in the court of the Last Judgment.[9] In God's court, he goes on to say, there will also be 'no pledyinge ne no sleighte'; that is, no lawyer to plead your case for you (a practice that was becoming increasingly important in English courts in Chaucer's time) and no chance of using trickery. God as judge can be neither deceived nor corrupted: he knows all our crimes, the Parson says, not only our actions, but even our words and thoughts.

The image of the Last Judgment as a court of law is important for an understanding of the average layperson's view of crime and justice in Chaucer's time. Medieval Christians viewed themselves as subject ultimately to a legal jurisdiction without limit, one that had full power to review their entire lives (including thoughts, words, and deeds that had gone unpunished by the secular and ecclesiastical authorities) and to impose eternal punishment. Moreover, in this Last Judgment, most people would be found guilty, to some degree; their main hope lay in the mercy of the Judge, which might be encouraged by the intercession of Christ or Mary as their 'advocate.'[10] The Retractions found at the end of most manuscripts of the *Canterbury Tales* provide evidence that Chaucer himself shared this view of the Last Judgment; Chaucer prays that he will find mercy on the Day of Judgment for all his 'giltes,' a Middle English word meaning both 'crimes' and 'sins,' and he includes among these 'giltes' a number of the *Canterbury Tales*; that is, those that show some sinful tendencies.[11]

This discussion of the religious dimensions of the concept of crime in the Middle Ages, necessarily brief though it is, should serve to indicate the interpenetration of religious and legal thought on many levels throughout the period. Concepts primarily associated with secular law – such as crime, punishment, and guilt – took on religious connotations in a society increasingly subject to the legal as well as moral jurisdiction of the church. In return, the medieval church saw itself and its role in society in increasingly legalistic terms. It is symptomatic of this process that in Chaucer's time the word 'law' could be used as a synonym for 'religion.' For example, in the *Man of Law's Tale*, the marriage of Constance, a daughter of the Christian emperor, to the Moslem sultan of Syria, is described as a means of increasing the dominion of 'the blessed law of Christ.'[12]

In *Law and Revolution: The Formation of the Western Legal Tradition*, Harold J. Berman argues that this interpenetration of legal and religious thought took on a new form in the eleventh century as a result of the movement he calls the 'Papal Revolution.'[13] He calls it a 'revolution' because the kind of change envisioned by Pope Gregory VII was a radically new vision: one single universal government patterned after the government of the world by God and attempting, so far as possible, to realize that government on earth. The name given to this vision was 'right order' (*rectus ordo*).[14] One of the fundamental principles of this 'right order,' according to Berman's analysis, was that it was to be a government not of men but of laws.

Behind this idea of the rule of law lay a fundamental medieval principle, 'the higher should rule the lower.'[15] As the heavens are higher than the earth and, according to the principles of medieval astrology, govern events on earth, so it is in the realm of human affairs. As God is set over men, so some men, by virtue of their God-given qualities or God-appointed offices, are set over others. All men, by virtue of the God-given superiority of their reason are set over all women, and all humanity (including women with their lesser share of reason) are set over the lower orders of creation, which were created for their use.

The reform envisioned by the supporters of the papacy was to translate this religious vision of 'right order' into political and legal reality, with the pope as supreme legislator and judge at its head, beneath him the church (reorganized into a fully articulated hierarchy of legal responsibilities), and below the church the legal authorities of various realms, subdivided within each realm into still smaller legal and administrative units such as cities and guilds. The smallest unit of governance is the household, presided over by the man of the house.

The 'right order' envisioned by the adherents of the papacy in 1075 was never realized perfectly in practice. In the years that followed, it had to come to terms with powerful lay authorities, notably kings, who refused to accept a vision in which their assigned status was below that of the lowliest member of clergy. In England, King Henry II continued to assert his royal supremacy over the church and attempted to consolidate his position by appointing as archbishop of Canterbury his friend Thomas Becket. In 1164, however, when Henry issued the Constitutions of Clarendon in an attempt to legislate into being the powers he claimed as king, Becket denounced the Constitutions as unjust and illegal usurpation of powers properly belonging to the church. The conflict between Becket and Henry II continued until 1170, when Becket was murdered, thus becoming the most famous martyr to the ideals of the Papal Revolution. Like many martyrs, Becket won a moral victory by his death. In response to the outrage caused by Becket's death, Henry II was forced to do public penance by walking barefoot to Becket's shrine at Canterbury, and he subsequently retracted those portions of the Constitutions of Clarendon which were offensive to the church.

Even after this compromise was reached, however, the conflict and its consequences were not forgotten in England. Becket's fame spread quickly, and his shrine at Canterbury became a favourite place for pilgrimages. It is worth noting that the company of pilgrims Chaucer describes in his *General Prologue* to the *Canterbury Tales* are following in the footsteps of the repentant Henry II, when they make their pilgrimage to visit the Canterbury shrine of Becket, whom Chaucer calls 'the holy blessed martyr.'[16]

The ideal for which Becket became a martyr, of one system of law reaching in ordered hierarchy from God down through the church and thence through the secular authorities to the individual household, thus came to co-exist with a considerable variety of practical applications. By Chaucer's time (c 1343–1400), there was a complex system of legal jurisdictions, competing as often as co-operating; there was much duplication and some conflict between the secular and ecclesiastical systems of justice. But the ideal of individual laws as part of a larger, divinely ordained, system of justice persisted. For Berman, one of the most important effects of the Papal Revolution was in the ideal it attempted to express: the ideal of reforming the world by means of law, law reorganized and rewritten where and when necessary but based on a consistent and coherent ideal of justice and bearing within itself the principles of its own further growth. It is this view of law, Berman argues, that forms the basis of a legal tradition that has dominated the Western world for the past nine hundred years or so, a tradition that is now increasingly under attack by a variety of rival theories of law.[17]

This ideal of law in general had important effects on the theory and practice of criminal justice in Chaucer's time. Punishment of acts of violence such as assault, murder, and rape, traditionally the province of the secular authorities, acquired a new moral and even religious significance. In punishing crimes, the secular authorities were viewed not merely as pursuing the limited practical goals of restoring the peace by providing a legal vehicle for retribution on behalf of the injured party; they were acting as agents of divine justice in exacting retribution on behalf of the violated order of justice itself. For the punishment of crime, even by secular authorities, was believed to play an important part in the gradual reformation envisioned by the Papal Revolution. Thomas Aquinas, in the context of a discussion of law that forms part of his *Summa Theologica* (1265–73), puts the church's view of the moral and religious mission of secular punishment in clear and straightforward terms: 'From being accustomed to avoid evil and fulfil what is good, through fear of punishment, one is sometimes led on to do so likewise, with delight and of one's own accord. Accordingly, law, even by punishing, leads men on to being good.'[18] This view of the divinely appointed mission of all those in authority to reform those who are subject to them by punishing their crimes gave new moral status to all secular authorities, including heads of households, who could be seen as acting on behalf of God for the good of those whom God had appointed them to rule.[19]

This medieval attitude towards criminal justice has little in common with many modern views on the subject. In his volume on *Criminal Law and Punishment* for the Clarendon Law Series, P.J. Fitzgerald notes, 'The claim of the courts to act as guardian of morals rings strange to modern ears.' Commenting on the view that secular justice is designed to act as an instrument of divine justice, Fitzgerald goes on to distinguish the modern from the medieval attitude: 'With Blackstone (Comm. IV.11) we may urge that atonement and expiation should be left to the Supreme Being.' Accordingly, Fitzgerald devotes a large part of his discussion to surveying other concepts as the basis for a modern rationale of criminal justice.[20] Objections like these against the medieval view of criminal justice are not new. They were heard even in the Middle Ages, not only in the protests of rulers like Henry II but also in fully reasoned alternative theories like those of Wyclif, who presented an argument on dominion and grace based on the assumption of a sharp distinction between the eternal order of divine justice and the temporal arrangements, by nature imperfect and pragmatic, necessary to keep public order. Wyclif's views were condemned as heretical, but they exerted wide influence in Chaucer's England.[21]

Berman's view of the relatively uniform ideal of law and justice held by canon lawyers and some other legal theorists associated with the church needs to be seen, I would suggest, in the context of other medieval views, not only the views of rival theorists but also the views of those who had direct personal experience of medieval justice in operation. This second group includes legal practitioners of various kinds as well as those laymen whose experience of justice was usually on the receiving end, who encountered the system of justice when they went to court to lay or answer charges in their own name. In England, where there was, as we have seen, a long legacy of conflict between English common law and canon law, those with practical experience of the courts would be especially likely to notice an absence of uniformity and coherence in these competing legal systems. As we can tell from the extant records of his life, most of which are legal documents of one kind or another, Chaucer himself had a variety of practical experiences of English law. Although he was not by profession a lawyer,[22] Chaucer served, together with other laymen and some professional lawyers, on the commission of the peace for the County of Kent from 1385–9 and on the commission of inquiry for the Court of the King's Bench in 1387. We also know that he had more than one encounter with the legal system at the receiving end; in addition to various civil actions, most of them involving real-estate, he was twice brought in on criminal charges: once in 1379, when he was accused in a rather unclear 'action of trespass and contempt' brought by a certain Thomas Stondon, and again in 1380, when he was accused of the rape of one Cecilia Chaumpaigne.[23]

In light of what we know of his many and varied encounters with English medieval justice, we may suspect that Chaucer had his own views on crime and justice and that his views were informed at least as much by personal experience as by theory. Although crime of all kinds plays an important role in many of the *Canterbury Tales*, Chaucer nowhere states his own views on the subject directly. In one area, however, the evidence seems clear. Chaucer's satiric descriptions of the greed and venality of various church officials in the *General Prologue* show that he could be a sharp critic of the claims of the medieval church to be an arbiter of justice. Perhaps his most direct and bitter attack on the administration of criminal justice by the ecclesiastical courts is the *Friar's Tale*. The friar tells the story of a summoner, an ecclesiastical official roughly parallel to the bailiff in the modern British system. The first lines of the friar's description of the summoner set the tone for the tale as a whole:

There was no slyer boy in all the land,
For he had subtly formed a gang of spies
Who taught him where his profit might arise ...[24]

The summoner uses lechers and prostitutes as his agents to tell him of the crimes of others, then blackmails these sinners by threatening to summon them to the archdeacon's court. The summoner is thus a man of many parts, counting theft, pimping, bribery, and blackmail among his talents, as he pursues his calling in the name of criminal justice. In the course of his duties, he meets a mysterious stranger whom he takes to be another summoner like himself because the stranger's account of his work has such a familiar ring:

My wages are extremely tight and small.
My master's hard on me and difficult,
My job laborious and with poor result,
And so it's by extortion that I live.
I take whatever anyone will give.
At any rate by tricks and violences
From year to year I cover my expenses.[25]

After he shakes hands and becomes the sworn brother of this stranger, the summoner learns the true identity of his new friend: the master he serves is not the archdeacon but Satan, and he himself is a fiend from hell.

In this tale, Chaucer's sharply critical view of criminal justice as practised by the ecclesiastical courts is fairly transparent, but in other tales his procedure makes his own views less easy to detect. His usual method is to let one of the members of his Canterbury pilgrimage tell a tale involving crime and the consequences that follow from it, leaving to his audience the task of deducing for themselves the view of criminal justice held by the character who tells the tale. Taken altogether, the *Canterbury Tales* embraces a wide spectrum of views on crime and punishment, wide enough to show that medieval views of this subject were anything but uniform. Where Chaucer's own views fit in this spectrum cannot be easily determined. Three tales that deal with interrelated questions, the *Man of Law's Tale*, the *Clerk's Tale*, and the *Wife of Bath's Tale*, provide evidence to suggest both that Chaucer was aware of the ideals of law and justice Berman associates with the Papal Revolution and that he did not accept these ideals uncritically or believe they could be easily realized in practice.

The main emphasis here will be on the *Man of Law's Tale*, because it represents a complex view of crime and punishment that Chaucer attributes to a representative of one of the highest branches of the legal profession of his time. The description in the *General Prologue* of the man who tells this tale makes it clear that he is no ordinary lawyer but a 'Sergeant of the Law,' that is, a member of the small and very prestigious Order of the Coif. This élite group was selected from among the most accomplished apprentices who had spent at least sixteen years studying and practising the law. The exclusiveness of the Order of the Coif to which Chaucer's Sergeant of the Law belongs may be judged by its numbers: during the entire reign of Richard II (1377–99), only twenty-one sergeants were created.

The elevated status of this élite group of lawyers appears from the description given by Sir John Fortescue in his treatise, *In Praise of the Laws of England* (1470): Sergeants had exclusive rights to plead in the Court of Common Pleas, all judges were selected from their Order, and their knowledge of common law was so highly regarded that they were often summoned to Parliament to decide difficult questions of precedent or legal principle.[26] But even in this élite group, the learning of a lawyer like Chaucer's Sergeant would have been outstanding, if we credit the claim Chaucer makes for him: 'He knew of every judgment, case, and crime/Ever recorded since King William's time.' The extent of this man's knowledge of legal precedent is astounding indeed; the records he claims to remember date from the accession of William the Conqueror in 1066. And as if knowledge of all legal cases recorded in the Year Books for the past three hundred years were not enough, Chaucer adds a further claim, 'And he knew every statute off by rote.'[27]

If these claims for the Sergeant seem exaggerated, they are. The kind of memory attributed to the Man of Law goes back further than the memory of the law itself: '"Legal memory" – the time before which the memory of the law does not reach – goes back to the coronation of Richard I, September 3, 1189.'[28] Moreover, it is unlikely that he could have known the contents, or even possessed copies of Year Books dating from William I; the extant Year Books recording cases begin only with the reign of Edward I in 1272.[29] Chaucer, however, was writing fiction, and one of his fictitious claims was that he derived all of his information about the people he describes in his *General Prologue* from conversations he had with them in the Tabard Inn in Southwark before they set off on their travels to Canterbury. In describing his own legal expertise, the Sergeant was apparently telling Chaucer what became popularly known as a 'Canterbury tale,' or, as we would now say, a tall tale.[30] Another of Chaucer's fictions is that he is a naïve reporter of the words of those he met at the Tabard and full of enthusiasm for what he hears. Chaucer presents himself as an average non-professional who stands in awe of the expertise the Sergeant claims for himself. The only overt sign he gives that he perceives a slight gap between the Sergeant's pretensions and his abilities is in his reaction to the Sergeant's claim about how busy his legal activities kept him: 'Though there was nowhere one so busy as he/He was less busy than he seemed to be.'[31] This apparently admiring portrait of the Sergeant is so lifelike that some studies have argued it is modelled on a real lawyer of the time; nevertheless, the exaggerated features are there to remind us that is not fact but fiction.[32] It is, indeed, the first time in the history of English literature that a member of the legal profession is portrayed as a fully developed character in a work of fiction.

Of course, lawyers like the Sergeant were a comparatively new phenomenon in the real world as well. The replacement of clergymen by laymen as legal professionals was a relatively recent development in Chaucer's time; the number of lay lawyers began to increase in the later thirteenth century, in part as the result of ongoing efforts of English kings, who continued the struggle begun by Henry II to extend the reach of royal justice and check the growth of the ecclesiastical courts. In the early fourteenth century, when judges began to be drawn from the order of sergeants, rather than from the clerks of the court, there was established, for the first time, a single legal career for laymen leading from advocacy up to the bench.[33] As Chaucer's description of his Sergeant makes clear, he was one of the very few who had reached the pinnacle of this career. Because of the Sergeant's unparalleled expertise in the theory and practice of the law, his tale has a special interest as representing what Chaucer took to be the 'professional' view of the issues involved in crime and justice.

In view of the Sergeant's professional expertise in legal precedent, it is not surprising that when his turn comes to tell a tale, he looks for precedents in the art of story-telling. As the authoritative source for these precedents the Sergeant fastens on Chaucer's own *Legend of Good Women*.[34] According to the precedent set by this book, a good story is the story of the suffering of a good woman, and, in telling the story of Constance, the Sergeant seems bent on outdoing Chaucer at his own game. The Man of Law's Constance, who is presented not only as good, but as the very model of Christian goodness, undergoes more suffering in the course of her long and tortuous tale than any of the women Chaucer describes in his *Legend*.

Constance, moreover, is both nobly born and beautiful. She is so beautiful that she attracts the love of a young sultan of Syria who has not seen, but only heard about her from the report of some merchants. And, as the only daughter of the Christian emperor of Rome, she is of such high birth that the future of the Christian empire depends on her marriage. By a nice twist of story-telling logic, it is just this combination of birth and beauty that causes her suffering. The sultan is so hopelessly in love with Constance, even before he meets her, that he agrees to convert to Christianity and abandon his Moslem faith. Although she has no desire for the match, her father the emperor insists that she marry the sultan because he and the pope see it as a means of enlarging the Christian empire. Again, Constance is the helpless victim of her own virtues; we have already been told that she is the very paragon of goodness, and goodness in a medieval woman means submission to the authority of those set above her in the scheme of divine justice. Thus, because she is 'good,' she submits to the will of her father, even though she herself is unwilling to marry the sultan. The logic of the lawyer's tale is relentless.[35]

Once arrived in Syria, however, Constance meets with another attitude towards law and a kind of woman very unlike herself. The sultan's mother is a devout Moslem, who is outraged by her son's apostasy from the faith and who conducts a kind of Islamic *jihad* in revenge. At the wedding feast, the sultan's mother arranges for a mass murder of all the Christians, not only those who are in Constance's retinue but even her own son and all those other former Moslems who received baptism along with him. She then pushes Constance out to sea in a rudderless boat. When the Man of Law denounces the sultan's mother vigorously as a 'serpent masked in feminity' he is ignoring the fact that, according to her own view of law and justice, she is following a logic as rigorous as his own. Like the Christian Saint Cecilia, whose story is included in the *Canterbury Tales* as the *Second Nun's Tale*, the sultan's mother views her religious faith as the highest law to which she owes allegiance, and she refuses 'thralldom' to any other faith. In sacrificing her feelings as a mother to her belief in her faith, the sultan's mother sees herself as a Moslem heroine, ready to 'die the death' rather than to 'depart From what that Faith has written in my heart.'[36]

It is one of many ironies in the *Man of Law's Tale* that the Man of Law appears oblivious to the fact that this declaration is a grotesque parallel to Constance's own role as Christian heroine, who goes through the rest of the story prepared to die for her faith. Successive episodes of the story show Constance drifting in her rudderless boat over a period of many years, driven from one hostile pagan shore to another, and suffering a series of unmerited trials from which she is repeatedly preserved by her faith in God. In the course of these adventures, problems in the internal logic of the story become increasingly apparent, so much so that gradually even the Man of Law himself begins to be aware of them. None of the sufferings of Constance are presented as trials of her faith, after the fashion of the story of Job. Instead, the Man of Law presents them as trials of the justice of God, and tries to explain why that justice seems to permit the punishment of someone who is innocent of all crime.

Sometimes it seems to the Sergeant that the story is merely an illustration of the operation of the fates written in the stars. But when he denounces the stars, his denunciation implicitly calls in question a fundamental axiom of the ideal of justice, that the 'higher should rule the lower.' At other times, he tries to see his story as merely an illustration of the harsh facts of life, especially the life of women. In this mood he makes Constance herself say, 'Woman is a thrall, Disposed and ruled over by men in all.'[37] Still another explanation he offers is the power of Satan, who, he claims, works through the sultan's mother as he worked through Eve and brought about the Fall of Man.[38]

As often as possible, however, the Sergeant tries to take the view of his story that is most in accord with the teaching of the church about the operations of divine justice. Like the good lawyer he believes himself to be, he asks himself, 'What law kept Constance then from drowning in the sea?' And he thinks he has all ready the answer to his own question:

God, to proclaim the wonders of His arm
By miracle through her, would have it so
And Christ who is the honey to all harm
Has chosen instruments, as well we know,
To work his purposes ...

But when he tries to explain what those 'purposes' are in this case, this expert in the law is forced to plead human ignorance: 'Our feeble sense grasps not the prudence of His providence.'[39]

In the source from which Chaucer took the tale he assigned to the Sergeant, the divine purpose of Constance's sufferings is clear enough. The story of Constance, as Chaucer found it, forms part of a chronicle of the growth of Christianity throughout history, written by a Dominican friar, Nicholas Trevet, for Princess Marie, daughter of Edward I, after she had entered a convent.[40] In this context the story plays a meaningful part because it tells how, after an aborted marriage to the sultan, Constance married another pagan king, Alla of England, whom she converted to the Christian faith. The child born of their union, in Trevet's version, ultimately became the 'most Christian of Roman emperors.'

In the Man of Law's version, however, the larger context of world history is absent, the end of the tale says nothing about the role of Constance's son in the growth of the power of Christianity, and the events are seen only from the perspective of the suffering Constance. In this context, Constance's marriage to King Alla is not part of some large scheme of divine providence, merely one happy episode in a sea of suffering, and even this episode is troubled by the hostility of Alla's mother, who forges a letter in Alla's name, commanding that Constance and her young child be set adrift again. Only later, after many years of still more suffering, are Constance and Alla reunited, and then their happiness is cut short by Alla's early death. The lesson of the Man of Law's long tale of the sufferings of a good woman is short and comfortless: 'Our felicities are of short life / And so it was with Alla and his wife.'[41]

As a result, far from justifying the ways of God to man, or, in this case, to woman, the tale the Sergeant tells raises the kinds of questions about divine justice that Trevet's version of the story was designed to answer. The Sergeant does believe in divine intervention in particular cases of outright blasphemy; the false witness who perjures himself by placing his hand on the Bible and accusing Constance of murder is struck so hard by the miraculous hand of God that his eyes pop out of his head and he falls dead on the ground. But when the Sergeant tries to understand the larger picture, to explain how divine justice could permit the suffering of such a paragon of goodness as Constance, he cannot find any answer. It is true that all who commit crimes in the story are eventually punished; even the Sultan's mother finally dies, executed by the command of the Roman emperor. But the Sergeant can find no justification for the unmerited sufferings of Constance, nor for the deaths of other innocent Christians such as those who died in the massacre at Constance's wedding to the Sultan. Worse still, it is not only that Constance is innocent; as the tale repeatedly shows, her very virtues, especially her submissiveness, are often the cause of the suffering inflicted by those who are her enemies.

The view of life in the *Man of Law's Tale* has little in common with the millenarian optimism that inspired the canon lawyers to envision the possibility of bringing about 'right order' on earth by following a pattern of justice laid up by God in heaven. Human law, as it appears in this tale, is as fallible as humans themselves, for it is created and administered by humans. Far from being the model of justice, ecclesiastical law is especially flawed, and the pope himself is fallible. The tale portrays the pope as disregarding one of the fundamental principles of canon law, when he arranges the marriage between Constance and the sultan without first assuring himself of Constance's consent.[42]

As for secular law, even when it tries to operate justly in accord with its own principles, it can convict an innocent person and let a guilty one go free. Forged letters often go undetected. A disappointed suitor almost succeeds in having Constance condemned for a murder he committed himself, because there are no eyewitnesses in the case, and he has planted the weapon, a bloody knife, in Constance's bed. Constance is saved, but only by a miracle of divine intervention, the hand of God which appears to strike the suitor dead as he perjures himself. Far from demonstrating the justice of human law, this divine intervention shows how often and how easily the practices of actual courts can lead to unjust convictions, when, as is more often the case, a miracle fails to occur.[43] Still another sign of the fallibility of human law is the way it varies from one culture to another. The sultan's mother is as strong a believer in the law of Islam as Constance is in the law of Christ. What appears to the Christian pope as the progress of the faith, by means of the conversion of the sultan, appears to the sultan's mother as sinful denial of the true faith, motivated merely by sexual desire.

The issues raised by the *Man of Law's Tale* suggest that the ideal of legal justice arising from the Papal Revolution as described by Harold Berman was not accepted unthinkingly by all members of medieval society. The fact that Chaucer assigns this tale, not just to a lawyer, but to a paragon of the legal profession of his time, shows that he meant the questions raised by the tale to be taken seriously.

It is not clear, however, how far we are meant to identify the Sergeant's views on these questions with Chaucer's own. In the introduction to the *Man of Law's Tale*, Chaucer has created a puzzle similar to the medieval logical paradoxes called *insolubilia* by making his Sergeant compare his tale with tales that Chaucer has told and distinguish the style of his own tale from 'Chaucer's' style: 'Though I plod on behind him, somewhat dim; / I speak plain prose and leave the rhymes to him.'[44] The problem is not just that the very lines in which he claims to be speaking in prose are themselves lines that rhyme. To make a fictitious character like the Sergeant criticize the 'rhymes' of the author of the very rhymed lines in which he speaks is to raise dizzying problems about the relations between the views of the character and the author who has created him.[45] Whatever we decide to make of this puzzle, we can see that Chaucer did not intend us to view his fictitious advocate the Sergeant as speaking for him in a simple and direct way. To arrive at Chaucer's own views, we would have to take into account all of the *Canterbury Tales* that deal with questions of crime and justice, including the one that Chaucer assigns to himself, the *Tale of Melibee*, an adaptation of a treatise by the thirteenth-century Italian jurist, Albertano of Brescia. (One reason why Chaucer's interest in the law has not yet received sufficient attention is that this tale has attracted few readers; in the translation by Coghill, it appears only in brief summary.) Even a necessarily brief account of two of the more familiar tales, however, will show how some of the fundamental questions of crime and justice raised in the *Man of Law's Tale* are further complicated and qualified when they are examined from other perspectives.

The *Wife of Bath's Prologue and Tale* raises in a radical form a question that is only indirectly implied in Constance's resignation to the position of woman in the scheme of medieval justice, as 'a thrall, disposed and ruled over by men in all.' In her prologue, the Wife of Bath attacks the very foundations of 'right order.' She claims that the view that women are naturally subordinate to men is not based on either divine justice or the inferior share of reason allotted to women by divine nature; this view is simply the result of the fact that all the books on these issues have been written by men. She rebels against all paternalistic authority, including the authority of books written by men, and in her tale proposes her own ideal of justice as an alternative to the ideal of 'right order' envisioned by men of the church.[46]

The Wife tells the story of a man who commits rape and is subsequently brought to trial, found guilty, and condemned to death. In real life, as Chaucer knew from personal experience, although statute law prescribed death for those found guilty of rape, conviction and capital punishment were uncommon. Many cases, like Chaucer's own, were settled out of court, on payment of a fine. A series of procedural requirements made it likely that an accusation of rape would not stand up in court, and even if the victim were successful in bringing a charge of rape, the defendant was usually prosecuted for the lesser charge of trespass. In those cases where there was an attempt to prosecute for the charge of rape, few juries after 1385 were willing to inflict capital punishment.[47] The successful prosecution for rape, literal application of statute law calling for capital punishment, and willingness of the jury to inflict the death penalty which appear in the *Wife of Bath's Tale* would have been seen by Chaucer's immediate audience not as a reflection of contemporary realities but as exaggerations appropriate to fiction, or perhaps relics of the harsh realities of the past. While the Wife herself sets the tale 'in ancient days,' the days of King Arthur and of 'fairy folk,'[48] she clearly regards it as an example of the superior form of justice women would contrive if they were given the power.

In the Wife's story of the trial and punishment of rape, the adjudication of the case is given over entirely to women. Although in his kingdom the customary penalty for rape is death, Arthur exercises his sovereign right as king to abrogate the severity of the law and he delegates authority in the case to Queen Guinevere and her ladies. This court of women agrees to remit all further punishment for the rapist knight if, in the course of a year and a day, he is able to learn the correct answer to the question, 'What is it that all women most desire?' This task is not simple. The knight must find an answer that will satisfy *all* the women of the court, and, as he discovers when he starts to inquire, women are by no means in agreement on this issue. Just before the allotted time is over, he meets an old hag who promises to give him the one universally satisfactory answer if he will promise in return to do whatever she next requires of him. (It is worth noting that even in fairyland, the principle of canon law, 'agreements must be kept,' is believed to be valid.)[49] The hag's correct answer is that women want 'sovereignty' most of all; they do not want any man to be above them. This answer saves the knight's life, but he is then forced to live out its full implications when the hag asks him to keep his promise and make her his wife.

The reformed rapist keeps his promise, but he cannot bring himself to consummate the marriage. When the hag fails in her attempts to use a moral lecture to persuade her new husband into performing his sexual duty, she then resorts to magic. She tells him she has the power to offer him two choices: he can have her ugly but faithful or beautiful but untrue. When in despair he says he will put himself wholly in her power and leave the choice to her, she announces that since she has finally achieved sovereignty, she will be both beautiful and true forever more.

The ending makes the story a model of poetic justice: a man who has violated a woman's body against her will is forced to submit to the will of women. Women make up the judge, jury, and counsel for the defence. And his punishment is not merely marriage, but total submission to the will of his new wife. As an example of an ideal principle of medieval criminal justice, the tale also has merit: it illustrates the principle quoted from St Thomas Aquinas that punishment makes people 'good.'

The poetic justice of the Wife's tale is so neat that it is possible to overlook the radical nature of the claim it makes for the Wife's kind of criminal justice. The Wife's vision of perfect justice on earth, once woman is granted unconditional sovereignty, is a parody of a number of medieval political and legal theories of absolute sovereignty that were proposed seriously in the Middle Ages. For example, we can see in her claim to offer full absolution from both the punishment and the guilt of his crime, on condition that he accept her as infallible sovereign, a fairy-tale variant on the similar claims of the pope.[50] The kind of submission represented by the reformed rapist as new-made husband is a parody of the submission traditionally recommended to wives: in accepting the wife's claim that she has power to remain beautiful forevermore, he is submitting not only his body and his will but also his reason to her authority. Any man who could so far abdicate his own powers of reason as to believe that his wife could remain forever beautiful would evidently be a big enough fool to believe that she would be true forever as well.[51] There is no question that Chaucer himself took the Wife's fairy-tale seriously as a fable of ideal criminal justice; the ending, like the ending of the *Man of Law's Tale*, deconstructs the ideal of justice the tale is told to support.

The last tale to be discussed here serves further to undercut the view of justice proposed by the *Wife of Bath's Tale* and to raise in a still different form some of the issues involved in the tale of the Man of Law. The Clerk of Oxford tells a story that takes up the issue where the Wife leaves off. In his tale, Walter, a young marquis of Lombardy, marries a poor girl named Griselda on the condition that she will grant him what the Wife of Bath would call unconditional sovereignty. Griselda agrees and lives up fully to her agreement. But instead of being content to live happily after, the marquis is moved to test the limits of his wife's obedience, by telling her it is his will to have their children, first the daughter, then the son, put to death. Just as submissive as Constance in the *Man of Law's Tale* or as the reformed rapist in the *Wife of Bath's Tale*, Griselda consents. She never argues with her husband and she never takes any measures to save her children. It is only when she finally also agrees to let him cast her out of the house so that he may take a new wife that Walter brings his experiment in sovereignty to an end. He brings back the children she thought had been killed, explains that he did not wish to cast her off after all, and claims that his only motive was to assure himself of her complete submission to his sovereign will.

The Clerk offers two morals to this unpleasant story, both of which serve as oblique comments on the tales of suffering and obedience told by the Wife and the Man of Law. The first moral is that the obedience of Griselda should be a model of the obedience we all owe to God.

> For since a woman showed such patience to
> A mortal man, how much the more we ought
> To take in patience all that God may do![52]

By a pattern we have seen in the other tales, however, the Clerk's tale itself calls in question the attitude towards divine justice the Clerk claims to be supporting. This moral would be more appropriate to the tale of Constance than to the tale of Griselda; unlike Constance, Griselda is forced not only to suffer but to perform injustice, to consent to criminal and unnatural acts, the murder of her own children. For the one act of homicide that Constance commits, the drowning of a knight who tries to rape her, she has the justification of self-defence (as well as the assistance of the Blessed Virgin Mary). But Griselda has no such justification for the murders she believes she is consenting to, except the vow of obedience to her husband. Griselda's obedience raises questions not only about the merits of absolute sovereignty but even about the fundamental principle that 'agreements must be kept.'[53] And unlike the model of criminal justice proposed in the *Wife of Bath's Tale*, the discipline to which one spouse subjects the other does not, in the *Clerk's Tale* teach the subject spouse how to be 'good.' Like the sufferings of Constance, this kind of discipline does not teach Griselda anything, because her obedience is already complete and demonstrated repeatedly in both words and actions. The testing of Griselda's obedience thus does not, by punishing her, make her 'good'; instead, her obedience to her husband makes her an accessory to what appears at the time to be the crime of murder.

The analogy underlying this moral, the husband as the image of God, is an analogy derived from the ideal of 'right order' described by Berman. But, as the *Clerk's Tale* shows, this ideal analogy does not hold in practice. The motivation for the rule of God may be ideal justice, but the motivation for Walter's actions is all too human. In terms of medieval psychology, it is the lust for power that Augustine called *libido dominandi*, which is endemic in all of fallen humanity and which, according to Augustine's analysis in the *City of God*, is bound to corrupt all human of power to some extent.[54] Far from illustrating a major premise of the ideal of 'right order,' that the husband's rule is modelled on the rule of God, the *Clerk's Tale* exposes the fallacy behind this premise, anticipating Lord Acton's well-known modern formulation, 'Power tends to corrupt and absolute power corrupts absolutely.'

The second moral proposed by the Clerk for his tale implies an alternative ideal of justice, based on the principle of the lawful right of resistance to unjust authority. In the prologue to her tale, the Wife of Bath described how she repeatedly refused to submit to any of her five husbands. In what he calls a 'song' dedicated to the Wife of Bath 'and all her sect,' the Clerk urges all 'noble wives' to avoid the humility of a Griselda, to take as their model the Wife of Bath herself and refuse to submit to the authority of their husbands.

> Arch-wives, stand up, defend your board and bed!
> Stronger than camels as you are, prevail!
> Don't swallow insults, offer them instead.[55]

The Clerk is not entirely serious in his recommendation; he announces before he begins this 'song' that he is no longer speaking in earnest. But behind his playful praise of the Wife's sturdy independence is the serious suggestion that unconditional obedience is no more likely to bring about ideal justice than is absolute sovereignty of the sort requested by the hag in the *Wife of Bath's Tale* and enjoyed by the husband in the *Clerk's Tale*. The Clerk is making a distinction between the views expressed by the Wife's tale and her prologue. The kind of sovereignty the Wife envisions for the married hag in her *Tale* is simply another form of the kind of tyranny practised by the husband in the *Clerk's Tale*. But the Wife's own natural instinct to rebel revealed in her *Prologue* – the very natural instinct which the church regarded as a sign that women need the rule of men – is seen by Chaucer's Clerk as a valuable basis for an important safeguard of the system of justice, the subject's traditional right to resist the authority of a tyrant.[56]

On the basis of these three cases from the *Canterbury Tales*, it is not possible to conclude with a systematic account of Chaucer's own views of crime and justice. Indeed, it appears that Chaucer was seriously doubtful about the value and practical application of any systematic view of justice such as the 'right order' promoted by the Papal Revolution. But we cannot be sure of Chaucer's own views on this matter, especially since he has cleverly arranged it so that each tale qualifies the views set forth in the others. My summary account here does not begin to exhaust the various ways in which Chaucer uses the accounts of crime in the *Canterbury Tales* to undercut and qualify one another. His own ideal of law, his views on its practical applications, and his personal attitude towards the ideal of 'right order' celebrated by Berman as the basis of the Western legal tradition, all remain elusive. He seems determined to avoid making, in his own voice as author, the kind of clear and authoritative pronouncements on these subjects that the medieval period called *auctoritates*.

One legacy of Chaucer to the Papal Revolution Berman describes is clear, however. In envisioning a discussion of justice that proceeds by means of tales which seem to contradict and qualify one another, Chaucer was following the method of the classic textbook of canon law, the *Decretum* of Gratian, also known as *The Concordance of Discordant Canons* (*c* 1140). In that work, Gratian established a habit of thought fundamental, not only to canon law but, as Berman argues persuasively, to other forms of legal thought as well. By setting over against one another conflicting rules of law, Gratian demonstrated his belief that by the use of reason some principle could be found to reconcile or adjust the contradictions or adjudicate the conflicting rights.[57] The example of Chaucer's *Canterbury Tales* suggests that a good many others in the period may have experienced this habit of finding conflicts and contradictions in the legal traditions and practices in which they lived to be a fundamental inheritance of the Papal Revolution. Chaucer provides evidence of the other side of the inheritance of medieval legal thought which Berman celebrates. In addition to a coherent ideal of law as 'right order,' the medieval legal tradition, as experienced by those like Chaucer who felt its effects in their daily lives, seems to have bequeathed to us a number of questions and doubts about various components of that ideal, questions and doubts that are being raised with increasing frequency in modern legal thought.

Notes

Patricia J. Eberle received her PHD from Harvard University in 1977. Her publications include notes for the *Man of Law's Tale* in *The Riverside Chaucer* and *Vision and Design in John Gower's Confessio Amantis*. She is now finishing a study, 'Self-Reflecting Mirrors: Interpretation Theory in Medieval Literary Visions.'

1 Joseph Allen Hornsby 'Chaucer and Medieval English Criminal Law and Criminal Procedure' in his *Chaucer and the Law* (Norman, Okla: Pilgrim Books 1988) 105–58, is the fullest discussion of crime in the *Canterbury Tales* to date. Hornsby discusses felony law, especially treason and rape, and aspects of criminal procedure as they are reflected in Chaucer's text; his bibliography includes full references to previous works on the topic. For a discussion of crime as a social and legal problem in the period, see J.G. Bellamy *Crime and Public Order in England in the Later Middle Ages* (London: Routledge & Kegan Paul 1973). On the larger subject of literature and law in medieval England see John A. Alford 'Literature and Law in Medieval England' *PMLA* 92 (1977) 941–51 and the basic bibliography of the subject: John A. Alford and D. Seniff *Literature and Law in the Middle Ages: A Bibliography of Scholarship* (New York: Garland 1984) esp items 187–236 on the law in Chaucer.

2 For an account of the difficulties created by medieval ways of defining and prosecuting crime, see *Proceedings before the Justices of the Peace in the Fourteenth and Fifteenth Centuries, Edward III to Richard II* ed Bertha Haven Putnam, with commentary by Theodore F.T. Plucknett. (London: Spottiswoode, Ballantyne & Co 1938). Plucknett notes, 'The legal vocabulary has changed so radically that the terms of modern criminal law cannot be applied as a general rule to medieval material ... It is only when trial takes precedence over pleading and process that

lawyers will tackle the problem of what facts will have to be proved in order to demonstrate that a particular crime has been committed – in other words, to frame a definition of that crime. In our period the trial holds a very minor place, however, and so we are dealing with material which contemporaries treated primarily from the procedural aspect' (cxxxiv). In these records of courts like the one Chaucer attended as a member of the commission of the peace, Plucknett points out that crimes were seldom defined as such; instead 'statements were made against a person in narrative form and a process issued against him, without giving a technical name to his crime and without disclosing (save in rare instances) which of the alleged facts constitute his crime' (cxxxvi).

3 For a good account of the complexities of procedure created by the overlapping of court jurisdictions during the later Middle Ages, see D.J. Guth 'Enforcing Late-Medieval Law: Patterns in Litigation during Henry VII's Reign' in J.H. Baker ed *Legal Records and the Historian* (London: Royal Historical Society 1978) 80–96.

4 *History of Criminal Law*, quoted in Theodore F.T. Plucknett *A Concise History of the Common Law* 5th ed (London: Butterworths 1956) 421

5 According to the *Latin Dictionary* of Charlton Lewis and Charles Short (1879; repr Oxford: Clarendon Press 1966), the word *crimen* is a contracted form of *cernimen*, meaning literally 'a judicial decision' (from *cernere*, 'to decide'). In classical antiquity, *crimen* was used in transferred senses as well, to refer either to the charge brought or to the crime committed. In later Latin (c AD 200–550), the transferred sense of 'crime' was extended to cover the Christian concept of sin; see eg, *Mediae Latinitatis Lexicon Minus* ed J.F. Niermeyer (Leiden: E.J. Brill 1976). The Middle English word 'crime' could be applied either to an act against the secular law or to a violation of religious prescriptions; see *Middle English Dictionary* part C6 ed Hans Kurath and Sherman M. Kuhn (Ann Arbor, Mich: University of Michigan Press 1960).

6 On the use of *crimen* to refer to sin see Morton W. Bloomfield *The Seven Deadly Sins* ([Lansing, Mich]: Michigan State University Press 1952 repr 1967) 97 and 377 n383. Other Latin terms, *culpa, delictum, peccatum,* and *vitium*, were also borrowed from legal language to apply to the religious concept of sin; on these terms see Lewis and Short *Latin Dictionary* and Niermeyer *Mediae Latinitatis Lexicon Minus*. Although words from other linguistic registers, such as medicine, were sometimes used metaphorically to describe sin as a disease (see Bloomfield 28) legal language provided the richest source of terms for the growing

language of sin in the Middle Ages. Medieval penitential use of *crimen* to refer to a habit of mind is an ancestor of the modern legal concept of the 'guilty mind' (*mens rea*), but differs from the modern concept in that the mental state alone could be viewed as 'criminal,' even in the absence of a guilty action. For a good discussion of the complexities involved in the modern legal concept of *mens rea* see Leo Katz *Bad Acts and Guilty Minds: Conundrums of the Criminal Law* (Chicago and London: University of Chicago Press 1987) 4–5, 165–209.

7 For a discussion of these points and their larger consequences, both in the Middle Ages and in modern times, see Harold J. Berman *Law and Revolution: The Formation of the Western Legal Tradition* (Cambridge, Mass, and London, England: Harvard University Press 1983) 186–94 and 598–9. The quotation translated by Berman from Lombard, '*Non enim consisteret peccatum, si interdictio non fuisset,*' is taken from *Sententiarum Libri Quatuor* Liber II Dist XXV.I, '*Quid sit peccatum*' in J.-P. Migne *Patrologia Latina* 192 (Paris: Garnier Fratres 1880) col 734.

8   That boldely dide execucioun
     In punysshynge of fornicacioun,
     Of wicchecraft, and eek of bawderye,
     Of diffamacioun, and avowtrye,
     Of chirche reves, and of testamentz,
     Of contractes and of lakke of sacramentz,
     Of usure, and of symonye also.
     But certes, lecchours dide he grettest wo;
     They sholde syngen if that they were hent;
     And smale tytheres weren foule yshent.

Unless otherwise noted, the translation of Chaucer's *Canterbury Tales* used throughout is by Nevill Coghill (Harmondsworth, Middlesex: Penguin Books 1951 and often reprinted); see pp 311–12 for the passage quoted. For some of the terms in the original Middle English, Coghill's translation is not quite precise enough: Chaucer's 'chirche reves' refers to theft of church property of any kind, not just spoliation of 'church endowment'; and Chaucer refers to 'lakke' rather than 'disregard' of sacraments, implying that the archdeacon, who conducted the ecclesiastical court for a local area, regarded not only acts of disrespect but also failures to observe any of the sacraments, most commonly confession and communion, as crimes. For the original Middle English text, see *The Riverside Chaucer* 3rd ed, gen ed Larry D. Benson (Boston: Houghton Mifflin 1987) p 123, ll 1303–10. References to this edition will be cited by the standard abbreviations to Chaucer's works and line numbers.

9 *ParsT* 164. For the meanings of the terms, see *Middle English Dictionary* part E3.

10 The idea of Christ as 'advocate' was based on the passage from Scripture, 'If any man sin, we have an advocate (*advocatum*) with the Father, Jesus Christ the just' (1 John 2:1). The idea of intercession as legal advocacy was later extended to include Mary and the saints as well. For a reflection of the idea of Mary as 'advocate' in Chaucer, see the *Second Nun's Prologue* 67–70 and *An ABC* 102–4. For the judicial meaning of *advocatus* in classical Latin, see Lewis and Short *Latin Dictionary*; in post-Augustan Latin, the meaning of the term as one who 'speaks for' (rather than merely giving advice to) a party in a lawsuit was well established. This is the sense from which the medieval Latin term is derived; see Niermeyer *Lexicon*.

11 The Retractions appear in Coghill 507–8, and in *The Riverside Chaucer* 328. For the range of meaning of *gilt*, see *The Middle English Dictionary* part G1, ed Sherman Kuhn and John Reidy; note that the plural use suggests that in the medieval period 'guilt' could refer, like 'crime,' to an individual instance as well as to a generalized state.

12 'Cristes lawe deere' *MLT* 237; Coghill 146

13 See Berman *Law and Revolution* 85–119. Charles Radding in *The Origins of Medieval Jurisprudence: Pavia and Bologna, 850–1150* (New Haven: Yale University Press 1988), disagrees with Berman's view that the 'Papal Revolution' was the principal cause for the changes in thinking about law that took place in this period and argues that many of these changes were the end product of a long process of development of the discipline of law in the period, a process that began with the appearance of a group of professional judges in the ninth century. He does agree with Berman, however, that 'the eleventh century marked the beginning of the modern western legal tradition'; see Charles Radding *A World Made by Men: Cognition and Society, 400–1200* (Chapel Hill: University of North Carolina Press 1985) 173. For a brief and authoritative account of the important changes in legal thinking and practice that began with the rediscovery of Justinian's *Digest* in this period, see Stephan Kuttner 'The Revival of Jurisprudence' in *Renaissance and Renewal in the Twelfth Century* ed Robert L. Benson and Giles Constable with Carol D. Lanham (Cambridge, Mass: Harvard University Press 1982) 299–323.

14 On 'right order' see Berman *Law and Revolution* 116–18.

15 For a discussion of this principle, with reference to the laws governing
the physical universe, see John Gower *Confessio Amantis* vols 2–3 of *The
English Works of John Gower* ed G.C. Macaulay, 4 vols EETS ES 82–3
(London: Oxford University Press for the Early English Text Society
1901) bk 7, iv, head note and ll 634–69. According to M.-D. Chenu, from
the middle of the twelfth century onwards, 'the "hierarchical"
conception of the universe would cast over men's minds a spell
comparable to that cast by the scientific mythos of evolution in the
nineteenth century'; see Chenu 'Nature and Man: The Renaissance of
the Twelfth Century' in *Nature, Man, and Society in the Twelfth Century:
Essays on New Theological Perspectives in the Latin West* ed and trans
Jerome Taylor and Lester K. Little (Chicago and London: University
of Chicago Press 1968; repr 1979) 23. Walter Ullmann discusses the
'fundamental' importance played by the title in canon law *'De maioritate
et obedientia,'* dealing with the relations of inferiors to superiors, in
medieval legal and political thought; *Law and Politics in the Middle Ages:
An Introduction to the Sources of Medieval Political Ideas* (Ithaca: Cornell
University Press 1975) 139. This concept of hierarchical order informs
the discussion of law in Aquinas' *Summa Theologica* 1–2, questions 90–7;
the very nature of law as Aquinas understands it involves this
relationship between 'higher and lower': it is 'an ordinance of a
superior *(praesidentis)* to his subordinates *(subditis)*, with the purpose of
making those subject to the law duly obedient *(ut subditi legi sint bene
obedientes)'* (1–2, q 92 a 1 ad 4, my trans).
16 Coghill, p 19; *GP* 1, l 17. For a summary account of the events of
Becket's life and some notice of the cult associated with his martyrdom
and his shrine, see Austin Lane Poole *From Domesday Book to Magna
Carta, 1087–1216* 2nd ed *The Oxford History of England* gen ed Sir George
Clark 3 (Oxford: Clarendon Press 1955; repr 1958, 1964) 197– 215. Poole
notes that each year, at Canterbury, the death scene of Becket was re-
enacted, and the legal issues involved were still remembered. For a
discussion of another legacy of Becket's opposition to the Constitutions
of Clarendon, the principle of 'double jeopardy,' see Martin L.
Friedland *Double Jeopardy* (Oxford: Clarendon Press 1969) 326–32.
17 Berman *Law and Revolution* 20–2, 25–41
18 '... per hoc quod aliquis incipit assuefieri ad vitandum mala et ad
implendum bona propter metum poenae, perducitur quandoque ad hoc
quod delectabiliter et ex propria voluntate hoc faciat. Et secundum
hoc, lex etiam puniendo perducit ad hoc quod homines sint boni.'
Summa Theologica 1–2, q 92a 2 ad 4 (Madrid: Biblioteca de Autores

Cristianos 1961–65) 2:600. The modern English translation is from *The 'Summa Theologica' of St. Thomas Aquinas* trans by the Fathers of the English Dominican Province, 2nd ed 22 vols (London: Burns, Oates, & Washbourne 1927) 8:27. Aquinas derives his conclusion from Aristotle, but it is worth noting a similar passage from the *Institutes* of Ulpianus quoted in the opening section of Justinian's *Digest* (1.1): 'we desire to make men good, not only by putting them in fear of penalties (*non solum metu poenarum*), but also by appealing to them through rewards ...'; see *The Digest of Justinian* 2 vols trans Charles Henry Munro (Cambridge: Cambridge University Press 1904) 1:3; and the edition of the Latin *Digesta* by Theodore Mommsen in *Corpus Iuris Civilis* 1 (Berlin: Weidmann 1893) 1. Modern theories of criminal punishment as rehabilitation have affinities with Aquinas' view.

19 A good example of this kind of thinking, which shows its consequences for the role of the head of the household, is the very influential treatise on government, *De regimine principum* by Giles of Rome, also called Egidius Colonna (*c* 1247–1316); book II, one third of the entire treatise, is devoted to 'The Government of the Family.' A modern edition of the French translation of Henri de Gauchi, made in 1296, includes discussion of the main ideas and the importance of the treatise: *Li Livres du Gouvernement des Rois* ed Samuel P. Molenaer (New York: AMS Press 1966).

20 P.J. Fitzgerald *Criminal Law and Punishment*, Clarendon Law Series (Oxford: Clarendon Press 1962) 82, 203. The medieval theory that the courts are, in a sense, guardians of morals, is still prevalent, however; it is frequently urged in obscenity cases, for example.

21 For a detailed account of this aspect of Wyclif's theory, see Michael Wilks 'Predestination, Property, and Power: Wyclif's Theory of Dominion and Grace' *Studies in Church History* vol 2 ed G.J. Cuming (London: Nelson 1965) 220–36, esp. 228–9.

22 The tradition that Chaucer had some professional legal training is accepted by Edith Rickert 'Was Chaucer a Student at the Inner Temple?' in *The Manly Anniversary Studies in Language and Literature* [no ed] (Chicago: The University of Chicago Press 1923) 20–31. D.S. Bland 'Chaucer and the Inns of Court: A Re-Examination' *English Studies* 33 (1952) 145–55, hesitates to accept it as more than a 'plausible theory.' Joseph Hornsby reviews the evidence in light of what has since been discovered about the nature of legal training in fourteenth-century England and the role of the Inns of Court and makes three decisive points: first, there is no good evidence that Chaucer was ever in

residence at one of the Inns; second, the Inns of Court in Chaucer's
time were places of residence, not institutions of learning; and third,
none of the records of Chaucer's legal activities show him performing
in a capacity that required professional legal training; see Hornsby
'Was Chaucer Educated at the Inns of Court?' *The Chaucer Review* 22
(1988) 255–68; repr in revised form in *Chaucer and the Law* 7–30.

23 For a collection of all the legal records remaining of Chaucer's life, see
Chaucer Life-Records ed Martin M. Crow and Clair C. Olson (Oxford:
Clarendon Press 1966). For records of Chaucer's service as on
commissions of the peace, see 348–63; for the charge of *raptus* see 343–7.
The charge of *raptus* has been discussed by P.R. Watts 'The Strange
Case of Geoffrey Chaucer and Cecilia Chaumpaigne' *Law Quarterly
Review* 63 (1947) 491–515, who argues that the records indicate that
Chaucer payed indemnification to avoid a trial, and by T.F.T.
Plucknett 'Chaucer's Escapade' *Law Quarterly Review* 64 (1948) 33– 6,
who argues that no evidence was offered for the charge and that
Chaucer was released from it. Other relevant legal records include the
records of an action of trespass and contempt brought against Chaucer
in the Court of the King's Bench (*Life-Records* 340–2), records of a case
of abduction in 1387, in which Chaucer served as justice *ad inquirendum*
(375–83), and records of a commission of inquiry into a robbery in 1390,
in which Chaucer lost his horse, goods, and twenty pounds from the
King's treasury. See also Hornsby *Chaucer and the Law* 20–30 for a
discussion of Chaucer's involvement with the law that is informed
by the most recent research on legal statutes and procedures of the
time.

24   A slyer boye nas noon in Engelond;
      For subtilly he hadde his espialle,
      That taughte hym wel wher that hym myght availle.
      (*FrT* 1322–4; Coghill 312)

25   'My wages been ful streite and ful smale.
      My lord is hard to me and daungerous,
      And myn office is ful laborous,
      And therfore by extorciouns I lyve.
      For sothe, I take al that men wol me yive.
      Algate, by sleyghte or by violence,
      Fro yeer to yeer I wynne al my dispence.'   (*FrT* 1426–32; Coghill 315)

26 For a detailed summary and critical evaluation of the extant
    information on the early history of the Order of the Coif, see J.H.
    Baker *The Order of Serjeants at Law* Selden Society, Supplementary

Series vol 5 (London: Selden Society 1984). Baker makes extensive use of Fortescue's work, but notes that it is not entirely reliable for the history of the order in the fourteenth century. Hornsby *Chaucer and the Law* 71 argues that the credentials given to Chaucer's sergeant are exaggerated and that in Richard II's reign sergeants at law did not have the status and expertise they had acquired by Fortescue's time.

27   In termes hadde he caas and doomes alle
      That from the tyme of kyng William were falle.

      ...

      And every statute koude he pleyn by rote.
      (*GP* 323–4, 327, and notes p 812; Coghill 28)
      The reference to 'termes' is a notorious crux: one possible interpretation is that he could recite in precise legal terminology all the cases and judgments since William the Conqueror; another interpretation takes the word to refer to the records of cases in the Court of Common Pleas (called Year Books), of which the Sergeant possesses a complete set. The Year Books, however, only recorded various pleadings, both successful and unsuccessful, not the eventual judgments or 'doomes.'

28   Sir Frederick Pollock and Frederick William Maitland, *The History of English Law before the Time of Edward I*, 2 vols (Cambridge: Cambridge University Press 1895) 1:82

29   On the Year Books see Albert C. Baugh 'Chaucer's Serjeant of the Law and the Year Books' in *Mélanges de langue et de littérature du moyen âge et de la renaissance offerts à Jean Frappier* 2 vols (Geneva: Droz 1970) 1: 65–76 and William Craddock Bolland *A Manual of Year Book Studies* (Cambridge: Cambridge University Press 1925).

30   For the expression 'a Canterbury tale (or story)' as equivalent to a tall tale, see J.A.H. Murray ed *A New English Dictionary on Historical Principles* 2 (Oxford: Clarendon Press 1893) 80; the earliest citation given for this usage is 1575, but it may well have been in use considerably earlier.

31   'Nowher so bisy a man as he ther nas, / And yet he semed bisier than he was' (*GP* 321–2; Coghill 28).

32   For the argument that the portrait was modelled on Thomas Pynchbek, a sergeant who was often justice of assize during the period 1376–88, see John Matthews Manly *Some New Light on Chaucer: Lectures Delivered at the Lowell Institute* (New York: Holt 1926; repr Gloucester, Mass: Peter Smith 1959) 147–57 and W.F. Bolton 'Pynchbeck and the Chaucer Circle in the Law Reports and Records of 11–13 Richard II' *Modern Philology* 84 (1987) 401–7; for the argument that in many ways

the portrait is designed to be viewed as an exaggeration, see Jill Mann *Chaucer and Medieval Estates Satire* (Cambridge: Cambridge University Press 1973) 86–7.

33 For the place of sergeants in the history of the legal profession, see Alan Harding *The Law Courts of Medieval England, Historical Problems: Studies and Documents* gen ed G.R. Elton no 18 (London: George Allen & Unwin 1973) 111–13 and Harding *A Social History of English Law* (Harmondsworth, Middlesex: Penguin 1966) 167–93.

34 Coghill 140–1; *MLT* 46–96

35 Two important discussions of the relation between the *Man of Law's Tale* and the law came to my attention after I had written this study. Paul A. Olson, in 'The Lawyer's Tale and the History of Christian English Law' *The Canterbury Tales and the Good Society* (Princeton: Princeton University Press 1986) 85–103, discusses the tale as Chaucer's critique of the Lawyer's 'absolutist vision of governing based on a kingship directed and protected by God,' and sees this critique as directed at the absolutist pretensions of Richard II. Carolyn Dinshaw, in 'The Law of Man and Its "Abhomynacions"' *Chaucer's Sexual Poetics* (Madison: University of Wisconsin Press 1989) 88–112, argues that 'The Man of Law ... incarnates patriarchal ideology and its expressed system of law' and his tale provides an opportunity of observing the limitations and inequities created by this system and ideology, especially for women.

36 'The lyf shal rather out of my body sterte / Or Makometes lawe out of myn herte!' (*MLT* 335–6; Coghill 148).

37 'Wommen are born to thraldom and penance / And to been under mannes governance' (*MLT* 286–7; Coghill 147). Chaucer's language is much stronger than the Coghill translation at this point, because it implies that there is an inherent connection between being 'under' in the hierarchical order and being in 'thraldom' or the state of a slave.

38 Coghill 149; *MLT* 365–71

39   God liste to shewe his wonderful myracle
      In hire, for we sholde seen his myghty werkis;
      Crist, which that is to every harm triacle,
      By certeine meenes ofte, as knowen clerkis,
      Dooth thyng for certein ende that ful derk is
      To mannes wit, that for oure ignorance
      Ne konne noght knowe his prudent purveiance.   (*MLT* 477–83;
      Coghill 153)

40 For a discussion of Trevet (also spelled Trivet) and the text of the portion of this chronicle that served as a source for Chaucer, see Margaret Schlauch 'The Man of Law's Tale' in *Sources and Analogues of Chaucer's Canterbury Tales* ed W.F. Bryan and Germaine Dempster (New York: Humanities Press 1958) 155–206.

41 '... litel while in joye or plesance / Lasteth the blisse of Alla with Custance' (*MLT* 1140–1; Coghill 172). Coghill's translation is more general than Chaucer's text, which makes no mention of 'our' felicities but simply says that 'the blisse' of Alla with Custance lasted only a 'litel while.' Coghill's version does, however, echo lines earlier in the text, which Chaucer borrowed from *The Miseries of the Human Condition (De miseriae humanae condicionis)* of Pope Innocent III:

O sodeyn wo, that evere art successour
To worldly blisse, spreynd with bitterness,
The end of the joye of oure worldly labour!
Wo occupieth the fyn of our gladnesse. (*MLT* 421–4; Coghill 151)

42 On the canon laws relating to marriage, see Berman *Law and Revolution* 226–30.

43 For a discussion of the relation between the trial scene in the tale and medieval English criminal procedures, see Hornsby *Chaucer and the Law* 145–8.

44 'Thogh I come after hym with hawebake. / I speke in prose, and lat him rymes make' (Coghill 141; MLT 96). The notes (854) give a brief account of the repeated attempts of Chaucer scholars to solve the problems created by this line. Many medieval *insolubilia*, such as the famous Liar paradox, involved problems created by self-reference in a similar way and were designed to test the limits of logical analysis; see Paul Vincent Spade *The Medieval Liar; A Catalogue of the **Insolubilia**-literature* (Toronto: Pontifical Institute of Mediaeval Studies 1975) and *Lies, Language and Logic in the Late Middle Ages* (London: Variorum 1988).

45 This device is a medieval equivalent of what modern theorists call the *mise en abyme* and, in a similar way, it raises the question of the truth function of a work of fiction. On the *mise en abyme* see Lucien Dällenbach *The Mirror in the Text* trans Jeremy Whiteley and Emma Hughes (Chicago: University of Chicago Press 1989).

46 The question of whether the Wife's ideal should be regarded as a feminist ideal *avant la lettre* has been raised repeatedly in Chaucer criticism; for a perceptive review of the issue by a modern feminist

critic, see Carolyn Dinshaw '"Glose/bele chose": The Wife of Bath
and Her Glossators' in *Chaucer's Sexual Poetics* 113–31.

47 See the full discussion of the law of rape in fourteenth-century
England, and its relevance for the *Wife of Bath's Tale* in Hornsby
Chaucer and the Law 115–20. Hornsby's account supersedes the discussion
of the crime of rape presented in the article by P.R. Watts cited in n23
above. Watts's study is based on twelfth- and thirteenth-century legal
treatises that prescribed the harsh punishments of blinding and death
by castration, and he does not take into account the three Statutes of
Westminster (1275, 1285, and 1382) nor the available records of actual
late fourteenth-century cases, which are discussed by Hornsby.

48 Coghill 299; *WBT* 857–9. There may well be irony in the implication that
capital punishment for rape, as assigned by the first Statute of Westminster (1275), is so rarely enforced in the late fourteenth century that
it seems to belong to the age of Arthur or the world of fairyland.

49 For a summary account of the canon law of contracts and the principle
pacta sunt servanda, derived from the principle of penitential discipline
that promises are binding, see Berman 245–50.

50 The terms 'infallibility' and 'sovereignty' do not have the same
meaning, as Brian Tierney points out in *Origins of Papal Infallibility
1150–1350: A Study on the Concepts of Infallibility, Sovereignty and Tradition in
the Middle Ages* vol 6 of *Studies in the History of Christian Thought* ed
Heiko A. Oberman (Leiden: E.J. Brill 1972) 2 and passim. The Wife
arrogates to herself powers that only the most extreme proponents of
papal absolutism in the later Middle Ages would endorse.

51 For a witty account of the irrationality of the alternatives offered by
the hag to her husband and the fairy-tale ending of the story, see
Theodore Silverstein 'Wife of Bath and the Rhetoric of Enchantment;
or, How to Make a Hero See in the Dark' *Modern Philology* 58 (1969–71)
153–73.

52   For sith a womman was so pacient
        Unto a mortal man, wel moore us oghte
        Receyven al in gree that God us sent;   (*CIT* 1149–51; Coghill 371)

53 As Berman notes, 'in order that morality might be safeguarded, it was
not only necessary that the promisor should have an object but that
this object should be reasonable and equitable' (*Law and Revolution* 247).
The obedience Griselda shows her husband obviously is neither
'reasonable' nor 'equitable' when it involves consent to what she
believes to be the murder of her children.

54 In the preface to book I, Augustine describes the central theme of the *City of God* as a contrast between the heavenly city, which is ruled with justice by God, and the city of the world, in which the so-called rulers are themselves the slaves of the 'lust for domination' (*dominandi libido dominatur*); see St Augustine *The City of God against the Pagans* vol 1 trans George E. McCracken, Loeb Classical Library (Cambridge, Mass: Harvard University Press and London: William Heinemann 1957; repr 1966) 12–13.

55   Ye archewyves, stondeth at defense,

     Syn ye be strong as is a greet camaille;

     Ne suffreth nat that men yow doon offense.   (*CIT* 1195–7)

The rhyme 'defense/offense' in Chaucer's text alludes more clearly to the right of resistance than is conveyed by Coghill's translation. For the full song, see *CIT* 1176–1212; Coghill 372–3. The reference to the 'secte,' as the note to line 1171 suggests, may well be to a legal *secta*, the group of persons who appear in a local court to support a plaintiff and attest the good faith of his claims; see also Hornsby *Chaucer and the Law* 36.

56 For a succinct discussion of the developments of this tradition in the political thought of the later Middle Ages, see Jean Dunbabin 'Government' in *The Cambridge History of Medieval Political Thought, c.350 – c. 1450* ed J.H. Burns (Cambridge: Cambridge University Press 1988) 493–8.

57 Berman *Law and Revolution* 144–9; see also Stephan Kuttner *Harmony from Dissonance: An Interpretation of Medieval Canon Law*, Wimmer Lectures 10 (Latrobe, Pa: Archabbey Press 1960). This method was borrowed from methods of solving contradictions in scholastic philosophy, as both Berman and Kuttner point out.

BRIAN PARKER

A Fair Quarrel (1617), the Duelling Code, and Jacobean Law

Though *A Fair Quarrel* was successful in its own day (1617–20) and is peculiarly appropriate for a collection considering the relation of law to literature, no one is likely to claim that it is a great play or one that might be revived successfully in the modern theatre. One obvious reason for this is the dated nature of its central theme, duelling and, more specifically, its hair-splitting concern with what constitutes a 'fair quarrel.'

Happily, duelling is one problem contemporary society no longer faces, but before examining what it involved in the early seventeenth century, I should like to suggest that the play has more general aspects that are not irrelevant at this time. To start with, there are communities in all major cities at this time where *macho* codes of status, family 'honour,' and vendetta can still be encountered. These can complicate the psychological grounds for certain crimes, as well as the mind-sets of litigants, witnesses, juries, judges, and advocates within a trial. Moreover, the basic situation in *A Fair Quarrel* offers a parallel to any legal situation in which there is a distinct gap between the legal code and what popular opinion or prejudice believe, so that the emotional position of everyone concerned is to some degree unstable. For example, in current divorce proceedings the demand for legal redress is often clouded by both parties' feelings of shame and desire for reprisal rather than fair dealing, and there may well be wide discrepancies among the lawyers involved in a particular case about the amount and type of latitude that is permissible within matrimony – a feminist counsel may have to argue before a judge who happens to be a Catholic conservative, for instance; or vice versa. In any such situation, one is likely to encounter the same divided sympathies, ambiguities, corruptions of language, recourse to white lies, and unconscious self-deceptions as Thomas Middleton and William Rowley explore in *A Fair Quarrel*.

Besides such general implications there is also a more specific reason why the play is appropriate for a legal-literary analysis. It is one of the very few literary works (of any period) that have been directly connected to major legislation at the very highest level. Because of *A Fair Quarrel*, Middleton became involved with no less personages than Francis Bacon (by then Lord Chancellor of England, and one of the most brilliant minds of the English Renaissance) and with the monarch, James I himself. A year after *A Fair Quarrel* was performed, Middleton 'ghosted' an anonymous pamphlet entitled *The Peacemaker* (1618) which was published under the direct aegis of the king and borrowed heavily from one of Bacon's speeches to Star Chamber to deny the very existence of the concept of a 'fair quarrel.' Since this connection of Middleton with Bacon and James is indisputable,[1] there is also a possibility that some connection may have existed before the play was written, and that *A Fair Quarrel*, like *The Peacemaker*, was intended to embody the government's vehement opposition to duelling. A priori, however, this seems unlikely, because the play is not clear enough for such a purpose; not sufficiently one-sided, that is to say, to provide efficient propaganda (as is proven by the wide divergences in critics' interpretations of it). On the other hand, it was certainly popular in performances at James's court – the 1617 title-page says 'it was acted before the King,' and the records indicate two more command performances in 1620 – and this popularity with James himself will have to be borne in mind when we consider the play's attitude to duelling.

Another reason why *A Fair Quarrel* is unlikely to be revived is that it is flawed artistically by a certain looseness of structure and by unevenness of style. These reflect the fact that the play was a collaboration between two men of widely different literary talent. William Rowley, who was mainly responsible for the play's farcical sub-plot, was best known in his own day as a comic actor, whereas his collaborator, Thomas Middleton, was a professional writer of the first rank who is now recognized as one of the most important and original dramatists of the generation that followed Shakespeare's. And as it is Middleton's contribution to the play and his probable relations with the court of James that we shall mainly be concerned with, it is appropriate to sketch in very briefly those aspects of his career that bear directly on *A Fair Quarrel*.

Middleton's father, a London builder, sent his son to Oxford, but his career there was abruptly terminated when his father's death left him with insufficient funds to complete his degree. This plunged Middleton immediately into an anomalous position in the very class-conscious London of the early seventeenth century. Though he was always careful to style himself 'gentleman' on the title-pages of his published works, his status as a professional writer – especially one working mainly for the theatres – placed him at the very edge of social respectability. Not surprisingly, his drama as a whole reflects an acute and painfully ironic sense of class conflict and of what the gentry of the early seventeenth century considered socially acceptable.

After his father's death, Middleton's mother quickly and rashly remarried, allying herself to a fortune-hunting 'captain' whose efforts to get control of her property soon involved the whole family in a maelstrom of suits and counter–suits about the marriage settlement, inheritances, family loans, and – very appositely for the play – the widow's sexual reputation. Thus Middleton learned a lot about the law from (as it were) the wrong side of the desk, and is often satirical at the expense both of lawyers and of the Jacobean rage for litigation. This interest was also fostered, more obliquely, by the audience he initially wrote for. The first half of his career was spent writing city comedies about the rising middle class of London, to be played by the two private boy companies (Paul's Boys and the Children of Blackfriars), both of which had close connections to the Inns of Court and habitually assumed that a large proportion of their audience would be law students and ambitious young hangers-on at court.

However, by 1613 the boy companies had virtually folded, and Middleton had to direct his attention elsewhere. One result was that he began to intensify his work for the guilds and rich merchants who controlled the city of London, composing pageants and entertainments for successive civic occasions and eventually becoming the city's official chronologer. This is pertinent to *A Fair Quarrel* because many of these city patrons were puritan in sympathy, and his connection with them not only throws light on Middleton's probable attitude to duelling – which the puritans unequivocally denounced – but also highlights a more pervasively 'puritan' aspect in Middleton's own character, at least in a negative sense.[2] Though he presents no positive assurance of the elect's salvation by grace, he seems to have had an almost Calvinist conviction of the universality of original sin and particularly of the human capacity for moral self-deception. Middleton's specialty, in fact, is the sardonic presentation of characters who refuse to recognize their own motives, of tricksters outsmarting themselves and hypocrites blundering to self-destruction in a fog of pious cant. This too is relevant to *A Fair Quarrel*, and, in particular, to the moral contortions of its nominal hero, Captain Ager, and to the concept of 'fair quarrel' in the play.

Besides the city, Middleton also began to write for the less socially exclusive adult companies, including Shakespeare's company, the King's Men. By 1616 these companies were dominated by a new fashion for tragicomedy – an anomalous mixed genre established particularly by Shakespeare's successors, Beaumont and Fletcher (both of whom were trained as lawyers), as well as by Shakespeare's own 'problem plays' and final 'romances.' And it is the mixed effect of this genre that *A Fair Quarrel* is designed to appeal to and exploit, requiring a sophisticated response that subsumes different, even contradictory, attitudes. The vogue for such transgressive effects is usually associated by social historians with the breakdown of traditional standards on all levels of seventeenth-century English life, and is often compared to the late twentieth-century Western taste for 'black comedy,' the 'absurd,' and self-referential 'camp.'[3]

The vogue of the *duello* was another symptom of this social breakdown, of which four aspects are relevant to *A Fair Quarrel*: the principles behind the custom of duelling; the reasons for its flare-up in the early seventeenth-century; the psychological stresses and logical inconsistencies inherent in its concept of 'fair' quarrel; and the government legislation aimed at suppressing duelling at the time that *A Fair Quarrel* was written.

As a method of settling disputes, duelling is essentially aristocratic, a holdover from more primitive periods in which it took one of two forms. The first of these was a pitched battle between private armies of retainers (as at the beginning of *Romeo and Juliet*). After the devastation of the Wars of the Roses (which was such a private struggle waged on a country-wide scale), the new royal house of Tudor determined to replace private armies with a centralized system of law, with the result that such pitched battles gave way to the personal *duello*. The other tradition of primitive combat remained relevant to the new vogue of duelling, however, because it involved the principle of personal 'trial by combat' between quarrelling nobles (as in the joust between Bolingbroke and Mowbray at the beginning of Shakespeare's

Richard II). This kind of trial depended on the belief that God would ensure victory for the rightful combatant, a belief that was, of course, utterly unfounded. 'May the best man win' was never more than a pious hope, and in practice duelling and trial by combat have a very high rate of error as modes of justice.

The duel involved other, more insidious aims than the deciding of specific quarrels, however. More widely and essentially, duelling became a method by which a social élite deriving originally from the warrior class tried to define its code of behaviour in order to keep standards up and, more crucially, keep interlopers out, in a rapidly changing society which threatened its identity and power base. Consequently, duelling was used not only to enable an individual to prove his right to belong but also to define what his personal place should be in the hierarchy of the élite. This element of personal aspiration found expression in the aristocratic code of 'honour' (a key term in both Renaissance literature and society),[4] which depended less on a man's private image of himself than on his public *reputation* among his peers. Even more precisely and narrowly, it depended on his reputation as a person of unquestionable courage who was ready to risk his life at the smallest challenge to his social standing. Because the whole system derived from medieval chivalry, soldiers were thought to be particularly touchy and competitive about such 'honour.' In the seven-ages-of-man speech in *As You Like It* (2.7.151) Jaques describes the typical soldier as 'Jealous in honour, sudden, and quick in quarrel,' and George Whetstone explains in *The Honorable Reputation of a Soldier* (1585) sig E2 recto: 'Englishmen are men of much desart, and therefore *Envie* and *Emulation* raigneth mightily among them' (and goes on to say that moderation of one's anger was neither common nor highly regarded by the English military class). Such an attitude motivates the play's opening quarrel between Ager and his colonel about whether a younger and less senior man, the Captain, can possibly be as highly esteemed for courage as his older superior, the Colonel. The confusion of standards here seems absurdly obvious to a modern audience, but its key is the way that *rank* in the early seventeenth century was identified with *honour*, which in turn was identified, for men at least, with a public *reputation* for *courage*.

Such a system has obvious illogicalities. There is no necessary equation between skill with weapons and either courage or a rightful cause; and the system was abused with equal ease by rogues who were expert with a rapier or by cowards willing to rely on noisy bluff. The latter were an especial nuisance in the early years of James's reign and are satirized as 'Roarers' in the sub-plot of *A Fair Quarrel*, reflecting the particular trouble they had caused in 1615, the year before the play seems to have been written. The hierarchical aspect of the system, moreover, was a temptation to the young, or those low down on the social ladder for other reasons (illegitimacy, lack of property), to raise their personal status like the 'fastest gun in town' by manufacturing quarrels with those socially above them or those with an acknowledged reputation for 'honour.' Such deliberate quarrels not only blurred the line between serious wrongs and trivial or nominal offences (especially 'giving the lie' – that is, flatly calling someone a liar – which was resented because it meant one was being treated as a social inferior) but also threatened to undermine traditional hierarchy itself, since an ordinary gentleman could call out and kill a great noble for a trumped up offence (unless the crown intervened, as it often found it had to).[5]

The way the system sabotaged its own premises can be seen, for example, in the progressive misuse of seconds. According to the duelling code, seconds were intended not only to make the practical arrangements for the duel and act as witnesses to fair play, but also, and primarily, they were expected to act as mediators, with a duty to try to compound the quarrel without recourse to fighting. In practice, however (as *A Fair Quarrel* demonstrates), seconds were more apt to be bloodthirsty partisans and inciters than pacifying mediators.

Even if the cause of a quarrel were trivial or specious, or the aggressor completely drunk or otherwise incapable of judgment, or the defendant an objector to duelling on grounds of religious conscience, there was immense public pressure to conform or risk having the very worst construction put on one's motives for refusing to fight. Thus Lawrence Stone reports that, 'Sir William Wentworth, who refused a challenge from the irascible Sir Thomas Reresby, had to submit while sitting on the bench at Quarter Sessions at Rotherham to being publically denounced as a coward, and having his ears pulled until they bled. It was small consolation that his assailant was fined £1,000 in Star Chamber, since King James pardoned the fine before it was paid.'[6]

It is just this element of social status that helps explain why duelling reached such crisis proportions in early seventeenth-century England: where, according to the statistics in Stone, the number of recorded duels and challenges leaped from only five in the decade of the 1580s to nearly twenty in the 1590s to a peak of thirty-three between 1610 and 1620, when *A Fair Quarrel* was written.[7] This is immediately understandable if we bear in mind that duelling was one means that the social élite used for self-definition. The traditional bases of feudal nobility – birth, estates, and war service – were deliberately undermined by the Tudors' creation of a new aristocracy (the 'new men') serving the centralized power of the crown. This process was accelerated by the accession of the foreign James I, bringing in his own Scottish nobility and, notoriously, creating powerful favourites loyal only to himself from among the handsome young indigents hanging around the court; and the strain was further compounded by the period's increasing switch from an arable to a mercantile economy, with consequent obliteration of the line between newly rich merchants climbing up the social ladder and impoverished small landowners sliding down it (a favourite theme in Middleton's city comedy). A major factor in the alarming increase of duelling, in short, was the social élite's own threatened sense of identity and exclusiveness: it mirrors the ruthless struggle for status among the parvenus and insecure establishment figures at James's foreign court.

There was also a second, technological influence on the boom in duelling, caused by a change in weaponry. The traditional sword-and-buckler – which according to Stone, was no more dangerous to life than all-in wrestling (an interesting comparison in the light of Chough, the foolish Cornish suitor in the sub-plot of A Fair Quarrel) – gave place to the much more deadly rapier, imported into England in the 1580s and firmly established as the aristocracy's favourite weapon by the 1590s. Its adoption in England was accompanied by an influx of Continental fencing masters, who set up academies in London to teach the skills and mystique of the new weapon and supplemented their personal instruction by a spate of hand-books (usually translated from the Italian) explaining the elaborate rules already worked out for duelling on the continent.[8] Perhaps the most influential of these many handbooks was the Practise, an adaptation of Girolamo Muzio's Il Duello (1550) which was published at London in 1595 by Vincentio Saviola, a famous swordsman in his own right who had established the most fashionable fencing academy in London during the last years of Elizabeth's reign.

The Practise is in two books, of which the first is an illustrated art of fencing, and the second (and more important for our purposes) a discussion of the proprieties to be observed in quarrelling, including a chapter entitled 'How Gentlemen ought to accept of any Quarrel, in such manner that they may combat lawfully.' The argument contains many absurdities: pedantries of punctilio, and hair-splitting between degrees of 'giving the lie,' for example, which Touchstone parodies in *As You Like It* (4.5); but the division between the two books reveals a more basic contradiction that strikes at the very heart of the rationale for duelling. Whereas book I pragmatically (and correctly) assumes that victory in a duel will depend mainly on skill with one's weapon, book II is wholly preoccupied with the justice of the *cause* for which the duel is being fought and the correct etiquette and *state of mind* to be observed in giving and receiving challenges.

This offers an important clue to the psychological, ethical, and legal concept of the 'fair quarrel' (or 'lawful combat') that is at the centre of Middleton and Rowley's play. Adapting the church's justification of a 'just war,' Saviola's very debatable contention in book II is that God will give victory to whichever combatant is the more righteous (and, concomitantly, will punish his opponent): 'For that God whose eyes are fixed even on the most secret and inner thoughts of our harts, and even punisheth the evil intent of men, both in just and unjust causes [NB], reserveth his just chastisements against all offenders, until such times as his incomprehensible judgement findeth to be most fit and serving to his purpose.'[9]

Saviola's conclusion, therefore, is that 'no man ought to presume to punish another, by the confidence and trust which hee reposeth in his owne valor; but in judgement and triall of armes, every one ought to present himselfe before the sight of God, as an instrument which his eternall majestie hath to worke with, in his execution of justice, and demonstration of his judgement.'[10] Therefore, Saviola argues, a duellist should not act hastily, in anger (as the Colonel does in the play), but should first submit himself to scrupulous self-examination, and only then coolly challenge (or accept a challenge, like Captain Ager) if he is completely sure of his moral grounds. His concern must not only be that his *cause* is just, however, but also (and this is very important for *A Fair Quarrel*) he must be sure that his own state of mind is impartial, neither vengeful nor self-aggrandizing; because Saviola is shrewd enough to perceive that human motivation can operate simultaneously at different and sometimes contradictory levels, so that combatants often challenge 'either for hatred or the desire for revenge, or some other particular affection: whence it cometh to passe, that many *howbeit they have right on their sides*, yet come to be overthrown' (my italics).[11] For example, he says quite specifically that a duellist must never fight to 'purchase honor' for its own sake (which, as I have argued, was a chief social motive for the duello), but only if he can see his antagonist as a general, public evil that must be eradicated for the common, not merely his own personal, good.

Thus, book II of Saviola's *Practise* attempts to invent a code of behaviour which will allow the results of a duel to be equated with providential justice, not just with chance, skill with one's rapier, or any other form of personal advantage; and Saviola emphasizes that, if a duellist is not this scrupulous, he risks an eternity of hell after death. In this he begins to overlap, of course, with some of the arguments of the opponents of duelling: intellectuals as diverse as the 'atheistic' (really deist) Sir Walter Raleigh, the Roman Catholic Earl of Northampton, and the puritans who dominated the city of London and were also an influential faction at James's court; not to mention King James himself who, living up to his motto 'beati pacifici,' had issued a proclamation against duelling in Scotland as early as 1600, three years before he became King of England – certain articles of which, we are informed, were 'pennit by his majesties awn self.'[12] In particular, there was the adamant opposition of Francis Bacon, first as attorney-general, then from 1617 on as the Lord Chancellor, who seems to have detested duelling as much for the feeble thinking behind it as for its waste of life and the challenge it offered to established law and order.[13]

The period 1613–18 saw a vigorous government campaign against duelling in which James, Bacon, and Henry Howard, Earl of Northampton, the Lord Privy Seal, all had a hand, and which ultimately involved Thomas Middleton. In October 1613, in direct response to a duel between two of his chief courtiers, the Earl of Essex and another of the Howard family, James issued his first mild general proclamation which prohibited the publishing of notices of duels.[14] At the same time, he asked his main legal advisers in the Privy Council for advice about how to suppress what was rapidly becoming a public scandal. Bacon's advice took the form of 'A proposition for the Repressing of Singular Combats and Duels,' which was not published at the time (though it can be found in *Bacon's Works*, ed James Spedding [1868] 11:397ff) but became the basis of his later, more important *Charge* to the Court of Star Chamber. Its characteristically practical recommendations were to punish *both* parties in the duel (not just the victor) as well as their seconds, and to lay charges as soon as a challenge was issued, instead of waiting until after the duel had taken place. Northampton's much cloudier advice took the form of two bulky folio-sized manuscripts (now in the British Library) and a shorter discourse called 'Duello

Foiled,' which are partly compilations of earlier writers against duelling and partly Roman Catholic homilies by Northampton himself on Christianity's prohibitions against revenge and against killing per se.[15]

The first public result of this Privy Council 'brainstorming' was *The Charge of Sir Francis Bacon, Knight ...* to the Star Chamber in January 1614,[16] when James seems to have instructed him as attorney-general to prosecute before the highest court in the land two nonentities (called Priest and Wright) as a test case that might provide a precedent for later infringements of the law by more important people. This *Charge* was published later in 1614, but before it reached print two other important legal documents had also appeared. The first was a second royal *Proclamation against Private Challenges and Combats ...* (February 1614),[17] which seems to have been co-authored by James and Northampton (the latter's long-winded obscure style is immediately distinguishable from Bacon's terse clarity); a few weeks later there appeared *A Publication of his Maties Edict and Severe Censure against Private Combats and Combatants*,[18] in which Northampton had an even larger share.

These constitute all the major legislation of the period, but they were not the sum of the matter by any means. Other forms of direct and indirect government intervention occurred right up to 1620, when the incidence of duelling began to diminish. For example, in a letter to the royal favourite George Villiers in 1616, Bacon writes:

> Yesterday was a day of great good for his Majesty's service and the peace of this kingdom, concerning duels, by occasion of Darcy's case ... I was bold ... to declare how excellently his Majesty had expressed to me a contemplation of his touching duels; that is, that when he came forth and saw himself princely attended with goodly noblesse and gentlemen, he entered into the thought, that none of their lives were in certainty [,] not for twenty-four hours [,] from the duel; for it was but a heat or a mistaking, and than a [giving of the] lie, and then a challenge, and then a life.[19]

And in February 1617 James went so far as to attend Star Chamber in person, where upon 'a case of challenge 'twixt two youths of the Inns of Court [ie, two young law students] ... he took occasion to make a speech about duelling,' the result of which was that both young men were fined the Jacobean equivalent of $50,000.[20] And finally, as was mentioned, in 1618, a year after the play had been published, an anonymous pamphlet entitled *The Peacemaker* appeared, 'ghosted' by Thomas Middleton but licensed for printing on James's personal instruction (conveyed by his secretary of state, Naunton, to the solicitor-general), with the verso of the first leaf bearing the royal arms with the initials IR (Iacobus Rex), the royal arms appearing again on the title-page with a 'Cum Privilego,' and the unsigned preface royally entitled 'To all Our true-loving and Peace-embracing Subjects' as though written by James himself.[21] In its arguments against duelling in part 4, this pamphlet drew directly on the recommendations and phrasing of Bacon's *Charge* to the Star Chamber in 1614, and it included a diatribe against tobacco (another of James's pet hates) which equated tobacco smoking with 'roaring,' as in the extra Captain Albo scene added to the Chough sub-plot of *A Fair Quarrel* sometime during the play's printing in 1617.

Though these various documents have different emphases and style (reflecting in particular the gap between Bacon, the terse, practical scientist, and Northampton, the wordy, scholastic theoretician), the arguments they put forward are essentially the same. Revenge, they invariably point out, is God's prerogative, and for Christians killing is a mortal sin, which the established church intends to enforce by denying Christian burial to any person killed in a duel and excommunicating any survivor. Combatants will also be punished by banishment or, where a duel has been fatal, by death, since, besides breaking religious law, duelling is an offence against the state, in that it exalts private justice above the government's and wastes the lives of an aristocracy whose valour should be wholly dedicated to the defence of the realm. Duelling is based, moreover, on a totally false concept of 'honour' – which it is the king's prerogative to define – and this false concept is encouraged by the 'vain discourses' of foreign hand-books and the perverse ignorance of public opinion. To risk one's life for 'contumely of words' or 'giving the lie' is to over-value what is trivial, and it is not true that such verbal insults escape existing law (as defenders of the *duello* claimed) since they can be appealed and judged in the earl marshal's Court of Chivalry. And, most important for our purposes, the government pronouncements emphatically deny that a duellist can make ethical discriminations that will enable him to fight a 'fair quarrel.' The 1614 edict is decisive on this point:

> ... the Lawes of the Kingdome proceed capitally against all those that are found to speed their enemies upon private quarrels in the Fields after a faire maner (according to the phrase) ... or without either protection by

the Court of *Chivalry*, or discharge by Parliament ... [and] we may conclude that boldness doeth rather begge, than Justice can finde any cause
to graunt impunitie upon a point that is so desperate.[22]

The only distinction the crown was prepared to make was between
an 'involuntary' challenge, made without deliberation under the stress
of the moment, and a deliberate, cold-blooded challenge, made with
malice aforethought. But significantly the government's emphasis was
precisely the reverse of that held by Saviola and the other theorists
of duelling, because, whereas these latter argued for a cool, self-con-
trolled decision to fight, the law insisted that 'all *challenges* in cold
blood, swarve from all prescription and forms of Justice that ever
were,'[23] thus codifying the indignant comment of Bacon's *Charge*: 'But
for a difference to be made in case of killing and destroying a man,
upon a fore-thought purpose, between foul and fair, and as it were
between single murther and vied [ie, aggravated] murther, it is but
a monstrous child of this later age, and there is no shadow of it in
any law divine or human.'[24]

Within this historical context, then, it is clear that *A Fair Quarrel*
was written to exploit a highly contentious social and legal issue of its
day in which there was a discernable gap between the law and public
opinion (at least among those who were most concerned, the aristocratic élite). The problem remains of deciding where exactly the play
itself stood on this issue. One school of modern critics (eg, C.L. Barber,
Fredson Bowers, Richard Levin, David Holmes, Carolyn Asp) takes
Captain Ager at face value in the light of the duelling code of the
time, and praises *A Fair Quarrel* for its scrupulous exploration of the
painful moral dilemmas faced by the Captain in trying to decide whether
to fight and by his mother, Lady Ager, in trying to decide whether
to lie about her chastity in order to prevent him. More recently, another group of critics (John McElroy, A.L. and M.K. Kistner, and one
of the play's recent editors, R.V. Holdsworth), perhaps better attuned
to Middleton's irony, has gone to the opposite extreme to claim Ager
as a hypocritical egotist and Lady Ager a kind-hearted but foolishly
self-deluding mother.[25]

A priori, as we have seen, it is more probable that *A Fair Quarrel*
is against duelling than for it: because of Middleton's puritan connections (and his ironical treatment of duelling in other plays), because
of the play's popularity with King James, and because James (and possibly Bacon) co-opted Middleton to write *The Peacemaker* pamphlet the

very next year. On the other hand, it is hard to go all the way with the debunkers. Though the final position of *A Fair Quarrel* is obviously anti-duelling, the problem is presented so that, instead of having a single, disapproving attitude drummed didactically home to them, the play's contemporary audience was cleverly drawn into the actuality of the dilemma by having to weigh a double response to the play. Middleton, in other words, is exploiting a mode of ironic tragicomedy, which assumes that the audience shares the same uncertainty of values as the play is exploring.

'Tragicomedy' is a notoriously slippery term because it can be used to designate plays as diverse in their effect as Shakespeare's *The Tempest* and his *Measure for Measure*. It is best thought of as a sort of sliding scale, at one end of which tragedy and comedy are related through such 'romance' elements as magic, pastoral convention, and supernatural intervention, while at the other extreme they are fused by a pervasive sense of irony that qualifies both genres, making comedy disturbing and sometimes savagely unfunny while tragedy is reduced in dignity and is often too obviously manipulated by the dramatist, too 'patterned,' to be emotionally cathartic.

Middleton writes tragicomedy in this latter ironic mode, with central moral uncertainties reflected at both the psychological and verbal levels of the play. Thus, besides mocking the vocabulary of duelling, *A Fair Quarrel* mocks the professional jargon of doctors (taken verbatim from a contemporary medical treatise); it sardonically represents the indirect, 'hinting' approach that characters adopt (rather like Shakespeare's Iago) when they are trying to achieve something they do not like to admit to – Ager outrageously probing his mother's chastity, for example, because the Colonel has angrily called him 'son of a whore,' or the Physician in the sub-plot trying to seduce by blackmail the pregnant heroine left in his charge; and Middleton himself exploits the ambiguity of certain key words. 'Fair,' for instance, which occurs twenty-six times in the play, can mean 'without trickery' when applied to a quarrel, or 'for a good cause,' or, on the contrary, 'a good excuse for aggression that has already been accepted for other reasons,' or, with a final cynical twist, 'because it entails a happy reconciliation without fighting at all'; and behind all these slippery usages float the ironic meanings of the word, 'plausible' and 'specious' (*OED*, fair, *adj* 5).

In order to illustrate this technique, I should like to concentrate on two aspects of the play which have the effect of making us see Captain

Ager's dilemma ironically, and thus prevent us from wholly sympathizing with his scruples. The first of these is the ironic parallels which are set up between the main plot (featuring the Captain, Lady Ager, and the Colonel) and two levels of sub-plot: the Jane story, in which her mercenary father and a blackmailing physician both fail to destroy her pre-contract to marry the impecunious Fitzallen; and the more farcical Chough-Trimtram scenes, with their concern for wrestling and 'roaring,' into which an extra dimension of parody is introduced by a curious added scene of the pimp 'Captain' Albo, his bawd Meg, and whore Priss. Secondly, I wish to apply to Captain Ager Saviola's shrewd distinction between concern for self-control in a just cause and the even more important question of the duellist's state of mind when he makes his decision to fight, recognizing that there may be egotistic motives (especially greed for 'honour') lying unrecognized by the person himself beneath an apparently scrupulous composure.

The use of double, triple, occasionally quadruple parallel plots is a common device in English Renaissance drama, and is employed for three main purposes. It can reinforce the pattern of the main plot by repetition; it can emphasize the seriousness of the main plot by providing comic parallels for contrast; or it can provide parallels that undermine, or at least call into question, the values of the main plot.[26] It has been frequently argued that the sub-plots of *A Fair Quarrel* function in the second of these ways, but, taking into account the play's social and legal background, it seems more probable that they function in the third. The way their irony works is most easily demonstrated by moving from the least important plot level – the added scene featuring Captain Albo, Meg, and Priss – through the original Chough and Trimtram farce scenes, to the serious secondary plot of Jane's resistance to her father, Russell, and her outwitting of the treacherous Physician.

The solitary Captain Albo scene seems to have been added sometime during the printing of the 1617 quarto, and, as it has no effect on the other action of the play and adds three new characters who do not appear elsewhere, its only possible purpose seems to be to provide a thematic comment by ironic parallels to the main plot. Both revolve round a 'Captain A' (with 'Albo' clearly a coward and fake) who is called upon to defend from verbal abuse the women under his protection, in Albo's case a mother-figure, the bawd Meg, and a sister-figure, the whore Priss, who are unambiguously immoral. Unlike the worthy Lady Ager, who tries to dissuade her captain from a duel, Meg

and Priss noisily insist that their captain fight on their behalf; whereas
Ager is only too eager (hence perhaps the name), Albo is *white*-livered
and ready to surrender; and the conclusion, in which they all get drunk
together, provides a comic reflection of the unlikely, euphoric conclusion of the main plot. Meg's song about men resigning their titles
of captain and commander to accept the role of pander comments
ironically on the treatment by both Captain Ager and the Colonel of
women in their care, and, as will be shown, also offers a parallel to
Russell and the Physician in the Jane plot.

The other scenes featuring Chough and Trimtram provide three
aspects of debunking parallelism. Chough's Cornish passion for wrestling, with its insistence on 'fair play' and a 'fair fall' and use of specialized jargon, provides a comically non-aristocratic version of the
duelling of the main plot. The duello code and the fencing schools
which propagated it are also parodied in Chough's involvement in the
Roaring School which teaches smoking and quarrelling techniques.
This school is run by one of the Colonel's ex-army friends who, we
are told, can find no other means of making a living in peace-time,
thus providing a comment on the inadequacy and mischievousness of
military habits transposed to civilian life. One of the main exercises
of the school is how to incite quarrels by slandering the female relations
of one's opponents with comically indecent names (a sister is to be
called a 'bronstrops,' meaning whore; a mother, a 'callicut,' meaning
bawd), and the whole ludicrous vocabulary of 'roaring' demonstrates
how aggression corrupts the very language (the lowest exemplum being
Trimtram's retort with a fart), with religious and death references
which are taken seriously in the main plot debased here to oaths and
comic epitaphs:

> *Here coldly now within is laid to rot*
> *A man that yesterday was piping hot:*
> *Some say he died by pudding, some by prick,*
> *Others by roll and ball, some leaf; all stick*
> *Fast in censure, yet think it strange and rare,*
> *He lived by smoke, yet died for want of air*   (4.1.205–10)

Finally, the treacherous obliqueness by which characters in both the
main plot and the secondary Jane plot try to betray their trust is parodied in the way that Chough, having promised not to say a word

about the fathering of Jane's apparently illegitimate child, cheats by craftily *singing* about it.

Chough's wrestling vocabulary allows an endless series of sexual double entendres, so that besides a parody of duelling in the main plot, it also provides a distortion of the main theme of the secondary plot, in which Chough is Fitzallen's rival for the hand of Jane. This secondary plot centres on two other ideas of 'honour,' in the sense of public reputation: the idea that a woman's 'honour' is her reputation for chastity, and the conviction of Jane's father, Russell, that 'worth' is only to be gauged by the money one possesses – a perverse standard that leads him to as ill-conceived 'care' for his daughter's financial future as his sister, Lady Ager's equally misdirected efforts to ensure her son's physical safety. At both this level and that of the main plot, the action revolves, in fact, around the dilemma of a child (Jane, Captain Ager) whose personal idea of 'honour' is jeopardized by a parent of the opposite sex with a quite different code of values; and in both plots, the resolution of the dilemma depends on the intervention of the sister of an enemy – Anne, the sister of the Physician who tries to corrupt Jane, and the Colonel's unnamed sister in the main plot, who sacrifices herself by marrying Ager in order to restore her brother's self-esteem.

The Physician's attempt to extort sexual favours by threatening to make public the birth of Jane's child is interesting not only for the oblique, hinting way he goes about it, but also for its demonstration of another corrupt 'guardian' figure – a doctor who is himself the disease – which is extrapolated by a minor set of parallels between doctors and soldiers, both of whom we are told, get their living by killing other men and obscure their actions by a specialized jargon. In this latter respect, the Physician's mealy-mouthed misuse of religious terminology is particularly significant, since Jane's complaint, 'Lord, what plain questions you make problems of!' (2.2.22),[27] could equally well apply to the dishonest scruples about duelling elaborated by both Captain Ager and the Colonel in the main plot.

The secondary plot also provides a fine illustration of one of Middleton's characteristic ironies in the way that both the manipulative Russell and the treacherous Physician are undone by their own too narrow cleverness. The Physician's attempt to shame Jane publically merely results in his own downfall and Jane's release from the danger of a marriage to Chough; and Russell's subsequent idea of tricking Fitzallen into marriage with a daughter he now thinks has born a child to someone else merely allows the two lovers to confirm publically the pre-contract they have already legally sworn to; while, by now pretending reluctance, Fitzallen also manoeuvres Russell into doubling his daughter's dowry, a promise he is forced to keep even when the truth about their pre-contract (and thus the legitimacy of their child) ultimately emerges. This sardonic conclusion of the secondary plot reflects that of the main plot almost exactly, with ironic parallels and inversions. Russell's switch from opposing Fitzallen to eager encouragement and bribery of him parallels the Colonel's swing from competition with Captain Ager about military worth at the beginning to competition with him about humility and material generosity at the end, with the manoeuverings about Jane's dowry in the secondary plot ironically inverting the 'potlatch' competition of the main plot in which, to express his contrition, the Colonel gives his sister a large marriage dowry, the Captain accepts the girl but tries to refuse the dowry, and the Colonel then insists that Ager accept an even larger sum (with parallels of phrasing between 'fair increase' and 'fair offering' further tying the two levels together).

Another interesting set of parallels between these plots is their casual mistreatment of *sisters*, though this is an element of *A Fair Quarrel* that might have been developed more clearly. Sisters are probably important to this play of martial and economic strife because in traditional iconography Peace was always emblematized as the 'sister' of Justice; thus, in the Dedication to *The Peacemaker* the final sentence reads: 'For peace that hath been a stranger to you, is now become a sister, a dear and natural sister; and to your holiest loves we recommend her.'[28] But, once again, it is an element that the play presents ironically. The Physician's attempt to misuse the good nature of his dependent sister, Anne, as a means to corrupt Jane has uncomfortable parallels with the way that the Colonel secures a spurious happy ending to the main plot by browbeating *his* sister into marrying Ager against her will, in order to secure his own sense of magnanimity. This sister does not appear until 4.1, and except for her reluctance to marry Ager and submission to her brother, is totally uncharacterized and even unnamed. Her significance is purely formal and symbolic, and the reconciliations at the end of the play follow an interestingly anticlimactic sequence. This dubious betrothal of Ager to the Colonel's sister is followed by the ironically materialistic triumph of Jane and Fitzallen, and this in turn is followed by the climactic embrace between Ager and the Colonel, which for the 'honour' code is clearly more important than the sacrifice of a hapless sister who expects 'the world [will] never show me joy again.'

Another person who sacrifices his sister is, of course, Russell, who causes grief for Lady Ager by deliberately fostering the quarrel between her son and the Colonel at the end of 1.1 in order to divert the Colonel's wrath from Russell's heartless treatment of his kinsman, Fitzallen. And this mistreatment of Lady Ager is of a piece with the Captain's own insensitivity to his mother's self-respect and feelings and the play's pervasive speeches of misogyny (which are delivered by Jane, Anne, and Lady Ager herself as well as by the male characters).[29] On every level of the play, in fact, the women are superior in feeling and conduct to the men, but they are constantly described as untruthful, lustful, and unreliable – charges that are only true of Meg and Priss (who are superior to Captain Albo despite this); and this fits with other suggestions in the play that bellicosity is the result of a denial of feminine values and misdirected sexuality in men, who, like the Colonel at the end, claim to have no 'mistress' but war. Such implications sit well with those of other plays by Middleton, whose analysis of human behaviour often strikingly anticipates that of modern psychiatry; but, like so many aspects of *A Fair Quarrel*, they are left tantalizingly undeveloped, only sketched in lightly. The only woman not ultimately victimized is Jane, but to hold her own she has to be as devious and untruthful as her mercenary father and her would-be seducer, the Physician; and her blithely conscienceless success in doing so throws into ironic relief Lady Ager's unsuccessful attempts to manipulate events by conscience-stricken lying in the main plot.

One last item in this ironic grid of correspondences that is easily overlooked in reading because it is buried in the theatrical structure, is that the play begins and ends in the house of the materialistic Russell, a setting which tends to undercut the 'honour' values of the main plot; so the way the Colonel 'forgives' Ager at the beginning merely in order that his needy kinsman may marry into city money, foreshadows the very materialistic way he expresses his spiritual contrition at the end by means of his sister's dowry, and places both actions in the context of the secondary plot's more frankly cynical attitude to money.

Besides these debunking parallels with other plot levels of *A Fair Quarrel*, there are also ironies within the main plot itself, a useful key to which is Saviola's distinction between having self-control in a 'just cause' and having a correct attitude of mind *beneath* that cause. Besides attacking duelling from beneath, as it were, by parallels of questionable behaviour in the other plots, A Fair Quarrel also attacks it from above by contrasting the Captain's egotism with his mother's unselfishness and, in a technique that is characteristic of Middleton, by having both the Captain and the Colonel use religiously charged vocabulary for self-aggrandizing states of mind that do not really rise above the non-religious attitudes of the duelling code.

Lady Ager is the most sympathetic character in the play – so much so that some critics have seen her as its tragic heroine[30] – yet even she is not untouched by irony. Most obviously, there is her rather foolish insistence on a quite unnecessary surgeon when she hears in 4.3 that her son has fought and survived a duel with the Colonel, a slightly hysterical over-protectiveness that was adumbrated in 1.1 when she tried to make him promise not to go off soldiering again. More subtle than this is the sickening switchback of ironies that Middleton presents, in classic tragicomic fashion, when Lady Ager lies about her chastity without managing to save her son from duelling, yet, when she then admits her innocence, merely provokes him into planning a second challenge of the Colonel. The irony here treads right along the line between comedy and tragedy, because though the situation is absurd, there is a strong sense of Lady Ager's agony of mind and selfless love for Ager, to which his egotism is incapable of responding in kind. Consequently, Lady Ager has to be kept silent after this scene: she does appear again at the end of act 5, as a witness of the betrothal of Jane and the reconciliation with the Colonel, but, despite her prominence in the play, she is given no more lines – because anything she could say would tip the very precarious balance of tone in the dénouement.

The Colonel is much more obviously and damagingly undercut. At the beginning he seems merely a copy-book example of the choleric, over-competitive soldier, but after he has been almost mortally wounded by Captain Ager he begins to use religious terminology which is sincere but never goes beyond the shallow duelling code itself in understanding.[31] It is less religious confrontation with death that changes the Colonel than the fact that, in line with the code, he thinks that having lost the duel to Ager proves he must be wrong – an admission without much sense or value when we recognize that he has always known that his slander of Lady Ager's chastity was unfounded. Moreover, the way he goes about rectifying the situation is also shown to be an extension of the 'honour' code. Not only does he sacrifice his sister against her will, with a materialistic emphasis on her dowry, as noted, but, even more revealingly, the vocabulary in which he talks about his change of heart reveals that he sees it as another competition, a struggle with Ager to see who can now seem the more generous and humble, and thus emerge a final 'winner.' The Colonel, in other words, is 'guilty of the final treason,/Doing the right thing for the wrong reason,' still wholly preoccupied with his personal reputation.

This is also true of Captain Ager, but in such a tricky, subtle fashion that he has often been admired by critics as truly noble in his scrupulousness. Actually, he is a brilliant example of Middleton's gallery of unconscious hypocrites and self-deceivers. Ager's self-control at first seems admirable, in contrast to the Colonel's choler, but it is gradually exposed as egotism: part of his self-image as a copy-book man of honour. As his mother points out, his groundless scruples about whether or not she has been adulterous show terrible insensitivity and disloyalty to her; and (rather like Hamlet) having delayed so long for conscience' sake, when Ager finally decides to act, he does so precipitously and rashly, with none of the self-control he prided himself on, and that Saviola requires.

The only time Ager uses religious terminology is after his mother's white lie, when, assuming his quarrel cannot be 'fair,' he trots out all the traditional Christian arguments against duelling. But as soon as he gets a personal excuse to fight, all these arguments disappear; and the illogicality of this is emphasized by the comments of his disgruntled seconds, who are amazed that he will now fight for being called a 'coward' when he refused to defend his mother's honour. They contrive, moreover, to send up the duel itself by their confused, 'sports reporter' commentary, which reveals their ignorance of the fencing expertise to which they have pretended; and the moral self-delusion of the Captain's victory is then exposed, when, still wrongly believing his mother an adulteress, he priggishly informs the wounded Colonel, 'Truth never fails her servant, sir, nor leaves him / With the day's shame upon him.' (3.1.165–6)

All the way through, if they are examined carefully, Ager's remarks to the Colonel reveal themselves as 'needling' and provocative: for example, the Colonel's 'son of a whore' insult is provoked by Ager calling him a 'foul-mouthed fellow' for his quite justified resentment of Russell's treatment of his cousin, Fitzallen; and at the end, there is something like regret in Ager's admission that the Colonel has 'put me past my answers.' Throughout he is 'eager' for the 'field' (his name puns on both words), because he sees it as an extension of the battlefield where he can add to his personal reputation for 'honour' – and this non-religious 'fierceness' (OED, eager, 5) is betrayed in the vocabulary with which he chides his mother for preventing the duel, the alacrity with which he fights on the excuse of 'coward,' and his wish to rechallenge the Colonel when his mother reveals that she has lied (which goes against even the duelling code, since a defeated opponent has already forfeited reliability). Even at the end, the Colonel only narrowly avoids another challenge from Ager in their competition of generosity.

To sum the Captain up, then: he is best understood as an illustration of the contradiction between the two books of Saviola's *Practise*: cold-bloodedly scrupulous about cause (as long as the attack is on his mother, not himself), but with an aggressive drive for personal honour underlying all his decisions, which Saviola condemns even when a cause is 'just,' a quarrel 'fair.'

King James and Bacon were quite right to welcome *A Fair Quarrel* to court as an anti-duelling play, therefore, and to ask its author to begin work on *The Peacemaker* more or less immediately. Yet the play is clearly no simple propaganda piece. It works indirectly via ironic parallels between its several plots and by exploiting the moral and psychological ambiguities within duelling's misappropriation of religious rhetoric.

The result is a tragicomic mixture in which the ostensible 'serious' level of debate is constantly undermined, but where that 'serious' level reflects so accurately the current confusions of 'honour' ideology that a Jacobean audience, for whom such ambiguities were real and unresolved, would be forced to react at both levels simultaneously. This ambiguity extends into the conclusion too, where, as in Shakespeare's so-called problem plays, a happy ending is provided which we feel uncomfortable about accepting.

Such a reading reveals *A Fair Quarrel* as a play about a controversial legal issue of its day which catches with extraordinary historical precision the social and intellectual insecurity of James I's court, but also exposes recurrent human patterns of hypocrisy and self-deception, as well as the moral confusions that arise when religious terminology is appropriated both by secular law and by a social code that aims to subvert it.

Notes

Brian Parker received his PHD from the University of Birmingham in 1958. An experienced actor, he has published many articles on English and Canadian drama, and has edited over ten plays, including Thomas Middleton's *A Chaste Maid in Cheapside* and Ben Jonson's *Volpone*. He is currently preparing a critical edition of Shakespeare's *Coriolanus* for the New Oxford Shakespeare.

1 Cf Rhodes Dunlop 'James I, Bacon, Middleton, and the Making of *The Peacemaker*' in *Studies in English Renaissance Drama* ed J.W. Bennett et al (New York: New York University Press 1959) 82–94, citing *Calendar of State Papers, Domestic* for 19 July 1618, and the original licence for the play in *Public Records Office* (SP 39:9[4]); also '*A Fair Quarrel, The Peacemaker*, and *The Charge of Sir Francis Bacon Knight*' in appendix E of David M. Holmes *The Art of Thomas Middleton* (Oxford: Clarendon 1970) 224–6.

2 See my 'Middleton's Experiments with Comedy and Judgement' in *Jacobean Theatre* ed J.R. Brown and B. Harris (London: Edward Arnold 1960) 178–99. Middleton's puritan bias and strong connections with the puritan merchants of London have been thoroughly documented in Margot Heinemann's *Puritanism and Theatre: Thomas Middleton and Opposition Drama under the Early Stuarts* (Cambridge: Cambridge University Press 1980).

3 See John F. McElroy *Parody and Burlesque in the Tragicomedies of Thomas Middleton* (Salzburg: Institut für Englische Sprache and Literatur 1972) 265–321, and Carolyn Asp *A Study of Middleton's Tragicomedies* (Salzburg: Institut für Englische Sprache and Literatur 1974) 103–47. A more general study of the ironic aspects of Jacobean tragicomedy can be found in Arthur Kirsch *Jacobean Dramatic Perspectives* (Charlottesville: University Press of Virginia 1972).

4 See C.L. Barber *The Idea of Honour in English Renaissance Drama, 1591–1700* (Stockholm: Almqvist and Wiskell 1957) and C.B. Watson *Shakespeare and the Renaissance Concept of Honor* (Princeton: Princeton University Press 1960).

5 The most recent overview of duelling is V.G. Kiernan *The Duel in European History: Honour and the Reign of Aristocracy* (Oxford: Oxford University Press 1988), which is useful for cultural background. See also A.F. Sieveking 'Fencing and Duelling' in S. Lee et al ed *Shakespeare's England* 2 (Oxford: Clarendon 1916) 389–407; Robert Baldrick *The Duel:*

A History of Duelling (London: Chapman & Hall 1965); F.W. Bowers
'Henry Howard Earl of Northampton and Duelling in England'
Englische Studien 71 (1937) 350–5 and 'Middleton's *Fair Quarrel* and the
Duelling Code' *Journal of English and Germanic Philology* 36 (1937) 40–65;
Baldwin Maxwell 'The Attitude toward the Duello in the Beaumont
and Fletcher Plays' in *Studies in Beaumont, Fletcher, and Massinger*
(Chapel Hill: University of North Carolina Press 1939) 84–106 and 'The
Attitude Toward the Duello in Later Jacobean Drama – A Postscript'
Philological Quarterly 54 (1975) 104–16; Sheldon P. Zitner 'Hamlet,
Duellist' *University of Toronto Quarterly* (1969) 1–18.

6 Lawrence Stone *The Crisis of the Aristocracy 1558–1641* (Oxford: Clarendon
1965) 246. Such arbitrary breaking of his own regulations reflects
James's belief that kingship was 'above the law'; this was the attitude
that eventually led to the Civil War of 1639.

7 Ibid 245

8 Such handbooks were published by Segar (1589), di Grassi (trans 1594),
Gyfford (1594), Saviola (1595), Norden (1597), Kepers (1598), Silver (1599),
Brisket (1606), and Seldon (1610).

9 *Vincentio Saviola, his Practise* (1594) Y5 recto

10 Ibid Z1 verso

11 Ibid Y5 recto

12 See A.W. Renton and M.A. Robertson *Encyclopaedia of the Laws of
England* 2nd ed 5 (London: Sweet & Maxwell 1907) 27–8.

13 In his 1614 *Charge* to the Court of Star Chamber (see n16) Bacon even
goes so far as to equate duelling with 'sorcery that enchanteth the
spirits of young men, that bear great minds, with a false shew, *species
falsa*' (401).

14 See *Stuart Royal Proclamations* ed J.F. Larkin and Paul L. Hughes 1, no
132 (Oxford: Clarendon 1973) 295–7.

15 Part of *Cotton Titus CI* and all of *Cotton Titus CIV*; the *Duello foil'd* is
reprinted (but misascribed) in Thomas Hearne *A Collection of Curious
Discoveries* 2 (1775) 225–42.

16 See James Spedding et al ed *Works of Bacon* 11 (1868) 399ff.

17 Larkin and Hughes *Stuart Royal Proclamations* 1, no 135, 302–8

18 STC 8498

19 *The Letters and Life of Francis Bacon* ed J. Spedding 6 (1872) 114. King
James was reacting to a challenge sent by Gervase Markham, a soldier
'well known of his valour' to his social superior Lord Darcy, about
which Bacon had addressed Star Chamber on 27 November 1616,

advising them 'that in all cases of duel capital before them, they will use equal severity towards the insolent murder by the duel and the insidious murder; and that they will extirpate that difference out of the opinion of men; which they did excellent well' (6, 114).

20 See Chamberlain's letter to Dudley Carleton 22 February 1617 in *Letters of John Chamberlain* ed N.E. McClure 2 (Philadelphia 1939) 54–5; also *Calendar of State Papers, Venetian* for 24 February 1617.

21 See Dunlop 'James I, Bacon, Middleton' and *The Works of Thomas Middleton* ed A.H. Bullen 8 (New York: AMS Press 1964) 319–46.

22 *A Publication of his Maties Edict and Severe Censure ...*, 1614 (STC 8498) 6–7

23 Ibid 8

24 Spedding *Works of Bacon* 11, 404

25 See Barber *Idea of Honour*; Bowers (36 *JEGP*); Richard Levin *The Multiple Plot in English Renaissance Drama* (Chicago: Chicago University Press 1971) 66–75; Holmes *Art of Thomas Middleton*; Asp *Middleton's Tragicomedies*; McElroy *Parody and Burlesque*; A.L. and M.K. Kistner 'The Themes and Structures of *A Fair Quarrel*' *Tennessee Studies in Literature* 23 (1978) 31–46; R.V. Holdsworth, introduction to his edition of *A Fair Quarrel* (London: Ernest Benn 1974).

26 Richard Levin's *The Multiple Plot in English Renaissance Drama* is the best study of this structural device (though I disagree with his actual interpretation of *A Fair Quarrel*).

27 *A Fair Quarrel* ed R.V. Holdsworth. For the Physician's misuse of religious terminology, see his comparison of his silence to a confessor's (2.2.40–2), or a seduction passage such as 3.2.32–6:

> we are not born,
> For ourselves only; self-love is a sin;
> But in our loving donatives to others
> Man's virtue best consists: love all begets;
> Without, all are adulterate and counterfeit.

28 Bullen 8:323

29 Cf 2.1.28–30; 2.2.188–9; 4.2.92–6; 4.3.8–11, 102–3

30 See for example Samuel Schoenbaum 'Middleton's Tragicomedies' *Modern Philology* 54 (1956) 7–19, and R.H. Barker *Thomas Middleton* (New York: Columbia University Press 1958).

31 For example:

> Oh, just heaven has found me,
> And turned the stings of my too hasty injuries
> Into my own blood!   (3.1.174ff)

Cf also 4.2.40ff.

JOHN D. BAIRD

Criminal Elements: Fielding's
Jonathan Wild

Jonathan Wild is a difficult book.[1] Those who warm to Fielding's lively presentation of mid-eighteenth-century life in *Joseph Andrews* and *Tom Jones* – the 'Roast Beef of Old England' school – are repelled by what they regard as a bleak thesis-novel. Those who enjoy Fielding's verbal irony in his most famous novels may find the radical ironies of *Jonathan Wild* too extreme for comfort. Authors of otherwise notable studies of Fielding's fiction find excuses for omitting *Jonathan Wild* from extended consideration, as being somehow outside the main line of development.[2] And those who are interested in *Jonathan Wild* in its relation to contemporary events, are faced with an uncomfortable historical puzzle: why should Fielding publish in 1743, a year after Sir Robert Walpole's defeat in the House of Commons and retirement from politics, a book which seems on first reading to be a rehash of earlier attacks on Walpole as a political Jonathan Wild, especially when Gay's *Beggar's Opera* had given that idea so brilliant a treatment some fifteen years earlier?

The circumstances which led to the writing and publication of *Jonathan Wild* have recently been illuminated by Martin C. Battestin in his new biography of Fielding. Battestin argues convincingly that Fielding had written a satirical attack on Walpole in the form of an account of Johnathan Wild by the spring of 1740; that Walpole then paid him to suppress it; and that in 1743 he published a revised version, greatly augmented by the Heartfree material, at a time when he was desperately short of money and compelled to include everything he had available in his three volumes of *Miscellanies*. Fielding continued to think well of the work, as is shown by his preparing the revised version which was issued posthumously in 1754. Battestin also shows that the equation of Walpole with Wild was a persistent device of satirists, and provides an example from 1747, when Walpole had been out of office for five years and dead for two. The character of Heartfree is a tribute to George Lillo (1693–1739), a London jeweller who became a successful playwright, greatly admired by Fielding for his high moral character.[3] Battestin's account is very helpful in explaining why the work is as it is, but there remain questions about the relation of *Jonathan Wild* to other literary works dealing with crime, and about historical and critical issues which it raises, which are the concern of the present essay.

The Life of Jonathan Wild the Great has only a tenuous connection with the actual life of Jonathan Wild. *That* has been told, in a work of remarkable historical research, by Gerald Howson.[4] Howson describes, with a mass of detail garnered from legal records, how Wild dominated the criminal activities of London for a decade before his execution in May 1725. Perhaps most important, Howson makes it clear that Wild, though a brilliant opportunist, was not an innovator; that in effect he stepped in to fill the void left by the retirement in 1713 of Sir Salathiel Lovell, Recorder of the City of London – that is, the senior judge of the City – who for some twenty years had run rackets essentially the same as Wild's, though from the other side of the bench. He also shows that Wild's demise made no essential difference; that after his death things continued much as before throughout the eighteenth century and on into the nineteenth.[5] Fielding's book shows no interest in Wild's activities as an episode in the history of crime.

Nor is Fielding particularly interested in the details of Wild's career. He provides Wild with wholly imaginary parents and an equally obviously fictitious early life, and he pays scarcely any attention to the systemic aspect of the historical Wild's enterprises. Of the many notable criminals who crossed Wild's path only Blueskin (Joseph Blake, known as 'Blueskin') and Roger Johnson appear in his narrative, and even these are only tenuously connected with their historical originals. Fielding's Blueskin, like the real Blake, attacks Wild with a knife, but he aims for the guts, not the neck. (It is a small change, but perhaps significant, if Fielding's Wild be taken to represent not the short and emaciated Wild of contemporary prints, but the gross figure of Sir Robert Walpole.) And Roger Johnson, who in actuality was a champion smuggler who ferried stolen goods to Holland, appears here as a prisoner in Newgate whose pre-eminence there Wild supersedes. Above all, Jack Sheppard, the greatest escape artist before Houdini, the hero of the London mob, whose destruction Wild engineered in November

1724 – a move which did much to lose him public sympathy, and in some degree led to his fall – Jack Sheppard makes no appearance at all. The copious and fascinating rogues' gallery which Howson lays out for us is almost entirely eliminated, to make room for the wholly fictitious story of Wild's campaign against the Heartfrees, just as Wild's six or seven wives – mostly *soi-disant* – are eliminated in favour of the fictitious Tishy Snap.

It may be helpful to contrast Fielding's procedure with those of Dickens and Scott. In *Our Mutual Friend*, Dickens' characters are all alike fictitious. The setting is contemporary, and we find ourselves at one point in the Great Ormond Street Hospital for Sick Children, but Dickens' basic claim is that his characters, though imaginary, represent actual types: that there are people like Gaffer Hexam and Rogue Riderhood, who engage in the kinds of activity that they engage in. Scott, in *The Heart of Midlothian*, takes as his starting point actual events, the Porteous riot and its consequences, but events of which many details are unknown. Into the familiar public record of these events Scott weaves some wholly fictitious characters, and gives fictitious actions to some figures who are historical. When these are important persons with living and important descendants (like the Queen and the Duke of Argyle), the added material is handled tactfully, and is such as would tend to enhance them in the eyes of an early nineteenth-century reader. Where, as in the case of George Robertson, history has little more than a name to offer, and that of no good odour, Scott is free to invent as his plot requires. The controlling principle is that fiction may extend history, supplement it, even humanize it, but it cannot change it. Fielding's procedure differs from Dickens' in that Jonathan Wild was a real person, whose execution eighteen years earlier was a notable event well within the recollection of most of his original readers. His procedure differs from Scott's, in that he substitutes fiction for history in his account of Wild. Indeed, Fielding deliberately violates not only history, but his readers' memories.

In one detail, however, Fielding does follow the record. Wild – the historical Wild – has a rather special distinction. He is the only felon named in Blackstone's *Commentaries*, appearing in the chapter 'Of Offences against Public Justice.'[6] It is a capital felony, without benefit of clergy, to take a reward under pretence of helping the owner to his stolen goods.

The famous Jonathan Wild had under him a well disciplined corps of thieves, who brought in all their spoils to him; and he kept a sort of public office for restoring them to their owners at half price. To prevent which audacious practice, to the ruin and defiance of public justice, it was enacted by statute 4 Geo. I. c. 11 that whoever shall take a reward under pretence of helping any one to stolen goods, shall suffer as the felon who stole them; unless he cause such principal felon to be apprehended and brought to trial, and shall also give evidence against him. Wild, upon this statute, (still continuing in his old practice) was a last convicted and executed. (132)

Compare Fielding: 'A learned judge particularly, a great enemy to this type of greatness, procured a clause in an Act of Parliament as a trap for Wild, which he soon after fell into. By this law it was made capital in a prig to steal with the hands of other people. A law so plainly calculated for the destruction of all priggish greatness, that it was indeed impossible for our hero to avoid it' (168).

Here, uniquely, it seems that Fielding's history and legal history coincide. But even here there is a problem. Fielding's brief summary irons out the incongruity that Blackstone finds mildly puzzling – '(still continuing in his old practice) was at last convicted' – the seven-year delay between the passage of a statute specifically aimed at Wild, and Wild's arrest and conviction. The statute was passed late in 1717, and Wild did not 'soon after' fall into the trap. Since in 1740, when this passage was probably written, Fielding had recently completed his reading for the bar and was about to become a practising barrister, he can hardly have been unaware of the date of the statute.[7] He is not, like Scott, weaving fiction to fit the facts, but adjusting a very few facts to fit a substantial body of fiction.

One may well wonder why Wild was allowed to continue in his evil courses for seven years after a statute was specifically directed at his criminal enterprise. Howson's account of the matter is convincing. He suggests that despite the irritation caused by Wild, which led to the passing of the Act, the authorities were willing to tolerate him because they had nothing better to put in place, and because his rule seemed to keep stealing within acceptable bounds. By 1725, however, Wild's power was beginning to threaten the authorities, and he was becoming greedier. In August 1724, he and his gangs of thieves followed the court to Windsor for an instalment of Knights of the Garter. (It was on this occasion that, according to one tradition, Gay made his acquaintance, and was inspired to write *The Beggar's Opera*.) Following the inevitable thefts, the stolen jewels were not returned shortly afterwards on payment of the expected ransom rates, but were returned only piecemeal at a much higher tariff, and in many cases not at all. The powerful were no longer willing to tolerate a recoverer of stolen property who could not or would not deliver the goods, and Wild's determination to see the popular hero Jack Sheppard hang led many of the general public to question his practice of 'thief-taking.' Once the mystique which surrounded him began to crumble, he became vulnerable. He appears to have been surprised by the vigour with which the authorities brought charge after charge until he was finally convicted. Howson suggests that rivalry between the magistrates of London and Westminster, and the fears of some corrupt magistrates that Wild might denounce them, may have been factors in the prosecution.

Jonathan Wild is not an easy work to categorize. A work of fiction it certainly is, but is it a novel? Where does it stand in relation to that shadowy line which divides the satirical novel, like Smollett's *Roderick Random*, from the narrative satire, like Swift's *Gulliver's Travels*? Fielding complicates the issue by calling his book, in the *Miscellanies* preface of 1743, 'the history of Jonathan Wild' (29); on the title page, for which Fielding was not necessarily responsible, it is called 'The Life of Mr Jonathan Wild the Great.' 'History' was a more flexible term than it is now; *Tom Jones* is officially 'The History of Tom Jones the Foundling.' At any rate, it seems clear from the opening of chapter 1 that the narrator – whom I am careful to distinguish from the historical Henry Fielding – is offering us a biography. The classical biographers, Plutarch, Nepos, and Suetonius, are the names explicitly invoked as models (39). Inasmuch as the first two share ethical aims, and the third gives personal details and scurrilous anecdotes, we may discern the influence of all three in Fielding's fiction. *Jonathan Wild* may best be defined as a fictitious narrative in a form strongly influenced by classical biography. Among its classical features are the accounts of the subject's ancestors and of his education, and the 'character' of the subject which follows the detailed account of his death. The 'character' of Jonathan Wild lacks one classical feature, however: a physical description of the man. This is because such particularity would interfere with the generalizing satirical purpose, which is very strong at this point; but a contributing factor may be that Wild's physical condition at the age of forty-two was not an inviting topic: 'truly *Jonathan's* Carcass was not worth such an Operation [dissection], for he was so contaminated by Venereal Performances with Lewd Women, that it was perfectly Rotten long before he died.'[8]

One stylistic feature of the ancient biography which plays an important part in *Jonathan Wild* is the use of the speech. Oratory was an important activity in ancient civilization, and the making of speeches was undoubtedly a vital element in every aspect of public life. Historians, notably Thucydides, gave a lot of space to speeches (often necessarily recomposing them, or making them up entirely) since these were both part of the historical record, and a way of revealing the attitudes of the major figures. They also contributed to the general analysis of the points at issue. The historian's views might be expressed as commentary upon the speeches. The ancient biographers used speeches in a similar way, and Fielding follows suit. Hence the formalization of speech throughout *Jonathan Wild*, and the absence of dialogue as is found in the majority of novels. Exchanges of views between characters tend to be turned into debates, with lengthy and rhetorically self-conscious presentations of views on each side, as in I.v, where Wild and the Count debate ambition. Where conversations are essential to plot, they are typically rendered in indirect speech, as for example in the scene between Wild and the Misses Doshy and Tishy Snap at the end of II.iii. Indirect speech enables the narrator to impose rhetorical self-consciousness on the plainly very un-Ciceronian and informal utterances of such characters. This stylistic proceeding is emphasized by the two passages of dialogue which are given in the original words of the speakers. These are written in the form of excerpts from a theatrical script; speeches are attributed to speakers, without narrative links. Both the 'dialogue matrimonial' between Jonathan and Laetitia in III.viii, and the 'dialogue between the ordinary of Newgate and Mr Jonathan Wild the Great' in IV.xiii are said to be transcriptions of shorthand reports made by persons who overheard the conversations (143, 205). They thus share the status of the letters to Heartfree in II.vii: documents inserted into the narrative; once again, a device with ample classical precedent.

Daniel Defoe's account of Wild, in his *True and Genuine Account of the Life and Actions of the Late Jonathan Wild*, makes a helpful contrast to Fielding's style.[9] There are no chapter divisions (a loss of shape as well as dignity), topics are taken up with only the loosest connection to the supposedly chronological scheme of the narrative, there are no speeches, no final 'character' of the subject, nor is any moral lesson given or implied. As he approaches the conclusion of this life of crime, Defoe writes: 'It has been a kind of comedy, or farce rather, all along, but it proved a tragedy at last' (250), and he repeats this idea in the last paragraph: 'Thus ended the tragedy, and thus was a life of horrid and inimitable wickedness finished at the gallows' (257). But Defoe makes no attempt to shape the life of wickedness according to the five-act structure traditional to tragedy. Defoe, of course, is not writing for a sophisticated literary audience, but for a literate but not classically educated person like himself; a tradesman or small business man, more familiar with the numbering of points in a sermon (cf 238, 240) than with the art of Roman biography. Both Defoe and Fielding, however, are careful to define 'canting' terms: in each case, the notional reader is assumed to be ignorant of the street culture being described.

This is not, of course, to say that Defoe's attitude to his subject is naïve or single-minded. On the contrary, the narrative voice is torn throughout between admiration of Wild's boldness and cunning, his manipulative skills, and his enormous success, and abhorrence of his egotism, brutality, and wickedness. The result is a tone of brisk jocularity: 'This Mrs Milliner as I am informed, is still living, so that Mr Wild has left several widows behind him at his exit, whether they go by his name or not, that he himself could not inform us' (231). Wild himself is characteristically referred to as Jonathan, which relegates him at once to inferior social status. Throughout, Defoe aims at a vivid account of contemporary events; Jonathan's end has been brought about in a very remarkable manner, 'such as history can not give one instance of the like, except lately, that of a murder at St Edmunds-Bury in Suffolk' (250) – a statement which neatly collapses all history into the last three months. Defoe's pamphlet, concentrating on its central figure and sharply contemporary in its tone, is clearly designed as a topical publication rather than a contribution to literature.

Fielding, literary by training and intending something more than an ephemeral publication, employs different methods. His reluctance to name places, for example, distinguishes *Jonathan Wild* from most crime reportage. We are told indeed that Wild's mother was Elizabeth, 'daughter of Scragg Hollow, of Hockley-in-the-Hole, Esq.' (44), and we hardly need a note to inform us that this was a place of low amusements and ill repute, but this is almost the only location actually named in the narrative of Wild's activities. He contemplates taking Mrs Heartfree to 'one of those eating-houses in Covent Garden, where female flesh is deliciously drest and served up to the greedy appetites of young gentlemen' (110), but decides to prosecute his designs in her home instead. He takes her to Harwich en route to Rotterdam (113), and his ensuing marine adventures take him to Deal (121). Various other geographic indications appear, but they are mostly large and vague: the American colonies, for example (44, 58), then of course the destination of transported convicts, and that large and remarkable tract of Africa where Mrs Heartfree has some of her most harrowing adventures. But in and around London, where most of the action takes place, locations are conspicuously lacking. Mr Heartfree briefly enjoys the liberties of the Fleet (148), but all we learn of Mr Snap's house, an important spot in this history, is that it is 'in a part of the town which chairmen very little frequent' (109); that is, a distinctly unfashionable district, despite the fashionable airs of most of its inhabitants. Tower Hill and Tyburn, the contrasted places of execution for traitors and for common criminals, are mentioned in an early speech of Wild's (52),but even Tyburn, the scene of our hero's apotheosis, is never named again. Defoe's narrative, by contrast, is not lacking in topographical details of London; we are told of Wild's lodgings, first in the Little Old Bailey, then in the Great Old Bailey (appropriately, between the law courts and Newgate); of a robbery at St Anne's church in Westminster; and the escape of Skull Dean, Mrs Wild's first husband, laden with fetters and under sentence of death, is made vivid by a characteristic touch of detail: 'he made his way as far as Giltspur Street towards Smithfield' (242). The only comparable touch in *Jonathan Wild* is when Wild meets Molly Straddle 'taking the air in Bridges Street'(91).

This prevailing silence as to specific places throws all the more emphasis on the one place that is named again and again: Newgate. The prison stands at the centre of the action, as it dominates the ethos of the novel. 'We will now repair to Newgate,' the narrator announces at the end of book III, 'it being the place where most of the great men of this history are hastening as fast as possible' (164); it is within these massive walls that justice is finally done to all the major characters, both the good and the bad. It is there that the Heartfrees are reunited, and the falsely accused jeweller is vindicated; it is there that Wild finally falls victim to the laws he has so long manipulated to destroy others. Fielding could hardly have shown more clearly the direct power of Providence, which strips away perjury and falsehood and unmasks the villain in the great sink of iniquity which stood so near to St Paul's Cathedral and so far from everything that building represents – a point underlined by the Christian inadequacy of the Ordinary, as Fielding presents him.

London in the early eighteenth century was full of prisons – Nokes gives a list of twenty-seven (266), a list not surprisingly derived from Defoe. Some of these were small, and some were principally debtors' prisons, but the total is still a large one. Newgate, as the largest and the destination of the most serious offenders, has a special symbolic status, as Defoe (again) makes clear in *Moll Flanders*. This status was confirmed in 1780, by the eagerness of the Gordon rioters to break down its doors and set the place alight – events memorably recreated by Dickens in *Barnaby Rudge*. It is not too much to say that Newgate was the centre, the holy place, as it were, of criminal culture for more than a century. In *Great Expectations*, written in 1861 but set in the 1820's, Dickens brilliantly recreates the Newgate cult, with its rites and its martyrs – one recalls the law clerk Wemmick's fingers encircled with mourning rings bequeathed by those clients who could not be saved from the gallows even by his employer, Mr Jaggers, and Pip's strange feelings of unease for hours after his visit to the prison which Wemmick called his 'garden' – the prisoners, like flowers, blooming only to be picked.

Just as Dickens presents Newgate as an infernal parody of mainstream society, so Fielding shows Newgate life as a parody of the outside world. This is clearly expressed in book IV, chapter iii, 'Curious anecdotes relating to the history of Newgate.' (The antiquarian tone of the heading emphasizes the topicality of the parallels.) Roger Johnson is the reigning head of all the prigs in Newgate; Wild, after covertly forming an opposition, publicly denounces him, and finally displaces him.[10]

> Newgate was divided into parties on this occasion, the *prigs* on each side representing their chief or great man to be the only person by whom the affairs of Newgate could be managed with safety and advantage. The *prigs* had indeed very incompatible interests; for, whereas the supporters of Johnson, who was in possession of the plunder of Newgate, were admitted to some share under their leader, so the abettors of Wild had, on his promotion, the same views of dividing some part of the spoil among themselves. It is no wonder, therefore, they were both so warm on each side. What may seem more remarkable was, that the debtors, who were entirely unconcerned in the dispute, and who were the destined plunder of both parties, should interest themselves with the utmost violence, some

on behalf of Wild, and others in favour of Johnson. So that all Newgate resounded with WILD *for ever*, JOHNSON *for ever*. And the poor debtors re-echoed *the liberties of Newgate*, which, in the cant language, signifies *plunder*, as loudly as the thieves themselves. In short, such quarrels and animosities happened between them, that they seemed rather the people of two countries long at war with each other than the inhabitants of the same castle. (173–4)

In this parable, the 'castle' of Newgate is England, the prigs are the politicians, and the debtors are the people, 'entirely unconcerned in the dispute,' and 'the destined plunder of both parties.' Unable to see the facts of their situation, the debtors take sides in a quarrel which, whatever the outcome, will leave them worse off than before. Even when a wise man among them points this out, they pay no real attention: 'This speech was received with much applause; however, Wild continued as before to levy contributions among the prisoners' (175). The self-interest of the powerful is disguised by a cloak of public-spirited rhetoric, here encapsulated in the phrase 'the liberties of Newgate'; but this pretence only works because the people are willingly self-deceived, and are thus accomplices in their own depredation. As Swift put it, happiness is the 'Serene Peaceful State of being a Fool among Knaves.'[11]

The people of England, like the debtors of Newgate, are collaborators in a fiction. The emptiness and futility of that fiction are demonstrated by the robes of office which Wild takes over from the defeated Johnson: a silk night-gown, an embroidered silk waistcoat, and a velvet cap. These garments are doubly fictitious. First, they are the informal, domestic costume of a gentleman. To wear them in Newgate is to claim that one is a gentleman in one's own house, relaxing, as it were; that one could go out if one could be bothered to change into something more formal. (Mr Dorrit affects similar attire when he performs his self-assigned role of Father of the Marshalsea Prison in Dickens' *Little Dorrit*.) Furthermore, the night-gown gives no warmth, the waistcoat is too big, and the cap makes his head ache. The clothes are manifestly not suitable for him, and betray his betrayal of the office he has misappropriated. Far from confirming his authority, they undermine it, and attract hostility from his victims. Fielding thus conveys the dynamic of political lying; always drawing the people in, yet always defeating its own ends.

The anticipation of George Orwell is obvious, both in the analysis of the power struggle – Wild condemns Johnson for wearing the special clothes, but immediately dons them himself (*Animal Farm*) – and in the idea of a language that means the reverse of what it says (*Nineteen Eighty-Four*). But Orwell's insights are conveyed in accounts of imagined societies, a farm run by animals, an England of the future. Fielding's insights, on the other hand, exploit a society that actually did exist, the world of Newgate prison, where the criminal elements no doubt feuded amongst themselves and preyed upon the unlucky debtors incarcerated with them. The demolition of Newgate and the disappearance of the system of criminal justice which is symbolized have dulled for modern readers the original revelatory force of Fielding's parable.

In the same way, the passage of time has dulled the reader's response to the criminal activities depicted in *Jonathan Wild*. Fielding could assume in his readers a background knowledge of offences and penalties which would help to shape their attitudes toward his characters. While a truly contemporary response of this kind is now irrecoverable, some insight into the way the crimes and punishments of Wild and his cronies were viewed in the mid-eighteenth century may be gained from a review of the relevant passages in Blackstone's *Commentaries*. Whatever the weaknesses of this treatise in the eyes of legal historians, Blackstone's attempt 'to make sense of the law for laymen'[12] has the advantage that it makes his work approachable for those who are not trained lawyers.

In book I, chapter iv, young Jonathan Wild makes his entrance into the world. It is appropriate that he should be committing two crimes at once. He, along with the Court La Ruse and Doshy and Tishy Snap, play cards together – an activity forbidden to all but gentlemen (except at Christmastime) by 33 Hen.VIII.c. 9, as Blackstone points out (171).[13] The Count – whom we may safely conclude, despite his title, is not a gentleman – regularly cheats at cards, and would therefore be amenable to prosecution under the statute 9 Ann.c. 14, which enacts, 'that if any person cheats at play, and at one time wins more than 10*l.* or any valuable thing, he may be indicted thereupon, and shall forfeit five times the value, shall be deemed infamous, and shall suffer such corporal punishment as in case of wilful perjury' (Blackstone 173). Rather than seek remedy at law, Jonathan's hands 'made frequent visits to the count's pocket' (49); that is, he engaged in a form of mixed or compound larceny, in this case, privately stealing from a man's person. This, if the value of the goods purloined exceeded twelve pence, was a felony without benefit of clergy by statute 8 Eliz.c.14; that is, 'a crime to be punished by forfeiture ... to which death may, or may not be, though it generally is, superadded' (Blackstone 98).

It is fitting that Wild should first step upon the stage, as it were, as a pickpocket, for at the end of his career, when he stands upon another stage beneath the 'tree of glory,' he leaves this world in the very act of picking a man's pocket. In law, at least, he had deserved hanging from the first moment he withdrew the Count's purse from the Count's person; here he is at the end, demonstrating the most admirable conservation of character to his last moment: 'Wild, in the midst of the shower of stones, etc., which played upon him, applied his hands to the parson's pocket, and emptied it of his bottle-screw, which he carried out of the world in his hand' (214).

Blackstone, in discussing pickpocketing, remarks – as so often – on the severity of English law; Blackstone – as so often – has a justification ready to hand: 'This severity (for a most severe law it certainly is) seems to be owing to the ease with which such offenses are committed, and the difficulty of guarding against them: besides that this is an infringement of property, in the manual occupation or corporal possession of the owner, which was an offence even in a state of nature'(241). With the first part of this comment Wild is in full agreement, as appears in his great speech in II.iv on the vanity of human greatness:'"Did I not misbehave in putting it into the power of others to outwit me? But that is impossible to be avoided. In this a *prig* is more unhappy than any other: a cautious man may, in a crowd, preserve his own pockets by keeping his hands in them; but while the *prig* employs his hands in another's pocket, how shall he be able to defend his own?"'(96). Picking pockets thus symbolizes the life of crime; he who perpetrates it is, by the act itself, made particularly liable to be its victim. To espouse such a life, as Wild's career in this version demonstrates, is to condemn oneself to an endless regress.

Wild next helps the Count to escape from Mr Snap's house. Escape from lawful custody is, of course, itself an offence, and Wild is guilty of at least a misdemeanour in assisting him (Blackstone 130–1). We are not told the nature of the accident which transports the young Wild for the statutory seven years to his majesty's plantations in America, at the conclusion of which he is back exactly where he started (58–9), ready to attempt a new type of adventure. He incites Bob Bagshot to rob the Count of his winnings at hazard. The robbery is not described, but it clearly is a robbery, an open and violent assault, as distinct from privately stealing: Bob is armed with pistols (59). Robbery requires violence or the threat of violence; the amount taken is immaterial (unlike the twelve-pence dividing line for privately stealing); and it is a felony without benefit of clergy (Blackstone 241–3).

Wild subsequently intimidates Bob, and gets another large part of the booty, by drawing his glittering hanger (robbery again). It is worth noting that mortally stabbing with a dagger, though done upon sudden provocation, was a species of manslaughter which, by statute of 1 Jac.i.c.8 was punished as murder. No murder is committed, and book I ends with Wild himself robbing an unlucky gambler (80).

With the appearance of the Heartfrees in book II, Wild moves in fresh directions. He conspires with the Count and others to rob Heartfree. Molly Straddle privately steals some of the proceeds; Wild, by coincidence being present when she tries to change a large banknote at Heartfree's place of business, compels Molly to swear an information against the recalcitrant Thomas Fierce. Fierce is duly arrested, but it takes more than Molly's perjured testimony to hang him, and his accomplice James Sly is persuaded to launch a pre-emptive strike and offer his information to the magistrate. This is the first of several conspiracies to have somebody convicted of a felony, one of Wild's most characteristic devices, and the climax of his campaign against Heartfree. In this case, of course, the prisoner is guilty as charged, but we are unlikely to think that Wild has behaved in a public-spirited manner. The usual punishment for conspiracy 'to indict an innocent man of felony falsely and maliciously' was imprisonment, fine, and the pillory. While most of Wild's conspiracies were to indict persons who were indeed guilty, his final scheme against Heartfree falls into this category of the accusation of the innocent. Perjury, like Straddle's here, and subornation of perjury, Wild's part in this transaction, are related offenses, and Blackstone explains the penalties for both. The punishment 'was antiently death; afterwards banishment, or cutting out the tongue; then forfeiture of goods; and now it is fine and imprisonment, and never more to be capable of bearing testimony'(137). Blackstone goes on to consider the question whether giving perjured testimony in a trial where the prisoner may be convicted on a capital charge should itself be a capital offence, and concludes that it should not: 'For to multiply capital punishments lessens their effect, when applied to crimes of the deepest dye; and, detestable as perjury is, it is not by any means to be compared with some other offenses, for which only death can be inflicted: and therefore it seems already (except perhaps in the instance of deliberate murder by perjury) very properly punished by our present law'(138).

Our concern in Fielding's narrative is chiefly with Wild's public acts and professional career, but we are allowed some glimpses of his private life. In book III he courts and wins Miss Tishy Snap. He writes a love letter to this 'most deivine and adwhorable creture'(140), and asks his associate Fireblood to deliver it. Miss Tishy at first breaks out in rage against Wild's impertinence, and refuses to accept the missive. Her dislike of the message, however, does not prejudice her against the messenger: '"But with you, young gentleman," says she, "I am not in the least angry. I am rather sorry that so pretty a young man should be employed in such an errand." She accompanied these words with so tender an accent and so wanton a leer, that Fireblood, who was no backward youth, began to take her by the hand, and proceeded so warmly, that, to imitate his actions with the rapidity of our narration, he in a few minutes ravished this fair creature, or at least would have ravished her, if she had not, by a timely compliance, prevented him'(141).

This is a remarkable passage. Fielding's verbal skill is shown by the reference to rapidity of narration, which, by emphasizing the fictive quality of what we are reading, and the absurd acceleration of foreplay and consummation which taking it seriously would entail, underlines the lack of concern we should feel for Miss Tishy's entirely supposititious chastity. The crucial word is 'prevent,' which is to be understood both in the usual modern sense, to stop someone from doing something, and in the older sense, current in Fielding's day, to meet beforehand, to anticipate something, as for example a wish or desire.

This masterly play on language is also good in law. In contrasting the Roman law of rape with the English, Blackstone remarks that the civil law punishes a man who abducts a woman from her parents or guardians whether she consents or is forced:

And this, in order to take away from women every opportunity of offending in this way; whom the Roman laws suppose never to go astray, without the seduction and arts of the other sex: and therefore, by restraining and making so highly penal the solicitations of the men, they meant to secure effectively the honour of the women. ... But our English law does not entertain quite such sublime ideas of the honour of either sex, as to lay the blame of a mutual fault upon one of the transgressors only: and therefore makes it a necessary ingredient in the crime of rape, that it must be against the woman's will.(210–11)

When Wild at last arrives in Newgate as a prisoner, he hopes that the keeper, his old friend, will treat him kindly: 'he promised himself not only a kind reception and handsome accommodation there, but even to obtain his liberty from him if he thought it necessary to desire it: but alas! he was deceived; his old friend knew him no longer, and refused to see him, and the lieutenant-governor insisted on as high garnish for fetters, and as exorbitant a price for lodging, as if he had had a fine gentleman in custody for murder, or any other genteel crime'(169). These were probably standard exactions; we see another, presumably less common kind when Mrs Heartfree appears as her husband is about to ride away from Newgate – be it noted, in a coach hired by his friend Friendly – to the place of execution. The commander of the sheriff's party is willing to allow a brief interview; five guineas from Friendly buys ten minutes. At the end of this period the commander urges Heartfree to act more like a man. In the end Friendly, whose ready money is exhausted, promises to return later with twenty guineas if the Heartfrees can have half an hour together. The commander then reveals that they can have as long as they like, for Heartfree has been reprieved. Twenty guineas for nothing clearly constitutes extortion: 'an abuse of public justice, which consists in any officer's unlawfully taking, by colour of his office, from any man, any money or thing of value, that it not due to him, or more than is due, or before it is due. The punishment is fine or imprisonment, and sometimes a forfeiture of the office' (Blackstone 141). Extortion is visited with no such penalties in *Jonathan Wild*, and here Fielding is faithful to the reality of his time.

The wheel comes full circle, and Jonathan Wild leaves the world as he entered it, picking a pocket. But there is one last offence, one committed by almost all the criminal characters in the book. As the ordinary, missing his bottle-screw, descends from the cart, 'Wild had just opportunity to cast his eyes around the crowd, and to give them a hearty curse' (214). This is the offence of common swearing and cursing,'taking God's name in vain in common discourse': 'By the last statute against which, 19 Geo.II.c.21 which repeals all former ones, every labourer, sailor or soldier shall forfeit 1*s.* for every profane oath or curse, every other person under the degree of a gentleman 2*s.* and every gentleman or person of superior rank 5*s.* to the poor of the parish; and, on a second conviction, double; and for every subsequent conviction treble the sum first forfeited; with all charges of conviction: and in default of payment shall be sent to the house of correction for ten days' (Blackstone 59).

This long and lamentable catalogue of wrongs in *Jonathan Wild* may be concluded by mentioning the drunkenness, a type of behaviour not uncommon in the novel, was punishable by a fine of five shillings, or six hours sobering up in the stocks (Blackstone 64); and that open and notorious lewdness, essentially the frequenting houses of ill fame, is equally common and equally liable to legal penalty. Blackstone adds, however, that since the Restoration of 1660, moral offenses have been left 'to the feeble coercion of the spiritual court, according to the rules of the canon law; a law which has treated the offence of incontinence, nay even adultery itself, with a great degree of tenderness and lenity; owing perhaps to the celibacy of its first compilers' (Blackstone 64).

There is, then, a great deal of typical crime in *Jonathan Wild*. But are there typical criminals, as there are in *Our Mutual Friend*? I think the answer, though subject to qualification, has to be no. Crimes are crimes however they are described, but the characters are figments of language only, and are rendered throughout by Fielding with a stylistic heightening which makes it very difficult for us to take them seriously as accurate representations of early eighteenth-century Newgate fodder. The persistent use of that favourite device of the time, the mock-heroic mode, in describing low actions and persons in a high style, emphasizes the gap between that which is described and the values implied by the language used for the description. At the same time, a reverse process comes into effect, suggesting (so to speak) that the low subject matter is not wholly undeserving of elevation. If such heightening is consistent and sufficiently prolonged, we tend to lose our grip on our context of judgment. This state of mind can be arrested at any time by a sharp anticlimax, which has the effect of resetting the reader's moral and aesthetic judgment; there is a good example at the end of IV.iii:'"And, should I speak in the language of a man who estimated human happiness without regard to that great-ness, which we have so laboriously endeavoured to paint in this history, it is probable that he never took (i.e. robbed the prisoners of) a shilling, which he himself did not pay too dear for"'(176). Here the narrator abandons for a moment the inflated rhetoric of the mock heroic in favour of plain language that brings the reader sharply back to the real values of everyday life, underscoring the brutal truth that corrupt empires are built on the extortion of small amounts from the poor and the defenceless. But such reset points are rare in *Jonathan Wild*; indeed, the constant false elevation is the thing many readers find wearing about the book. A similar technique, with different effect, is found in Pope's *The Rape of the Lock*. Pope's epic treatment of a silly quarrel certainly underlines the folly of the squabble, but in its consistent heightening it also helps us to see the universality of such folly, and our own participation in it.

Far different is Fielding's purpose. In *Jonathan Wild* the heightening of style and the persistent reversal of values stress moral ambiguity, especially the contrast between the values as we acknowledge publicly and the values we really live by. Do we really believe in honesty and hard work, or do we in fact admire success, however obtained? Is it the urgings of piety or the imperatives of power that direct or lives? Wild's actual life is not interesting to Fielding, but Wild's actuality is vital to him. Wild really did direct the thieves and catch them, plan the burglaries, and recover the goods. What's more, he enjoyed a high reputation for doing so.

It is this elevation of Wild that makes him the supreme symbol of a society that has cut adrift from its moral moorings, a society which cannot tell the difference between right and wrong. It would therefore be a mistake to regard this book simply as a belated and unoriginal attack on Sir Robert Walpole which was published only because of the author's pressing financial need. Walpole had been forced into retirement, but his successors continued to employ his corrupt methods of government. In its revised and extended form, *Jonathan Wild* is directed against politicians who deal daily with authority and too often misuse it for private ends; it is directed too at those who tolerate them, believe what they say, and repeatedly vote for them. It is directed at the corrupt legal system that a corrupt society deserves and gets. The importance given to those tedious Heartfrees is intended precisely to make explicit the contrast between those who have elected to live in the world of Wild, which is governed by force and fortune, and those who live with the Heartfrees in a world governed by divine providence.

Jonathan Wild is not Fielding's most lovable book, but it is the one in which he expresses in its starkest form his view of a society which has abandoned principle in favour of personal gain – take the money and run – and which therefore, like Wild, must sooner or later face the ultimately self-destructive consequences of its folly.

Notes

John D. Baird received his PHD from Princeton University in 1970. His publications include *Editing Texts of The Romantic Period* and volume 1 of *The Poems of William Cowper* for Oxford University Press; he is currently editing a second volume of Cowper's poems.

1 All page references to Henry Fielding's *Jonathan Wild* and to Daniel Defoe's *Genuine Account of the Life and Actions of the late Jonathan Wild* are to the edition by David Nokes (Harmondsworth: Penguin 1982).

2 E.g. Robert Alter *Fielding and the Nature of the Novel* (Cambridge: Harvard University Press 1968); J. Paul Hunter *Occasional Form: Henry Fielding and the Chains of Circumstance* (Baltimore: Johns Hopkins University Press 1975). The best discussion of *Jonathan Wild* is that found in C.J. Rawson *Henry Fielding and the Augustan Ideal under Stress* (London: Routledge 1972).

3 Martin C. Battestin with Ruthe R. Battestin *Henry Fielding: A Life* (London: Routledge 1989) 281–3, 372, 206–7

4 *Thief-Taker General: The Rise and Fall of Jonathan Wild* (London: Hutchinson 1970)

5 Readers of Virginia Woolf's *Flush: A Biography* (London: Hogarth Press 1933) will be aware of a Victorian variant on Wild's lost property office: the stealing of dogs for ransom. Flush was Elizabeth Barrett's spaniel, twice stolen and twice redeemed from the dog-nappers.

6 William Blackstone *Commentaries on the Laws of England* IV (Oxford: Clarendon 1769; photorepr 1966)

7 Battestin 271–2, 281

8 Alexander Smith (pseud?) *Memoirs of the Life and Times of the Famous Jonathan Wild* (London 1726; repr New York: Garland 1973) 22

9 The pamphlet reprinted by Nokes was first ascribed to Defoe by William Lee in *Daniel Defoe: His Life and Recently Discovered Writings* 1(London: Hotten 1869)xlix. It appears as no 471 in John Robert Moore *A Checklist of the Writings of Daniel Defoe* 2nd ed (Hamden, Conn.: Archon 1971) 196. It continues to be accepted as the work of Defoe by scholars; eg, Paula R. Backscheider *Daniel Defoe: His Life* (Baltimore: Johns Hopkins University Press 1989) xiv, 490–1.

10 Battestin points out that in this episode Johnson represents the fallen Walpole, and Wild his successful adversary, William Pulteney (338).

11 *A Tale of a Tub* ed A.C. Guthkelch and D. Nichol Smith, 2nd ed (Oxford: Clarendon 1958) 174

12 S.F.C. Milsom *The Nature of Blackstone's Achievement* (London: Selden Society 1981) 12
13 Scofflaws like Wild would pay little attention to the statute of 1541, but it had considerable effect upon the law-abiding; W. Gurney Benham, in *Playing Cards: History of the Pack* (London: Ward Lock 1931), notes that because of it 'cards up to a comparatively recent period were regarded as an almost essential part of Christmas revelry' (26).

JANE MILLGATE

Scott and the Law: *The Heart of Midlothian*

Walter Scott was both a man of law and a man of letters. In virtually every one of his novels, and even in some of his poems, the law makes its presence felt. Lawyers of all kinds figure in his cast of characters, occasionally as protagonists, more often as facilitators or impeders of the action; at other times they act as interpreters of that action, reducing it to retrospective order. The activities of proving, explaining, reconstructing, assessing probabilities, and coming to conclusions and judgments are integral to the way Scott's plots function, and it is remarkable how often in his novels legal right endings coincide with narrative right endings.

Scott was in a sense born to the law. His father was a solicitor, or, to use the Scottish term, a Writer to the Signet, and in March 1786 the fourteen-year-old son was indentured to the father for a five-year apprenticeship. From the outset of his son's legal training the elder Scott probably cherished the ambition of seeing one who was so much more extrovert, flamboyant, and articulate than himself proceed beyond the sphere of Writer to that of Advocate (or barrister), and in the winter of 1788 the younger Scott was sent to the university. He did not think much of the lectures offered there on the Roman, or civil, law, but admired those on Scottish municipal law given by David Hume, nephew of the famous philosopher. He even went to the trouble of making for his father a fair copy of the lecture notes he took down in Hume's classes – though it is difficult to say whether this was a mark of filial devotion, an attempt to appease his dour and demanding parent, or simply a proof of attendance. His father's comment on receiving the gift is reported to have been that it afforded 'very pleasant reading for leisure hours.'[1]

Scott played a leading role in the extra-curricular life of the university, especially in the Speculative Society, the most important of the Edinburgh debating clubs, with a membership consisting largely of law students and young lawyers. (It is perhaps relevant to *The Heart of Midlothian* to note that the questions debated by the society during the period of Scott's active membership included, on 26 November 1793, 'Ought any crimes to be punished with death?' and, on 16 February 1794, 'Is mercy incompatible with strict law?')[2] He successfully completed all the stages necessary for admission as an advocate, assuming the gown in the summer of 1792, just prior to his twenty-first birthday, and then practised as an advocate with reasonable success for the next fourteen years, appearing in criminal cases before the Court of Justiciary both in Edinburgh and on circuit, and before the Court of Session in Edinburgh in various equity cases; he was also involved in two appeals to the House of Lords.[3]

Scott even argued before the General Assembly of the Church of Scotland a case in which he defended the Revd Mr John M'Naught, minister of Girthon, against charges of 'habitual drunkenness, singing of lewd and profane songs, dancing and toying at a penny-wedding with a "sweetie-wife" (that is, an itinerant vender of gingerbread, &c.), and moreover of promoting irregular marriages as a justice of the peace.'[4] It is hardly surprising, given the number and specificity of the items in the indictment, that Mr M'Naught was found guilty and deposed from the ministry. All the cronies of Scott's student days were in court on this occasion, and we get some sense of the flavour of that companionable group, many of whom were to remain his life-long friends, from the account of the proceedings in Lockhart's biography of Scott:

> He began in a low voice, but by degrees gathered more confidence; and when it became necessary for him to analyse the evidence touching a certain penny-wedding, repeated some very coarse specimens of his client's alleged conversation in a tone so bold and free, that he was called to order with great austerity by one of the leading members of the Venerable Court. This seemed to confuse him not a little; so when, by and by, he had to recite a stanza of one of M'Naught's convivial ditties, he breathed it out in a faint and hesitating style; whereupon, thinking he needed encouragement, the allies in the gallery astounded the Assembly by cordial shouts of *hear! hear! – encore! encore!* They were immediately turned

out, and Scott got through the rest of his harangue very little to his own satisfaction.[5]

The young advocate enjoyed the patronage of the head of the Scott clan, the Duke of Buccleuch, and it was through the Duke's intervention that he was appointed sheriff, or resident magistrate, of Selkirk in December 1799, holding that office until his death in 1832. Much of the business of the Sheriff's Court was in fact carried on by the sheriff substitute, but Scott himself gave judgment in a good many cases over the years and was also actively involved in the sheriff's duties at election times. The cases Scott handled – sometimes on the basis of actual court hearings in his presence, sometimes on the basis of written submissions only – were both criminal and civil; rural crimes such as poaching or illegal fishing figured quite frequently, as did cases relating to the ownership of land or disputes between landlords and tenants. Scott's judgments – according to their early twentieth-century editor who was himself a sheriff of Selkirk – were characterized by their 'succinctness and lucidity,' while Scott himself 'was strict in the matter of regularity of procedure in the cases before him.'[6]

His office as sheriff of Selkirk did not preclude Scott's continuing to practise as an advocate, nor did he in fact give up that practice until 1806, when he accepted an appointment as one of the principal clerks to the Court of Session, the supreme civil court in Scotland.[7] This was a well-paid position, but Scott did not begin to enjoy its salary until 1811, since for the first few years he was doing the work of a retired clerk who continued to receive the emoluments in return for Scott's being guaranteed the reversion of the office. Even with the salary, however, it was by no means a sinecure, since daily attendance at court was required during the legal terms. As senior officials of the court the principal clerks did not themselves take down verbatim all that was said or submitted, but they had to follow the proceedings closely and continuously in order to ensure that correct procedures were followed and to be capable of writing up the decision of the judges in the form of a summary, or interlocutor, which was then entered in the court record.

Scott did not retire from his clerkship until the summer of 1830, two years before his death. He had been offered a judgeship, also in the Court of Session, in 1826, but by that time a financial crash had resulted in the bankruptcy of his publishers and his own ruin, and his overriding concern was to earn enough by his writing to pay off all of his creditors:

to become a judge would, he felt, restrict the kind of writing he could do and allow him even less free time than the clerkship. He would, however, have accepted a judgeship in the Court of Exchequer had that been offered to him in 1826. The duties involved in serving on the bench of that court, which dealt with revenue matters, were far less onerous than those of the Court of Session, and Scott had dreamed of becoming one of the Barons or Exchequer as early as 1807 and engaged in an active campaign for such a position in 1816–17.[8] It was not to be, however, and Scott continued to pursue his twin careers to the point of total exhaustion until illness intervened: he can, in fact, be said quite literally to have died in the attempt to clear his name and reimburse his creditors.

These details of Scott's experience as a lawyer may serve to demonstrate just how thorough and continuous was his immersion in the legal life of Scotland, and how familiar he became with every aspect of the practice of the law, from the initial drudgery of copying legal papers in his father's office, to the taking down of depositions, to the examination of all the written evidence in a case, to the summarizing of judgments and their legal bases, and to the delivery of judgments themselves. Looking through the records of the Court of Session, the first case I came upon in which Scott, acting as clerk, composed the interlocutor rather disappointingly concerned the ownership of some stolen bullocks which had been subsequently sold at market.[9] Many of his later cases, however, did turn on the kinds of questions about inheritance he was fond of using as devices in his own plots. One case in particular, that of Rutledge against Carruthers, involved legitimacy, inheritance, and entail, and in the judgment given 20 January 1810 the court refused to allow evidence of family likeness to go to proof, 'being of opinion that the circumstance of resemblance was too much a matter of fancy, and loose opinion, to form a material article of evidence.'[10] This particular case was appealed back to the court in 1812, and the record of the decision reached at that time is one of the longest for this period. The case was subsequently appealed to the House of Lords.[11] Fascinating though it is to find Scott involved in a case of this kind, and to acknowledge its affinities with the recognition scenes in novels such as *The Antiquary* or *Guy Mannering*, it has to be said that Scott hardly needed to go to the law courts simply to find the stuff of his plots: lost heirs who need to prove their paternity have been occurring in stories for almost as long as people have been telling them. What he chiefly gained from his experience as advocate, clerk, and sheriff was his grasp of all the ways in which the law pursues its activities of demonstrating, proving, explaining, narrating, and plotting, his understanding of the law as an historically evolving system, his permanent concern with issues of truth and justice and their not always straightforward relationship with legality, and above all, perhaps, that profound insight into the Scottish character which he gained from all those years of reading and listening to evidence.[12]

Although one can to some extent account for the pervasiveness of the law in Scott's writings by reference to his own background and training, one also needs to take into account the place of the law in Scottish life and in the national consciousness of Scotland as a country. When Scotland lost her parliament at the time of the Act of Union with England in 1707 the two institutions which were absolutely protected under the new settlement were the legal system and the church – although there was also a provision with respect to the distinctiveness of Scottish education. With parliament gone, the lawyers quickly moved into the power vacuum in Edinburgh society, and the courts became the focus of much of the intellectual and political energy of the country. To this day many things in Edinburgh are still controlled by lawyers, and the Scots have an exceptional knowledge of and fascination with all things legal. As the years went by, the law and the church also accreted to themselves a great deal of the nationalist sentiment which survived the Union, and it is of some interest in this respect to read Scott's recollections of those university lectures on Scottish law given by David Hume.

Scott admired Hume for the 'penetration and clearness of conception' with which he presented the Scottish law at the end of the eighteenth century as a system 'formed originally under the strictest influence of feudal principles' but then 'innovated, altered, and broken in upon by the change of times, of habits, and of manners, until it resembles some ancient castle, partly entire, partly ruinous, partly dilapidated, patched and altered during the succession of ages by a thousand additions and combinations, yet still exhibiting, with the marks of its antiquity, symptoms of the skill and wisdom of its founders.' Hume's emphasis on the historical development of the law left a lasting impression on Scott, as did the clarity with which Hume demonstrated how the antiquarian puzzle presented by this ancient fabric was none the less susceptible of being 'analyzed and made the subject of a methodical plan by an architect who can understand the various styles of the different ages in which it was subjected to alteration.' And at this point in his recollections Scott praises his old professor for having been just such an architect, capable of steering between 'fanciful and abstruse disquisitions' on the one hand and 'dry and undigested detail' on the other, 'tracing clearly and judiciously the changes which took place, and the causes which led to them.'[13]

The historicist perspective and structural insight which Scott so admired in Hume's lectures was a product of general Scottish Enlightenment thought. The notable thinkers of eighteenth-century Edinburgh, that Athens of the North as it liked to consider itself – men such as the philosophers Adam Ferguson and Dugald Stewart, the historian Alexander Fraser Tytler, and the lawyer David Hume – always discussed the law in terms of its function within particular societies and periods.[14] Rather than depending wholly on the rationalist arguments that were associated with the idea of natural law and derived the case for particular laws exclusively from absolute and timeless principles, they tended to see the laws of a country as the product of particular political, cultural, and social forces existing and developing over time, as devices designed to maintain peace and order within a particular state of society.[15] And this remained Scott's own basic perception. For him the law was to be read and interpreted not as an atemporal system but as an historical construct, something that had evolved over time; any reform or change ought therefore to be carried on in an organicist spirit, so as to recognize the process by which the system had grown.

Not surprisingly, he had a particular abhorrence of reforms based on simple-minded analogies with English legal practice and aimed at producing an appearance of parallelism or symmetry between the two parts of Great Britain. Writing in 1810 of a scheme for radical reform of the Court of Session that in his opinion had been rightly abandoned, he commented on the would-be reformers' culpable disregard of 'the genius and characteristics of the law of Scotland' and their lack of 'deference ... to the unalterable habits of the people.' He did not wish to be understood to mean 'that a superstitious regard for antiquity ought to stay the hand of a temperate reform,' but reminded his readers that 'to justify a legislator in imposing on one nation the code of law ... [and] forms and procedure ... that prevail in another, it is not enough that they have been found practically good in the country from which they are proposed to be transplanted. ... It is only in its natural soil, where it has long been planted, that the tree can be expected to flourish.'[16]

This essentially conservative position, diachronic rather than synchronic in its perspective, and acutely sensitive to national as well as to temporal distinctions, can be easily recognized in the pages of *The Heart of Midlothian*. Scott is very severe on the statute against child murder under which Effie Deans is condemned because it offends against what he sees as a fundamental principle of justice – the presumption of innocence until guilt is proved. But in dealing with the statute (which had been repealed by his own day) he also makes the reader aware of the social, religious, and cultural circumstances of seventeenth- and eighteenth-century Scotland which brought it onto the books and kept it there until the early years of the nineteenth century.

The Heart of Midlothian features two plots, the first of which begins with two men sentenced to death for smuggling and attacking revenue officers; one escapes but the other is hanged. At the execution an officer of the law orders his men to fire on what he sees as a threatening crowd and innocent bystanders are killed, an action for which he is subsequently condemned to hang in his turn; although he is reprieved by a pardon from the crown, he is dragged from the prison by a lynch-mob which refuses to acknowledge the justice of the pardon and appoints itself his rightful executioner. Alongside this public plot of the Porteous riots runs a private plot involving another capital charge, that of child murder, on which Effie Deans is convicted at the end of a trial which is recounted in some detail.

Curiously enough, however, these crimes, though prominent as events in *The Heart of Midlothian*, are not themselves its central focus. There is very little of the whodunit about the novel. We know from very early in the action who has organized the attack on the prison and the hanging of Porteous; we also know that Effie has not killed her child, that Robertson is its father, and that Meg Murdockson is responsible for its disappearance. The only mystery concerns the fate of the child, and this is given little prominence until the very end of the book. The functioning of the law itself is presented in considerable detail, but the penal system as it then existed is not exposed to abstract criticism or general challenge. Some of the agents of the law are venal or insensitive, but the charging and trial of Porteous are shown as being carefully and properly handled, and the extensive presentation of the trial of Effie Deans leaves little ground for complaint about either the manner of the investigation or the conduct of the court.[17] The matter is treated by almost all concerned with proper dignity and decorum, mixed indeed with considerable tenderness and sympathy for Effie and her family.

In both the case of Porteous and that of Effie Deans the problem with the law seems to be that it is curiously beside the point. The Porteous conviction and subsequent pardon, though legally proper, are unacceptable to the people of Edinburgh, and Effie's guilt, though perfectly proved in accordance with the statute under which she is charged, is both unacceptable to her sister Jeanie and incompatible with ideas of natural justice shared by figures as divergent as Mrs Saddletree, the Duke of Argyle, and the reader. The earlier episode of Wilson's attack on the revenue officers displays some of the same characteristics in that many members of the local community share Wilson's own assumptions about the excise laws. While the law is presented as going perfectly through its motions, other processes and other systems of value simultaneously deny the validity of those motions, thus creating a fundamental sense of instability in the novel's world.

To use 'world' in the singular in this way may be itself misleading. The novel presents a whole series of small and ordered but very separate systems, each operating in accordance with its own conventions and rules. The smallest of these distinct worlds is that of Davie Deans, a kingdom with perhaps only two legitimate inhabitants, Davie himself and his daughter Jeanie, and even Jeanie's absolute loyalty to the Deanite code is suspect. The criminal world of Edinburgh and the Great North Road is a considerably larger realm, and within it a figure such as Ratcliffe has a certain power; he can issue a safe conduct which will protect Jeanie, at least to a limited extent. The legal world of Edinburgh has its own system and private language, a language for which Saddletree acts as an interpreter who only darkens meaning and makes what he would explain and justify seem merely the more puzzling and irrational. At the apex of privilege and power is the world of the royal court in London, where queen and duke fence and spar and a system of political and personal relationships and obligations exists of which Jeanie can have no knowledge – with the result that she contravenes some of its most sacred taboos as soon as she opens her mouth. In the country of Argyle the law of the land does not run unless it pleases the Duke that it should do so, and men can be strung up at the door if that seems appropriate to the somewhat distorted notions of feudal justice held by the Duke's local representative.

But powerful though certain people may be in these various worlds, external forces of violence and disruption, owing allegiance to different codes, are always ready to force their way in, break down the doors, take the law into their own hands, execute their own capital punishment. The Queen is powerless to protect the man she has pardoned and tells Jeanie in her bitterness that even if she does pardon Effie the Scots will probably hang her out of spite. The strong door of the Tolbooth cannot protect those it restrains. The mob at Harrabee, not sated with the hanging of Meg Murdockson, seeks out and destroys her mad daughter. Up in the mountains of Argyle a tolerated criminal, judging that the conventions by which he has previously been allowed to operate without challenge have been contravened, thinks himself licensed to attack and kill a distinguished visitor who has himself been a smuggler and outlaw in earlier days.

To understand the peculiar impact on the novel's first readers of all this only partially controlled violence and disorder one has to remember the historical circumstances that prevailed both at the time of its publication and at the date of its action. In 1818 the Napoleonic Wars were only three years in the past and the memory of the French Revolution and all the horrors of the Reign of Terror still very fresh in the xenophobic imagination of the British public.[18] Moreover the post-war economic crisis had begun to produce class violence of a new kind in Britain itself, mass demonstrations by the poor and disenfranchised were striking fear into the hearts of the respectable classes, and the situation was clearly deteriorating in a way that would lend a sense of inevitability to its culmination in the authoritarian violence of the so-called massacre of Peterloo in the following year. The action within the novel is poised at a moment between the last two great conflicts on British soil, the Jacobite uprisings of 1715 and 1745, and the populace of Scotland is depicted as anything but satisfied with a Union settlement that had deprived them of their independence and parliament and now seemed to be threatening their legal system as well.

Scott's depiction of the mob at the door of the Tolbooth carries what would have been for his first audience unmistakable overtones of both the French Revolution and contemporary radical disturbances, and it does nothing to diminish the uncomfortable nature of this episode that the mob is shown as acting with discipline and unified purpose:

They eagerly relieved each other at the labour of assailing the Tolbooth door: yet such was its strength, that it still defied their efforts. At length, a voice was heard to pronounce the words, 'Try it with fire.' The rioters with an unanimous shout, called for combustibles, and as all their wishes seemed to be instantly supplied, they were soon in possession of two or three empty tar-barrels. A huge red glaring bonfire speedily arose close to the door of the prison, sending up a tall column of smoke and flame against its antique turrets and strongly grated windows, and illuminating the ferocious and wild gestures of the rioters who surrounded the place, as well as the pale and anxious groups of those, who, from windows in the vicinage, watched the progress of this alarming scene. The mob fed the fire with whatever they could find fit for the purpose. The flames roared and crackled among the heaps of nourishment piled on the fire, and a terrible shout soon announced that the door had kindled, and was in the act of being destroyed. The fire was suffered to decay, but, long ere it was quite extinguished, the most forward of the rioters rushed, in their impatience, one after another, over its yet smouldering remains. Thick showers of sparkles rose high in the air, as man after man bounded over the glowing embers, and disturbed them in their passage. It was now obvious to Butler, and all others who were present, that the rioters would be instantly in possession of their victim, and have it in their power to work their pleasure upon him, whatever that might be.[19]

Butler and those other 'pale and anxious' watchers at the windows are the reader's representatives as helpless observers in this episode of the storming of the Heart of Midlothian, but in a later scene the terrifying effects of such violence are rendered even more vivid by the fact that the powerless witness is Jeanie, heretofore such a figure of strength. She has moved unmolested through the world of crime to arrive in the presence of the Queen herself, and there in an act of single moral combat she has wrested the life of her sister from the sovereign's grasp by the force of her own impassioned speech. The encounter of Jeanie and her companions with the mob at Harrabee is doubly disturbing because all has apparently been going so well. Jeanie's return to Scotland is quite different from her dangerous and solitary journey down to London; she now travels in all the security afforded by the Duke of Argyle's carriage and in the company of his representative. But suddenly the carriage is surrounded by a mob going to see 'a domned Scotch witch and thief get half of her due' (389). In the distance, clearly visible not only to the enthralled gaze of Mrs Dolly Dunton but also to the appalled and powerless Jeanie, can be seen 'the outline of the gallows-tree, relieved against the clear sky, the dark shade formed by the persons of the executioner and the criminal upon the light rounds of the tall aerial ladder, until one of the objects, launched into the air, gave unequivocal signs of mortal agony, though appearing in the distance not larger than a spider dependent at the extremity of his invisible thread, while the remaining form descended from its elevated situation, and regained with all speed an undistinguished place among the crowd' (390). This is truly a nightmare vision, cruelly mocking the achievement of Effie's rescue from a similar fate. And it is rapidly followed by the mob violence which results in the death of Madge Wildfire, Effie's poor mad alter ego. As Madge is dragged off by the rabble Jeanie hears her half promise to tell what happened to Effie's child, but cannot reach her in time. It is hard for Jeanie or the reader to feel completely comforted by the apparent restoration of the laws of natural justice in the pardoning of Effie, when that pardon is undercut by an episode such as this.

It is scarcely less disturbing that Jeanie should carry out as her final major action in the novel the release of her nephew, the parricidal Whistler. He escapes hanging only to be carried off to slavery in America, where he completes his career by murdering his inhuman master and moving completely beyond the realm of law and organized society into the savage world of the Indians. *The Heart of Midlothian* has its lost-heir plot after all, but it is a parodic inversion of that plot as it occurs in novels such as *Guy Mannering* or *The Antiquary*, and the ironic transformation must have been fully registered by readers familiar with those earlier novels and their conventions. The romance endings of Scott's earlier novels used the recognition and restoration of the rightful heir and his subsequent marriage to symbolize regeneration for the entire community. It is hard to imagine anything more disruptive of such a pattern of meaning than the expulsion of the Whistler from the realm of civilization and his consignment to an isolated and murderous exile.

Jeanie herself is compared both to the Lady in Milton's *Comus* and to Christiana in *The Pilgrim's Progress*, both characters of resolute chastity and purity under siege. She is the heroine of truth, and her integrity and personal intactness are absolute. She will not lie to the court, even though the lawyers expect, and even hope, that she will do so. She moves through a world of violence, sin, and crime, and requires of those she encounters that they contribute, at least for a time, to the enactment of her own ethical vision. Within certain limits she is completely effective, and her success in altering the workings of justice is another factor undercutting the operation of the law in the novel. But she can only do so much; she can rescue Effie from the gallows and compel the Duke of Argyle and the Queen to acknowledge that a law which operates on the presumption of guilt rather than of innocence is a bad law: 'It seems contrary to the genius of British law ... to take that for granted which is not proved, or to punish with death for a crime, which, for aught the prosecutor has been able to show, may not have been committed at all' (351). But what she has in fact demonstrated, as the Queen herself notes, is merely 'a very good argument for annulling the Act of Parliament,' which 'while it stands good, [cannot] be admitted in favour of any individual convicted upon the statute' (366).[20] Effie is pardoned in the teeth of the law, and the law itself remains on the books unamended.

And even for Effie herself, all that the pardon gains is time – time to repent, time to find her own salvation. The glimpse we have of her later in the novel gives no indication that she has in fact used this opportunity to achieve salvation as it would be understood either by her father's religion or by Jeanie's. Her final retreat into a convent is accompanied by no assurance that she has found peace or comfort. The condition of exile is imaged more melodramatically in the fate of her son, but it is sufficiently real for Effie herself. She remains as she described herself in that fleeting encounter before she went off with Staunton in the smuggler's vessel, unable to come home again to the family world of Jeanie and her father, condemned to remain 'a banished outlawed creature' (443).

This account perhaps makes the novel sound bleaker than it truly is by giving insufficient weight to the sheer force of Jeanie's own moral power, religious assurance, and truth, or to that image of pastoral happiness projected by the Highland Arcadia to which she, Reuben, and their children are allowed to retreat. But Jeanie perhaps shares something of the fate of the law in this novel in that the processes of the larger public world remain curiously unaffected by the exercise of her power. Her own husband and children can up to a point be secured and nurtured, but her sister, her brother-in-law, and her nephew all fall outside the circle of her protection. We may even be slightly troubled by the glimpses we are given of her children's futures, by the fact that 'David received a commission' in the army, astonishing his peers by 'the rapidity of his promotion,' while 'Reuben followed the law, and rose more slowly, yet surely,' and Effie's namesake, Euphemia, came into a fortune 'augmented by her aunt's generosity' – a dowry which, 'added to her own beauty, rendered her no small prize,' so that she eventually 'married a Highland laird' (506). Such worldly successes seem destined to take the children far beyond Jeanie's protective power, out of Arcadia and back into the time-bound world of violence, legality, and social aspiration.

Jeanie's character and personal situation have commonly been treated as the central issues in the novel, but it is by no means clear that this is, in fact, the most fruitful line to pursue. That is not to say that we should in any way underestimate Jeanie's anguish: we are invited by textual allusion to relate her situation to that of Cordelia in *King Lear* or of Isabella in *Measure for Measure*, and such analogies certainly serve to elevate the moral seriousness of her predicament. But what emerges so clearly is the extent to which her psychology and religious and cultural background, as so plainly exhibited throughout the novel, quite simply make it impossible for her to do anything other than tell the truth at Effie's trial. Far more complex and problematic than the personal moral issue for Jeanie, surely, are the general questions of the relationship between legality and justice and the degree to which historical, social, and cultural circumstances can and should affect the development of the law and its application.

The question of capital punishment and its appropriateness to particular crimes is raised here, though no simple answer is provided. We know from external evidence as well as from some comments within the novel that Scott believed in capital punishment and, indeed, in public execution, as a deterrent. That is not to say that he considered capital punishment an appropriate penalty for all the crimes to which it was assigned in his day, and he certainly did not endorse the particular statute of child murder at issue in the novel, a statute which had required the prosecution to prove, not that murder had in fact been done, but merely that the living child could not be produced and that the mother had failed to alert those who might appropriately assist her at its birth. Mr Saddletree calls this 'a beautiful point of presumptive murder' (52–3) and 'rather a favourite of the law, this species of murther being one of its ain creation' (55). To which Mrs Saddletree responds, 'Then, if the law makes murders ... the law should be hanged for them; or if they wad hang a lawyer instead, the country wad find nae faut' (55). Scott insists that we view the statute in the context of seventeenth- and eighteenth-century Scotland, and especially of that fear of public shame in front of the kirk-session which led young women to conceal their pregnancy and fail to make appropriate preparations. His presentation of the circumstances of the times makes the logic of the statute's introduction clear while none the less indicating that an alternative remedy perhaps lay in another quarter, with kirk rather than with the legal system.

This question is not analysed in the abstract, but like so much else it is commented upon through the novel's analogical structure. In a very small episode late in the novel we are given a conversation between Reuben Butler, as minister of the parish of Knocktarlitie, and Duncan of Knockdunder about punishing Ailie MacClure of Deepheugh as a witch. It is Duncan, the native of the parish, who draws Butler's attention to the cultural circumstances that should be weighed against the church's precepts with respect to fortune-telling. Duncan understands far more about Highland customs and practices than the lowlander Butler, and points out that the old woman 'only spaes fortunes' and ought not to be exposed at kirk-session for fear that the 'poys take hould on her to duck her in the Clachan purn' (457). The episode alludes to a number of earlier elements, not least the fate of Madge Wildfire, killed after being ducked for a witch; it also offers an example of the effect of exposure at the kirk-session and so is related to the statute against child murder. Butler's appropriately 'enlightened' response is clearly endorsed by the text: 'he had not attended to the risk of ill usage which the poor woman might undergo at the hands of the rabble, and ... he would give her the necessary admonition in private, instead of bringing her before the assembled session' (457). As interpreter of the law of the kirk and minister of the parish, Reuben's conduct here serves as a small-scale model of Scott's ideal of the administration of justice in the larger sphere. The law is the product of cultural and social circumstance, and its effective administration and reform require a full understanding both of the principles of justice and the workings of the society within which that justice is in practice to be applied.

Notes

Jane Millgate's publications include *Macaulay; Walter Scott: The Making of the Novelist*; and *Scott's Last Edition: A Study in Publishing History*.

1 J.G. Lockhart *Memoirs of the Life of Sir Walter Scott, Bart.* 7 vols (Edinburgh: Robert Cadell 1837–8) 1:184

2 G. M'Donald *Life of Sir Walter Scott, Bart. with Notices of his Works, &c* (London: Jones & Co. 1838) 39

3 For a survey of Scott's practice as an advocate see T.P. McDonald 'Sir Walter Scott's Fee Book' *Juridical Review* 62 (1950) 288–316.

4 Lockhart 1: 224; Lockhart supplies extensive quotations from Scott's law papers in which the case for M'Naught's defence is made, 1:224–7; the original papers bearing Scott's ms additions are in the National Library of Scotland, ms 1627.

5 Lockhart 1:227–8

6 John Chisholm *Sir Walter Scott as a Judge* (Edinburgh: W. Green & Son 1918) 5, 6–7

7 When Scott first entered on his clerkship, the Court of Session was still undivided; the fourteen ordinary Lords of Session could hear cases individually and pass judgment, but if that judgment was appealed to the full court then the hearing took place before all fifteen judges, including the Lord President, sitting together. Henry Cockburn describes the situation as it prevailed in his own and Scott's youth: 'a mob of fifteen judges, meeting without previous consultation, and each impatient for independent eminence, and many of them liable to be called away and to return irregularly in the course of the same day'; see *Memorials of His Time* (Edinburgh: Adam and Charles Black 1856) 129. Scott's own somewhat more cautiously phrased comment on the sittings of the fifteen is in keeping with Cockburn's: 'a court of fifteen men trained to polemical habits from their youth, is more fitted for the dexterities of a popular debate, than for the gravity and decorum of judicial deliberation'; in 'View of the Changes Proposed and Adopted in the Administration of Justice in Scotland' *Edinburgh Annual Register, 1808* (Edinburgh: John Ballantyne and Co. 1810) 344. The structure of the court was changed in 1808, and henceforth it was divided into an Outer House in which the seven junior Lords of Session heard cases at first instance, and an Inner House in two Divisions where appeals were heard. In his later years Scott served as Clerk of Session in the First Division of the Inner House, which was presided over by the Lord President. Cases could be appealed from the Court of Session to the House of Lords, but the conditions under which this was allowed were made more restrictive as a result of a commission to inquire into the administration of justice in Scotland – a commission that was appointed in 1808 and for which Scott acted as secretary. An important incentive

for the pursuit of such appeals was removed; penalties imposed by the
Court of Session were henceforth immediately enforceable, whereas
before the reform they did not have to be paid until all avenues of
appeal had been exhausted.

8 See *Letters of Sir Walter Scott* ed H.J.C. Grierson 12 vols (London:
Constable 1932–39) 4:309–17 and 9:441–2.

9 *Decisions of the Court of Session, from November 1801 to November 1807*
collected by J.H. Forbes and John Jardine (Edinburgh: Bell & Bradfute
1808), interlocutor of 17 June 1806

10 *Decisions of the First and Second Divisions of the Court of Session, from
November 1808 to November 1810*, collected by J.H. Mackenzie et al 2nd ed
(Edinburgh: Faculty of Advocates 1815) 528

11 The House of Lords referred the case back to the Court of Session for
review and 'to do as is just': *Decisions of the First and Second Divisions of
the Court of Session, from November 1815 to November 1819* collected by J.
Campbell et al (Edinburgh: Manners and Miller 1821) 768. The case was
finally decided on 16 December 1819 when the Court of Session, having
reviewed the earlier interlocutor and supplementary memorials from
the parties, sustained the original judgment; see *Decisions of the First and
Second Divisions of the Court of Session, from November 1819 to November 1822*
collected by J. Wilson et al (Edinburgh: Manners and Miller 1825) 72.

12 To the end of his life Scott maintained a lively awareness of the
linkage between the actual workings of the law and the stuff of his
fiction. On 5 December 1828 his publisher Robert Cadell noted in his
diary: 'Sir Walter Scott called & gave me a note to append to the
Antiquary on a Law discussion this day in the first division of the
Court' (NLS ms 21018, f 52). The note duly appeared in the 1829 edition
of *The Antiquary*, where Jonathan Oldbuck's ingenious celebration of
the superiority of Scots over English law with respect to imprisonment
for debt – in Scotland the offence was not the debt itself but rather the
refusal to obey the royal command to repay it – was annotated with a
reference to the case of *Thom* v *Black* before the Court of Session on 5
December 1828 (*Waverley Novels* 48 vols [Edinburgh: Cadell & Co.
1829–33] 6:243–4).

13 Autobiographical fragment composed by Scott 1808–10, Lockhart 1:58–9.
In using the 'ancient castle' metaphor to characterize the state of the
Scottish law Scott is echoing a famous passage in book III, chapter 17 of
Blackstone's *Commentaries* on the English law: 'Our system of remedial
law resembles an old Gothic castle, erected in the days of chivalry, but

fitted up for a modern inhabitant. The moated ramparts, the embattled towers, and the trophied halls, are magnificent and venerable, but useless, and therefore neglected. The inferior apartments, now accommodated to daily use, are cheerful and commodious, though their approaches may be winding and difficult' (Sir William Blackstone *Commentaries on the Laws of England* [London: A. Strahan 1787] III, 268).

14 Ferguson was the father of one of Scott's closest friends, while Stewart and Tytler, like Hume, were among his teachers at Edinburgh University.

15 For a general discussion of Scott's debt to the so-called commonsense philosophers of eighteenth-century Edinburgh, see Duncan Forbes 'The Rationalism of Sir Walter Scott' *Cambridge Journal* 7 (1953) 20–35. For a discussion of the legal ideas current in eighteenth-century Scotland and the particular historicist dimension that distinguished Scottish Enlightenment thinking from the more exclusively sociological conceptions of Montesquieu, see Peter Stein, 'Law and Society in Eighteenth-Century Scottish Thought' in *Scotland in the Age of Improvement: Essays in Scottish History in the Eighteenth Century* ed N.T. Phillipson and Rosalind Mitchison (Edinburgh: Edinburgh University Press 1970) 148–68. This essay draws on two earlier articles by Stein in the *Juridical Review* for 1957 and 1963.

16 *Edinburgh Annual Register, 1808* 345–53. Scott is here following the advice of his teacher David Hume as to the need for 'the greatest diffidence and caution in comparing the laws of different countries, even when both are fully known to us' (*Commentaries on the Law of Scotland, Respecting the Description and Punishment of Crimes* I [Edinburgh: Bell & Bradfute 1797] xliii).

17 Documents relating to the actual criminal proceedings against the smugglers Wilson and Robertson, Captain John Porteous, and various suspects charged with participation in the murder of Porteous, were published by Scott's publisher Constable immediately after the novel's first appearance, in the wake of its great success. Scrutiny of this collection provides interesting evidence of Scott's use of actual legal-historical materials and of the ways in which he transformed those materials for his own novelistic purposes. See [Charles Kirkpatrick Sharpe comp.] *Criminal Trials, Illustrative of the Tale Entitled 'The Heart of Mid-Lothian,' Published from the Original Record* (Edinburgh: Archibald Constable and Co. 1818).

18 It is interesting in this context to read Scott's own accounts of mob violence during the French Revolution in the first volume of his *Life of Napoleon Buonaparte* 9 vols (London: Longman 1827).

19 *The Heart of Midlothian* ed Claire Lamont (Oxford: Oxford University Press 1982) 64. This World's Classics edition of the novel is the most carefully prepared of those currently in print; it is based on the 'magnum opus' edition of the novel produced by Scott at the end of his life and first published in 1830. Subsequent references are incorporated, within parentheses, in the text.

20 Scott nowhere mentions that a somewhat similar statute had existed in English law from 1624; this was directed against the 'many lewd women that have been delivered of bastard children, [who] to avoid their shame, and to escape punishment, do secretly bury or conceal the death of their children' (21 Jac. I. c.27). The English law decreed that a mother who concealed the death of a bastard child and could not 'make proof by one witness at the least, that the child (whose death was by her so intended to be concealed) was born dead' would be liable to capital punishment. Objections were subsequently made to this statute on grounds similar to those invoked by Scott in criticizing the Scottish law: that it required the accused to demonstrate innocence and that in effect concealment had become in itself a capital offence. According to Peter C. Hoffer and N.E.H. Hull, by the beginning of the eighteenth century a defence citing preparations for the birth of the child was usually successful in the English courts, but despite a strenuous attempt by Edmund Burke and Charles James Fox to have the statute repealed in 1772 it remained on the books until 1803; see *Murdering Mothers: Infanticide in England and New England 1558–1803* (New York: New York University Press 1981) 87.

The Scottish act 1690 c.21 was entitled an 'Act anent Murthering of Children' and was not confined to the mothers of bastard children. The wording of its preamble contained none of the English act's references to 'lewd mothers' and expressed much greater concern with the danger which the simple concealment of pregnancy constituted for unborn children, those 'innocent Infants, whose Mothers do conceal their being with Child, and do not call for the necessary Assistance in the Birth, whereby the new born Child may be easily Stifled, or being left exposed in the condition it comes to the world, it must quickly perish.' The grounds of proof were more clearly and explicitly stated in the Scottish act than in the English: 'if any woman shall conceal her being with Child, during the whole space, and shall not call for, and make use of help and assistance in the Birth, the Child being found dead, or amissing, the Mother shall be holden and reputed the Murtherer of her own Child.'

When the English act was repealed a penalty of two years' imprisonment was substituted for the crime of concealing the birth, a similar penalty being imposed for concealment when the Scottish act was repealed in 1809. The new Scottish statute repeated exactly the conditions under which the old one had applied: that if 'any Woman ... shall conceal her being with Child during the whole Period of her Pregnancy, and shall not call for and make use of Help or Assistance in the Birth, and if the Child be found dead or amissing, the Mother being lawfully convicted thereof, shall be imprisoned for a Period not exceeding Two Years' (49 Geo. III. c.14). In the note on child murder composed for the 1830 edition of the novel the alteration in the Scottish law is wrongly assigned to 1803. Scott had apparently been unsure of the exact date at the time of writing the note and left a blank space in his manuscript; whoever checked the date wrongly supplied that of the repeal of the English law (*Waverley Novels* 12:21; Scott's interleaved set containing his manuscript revisions, NLS ms 23009, interleaf between 96 and 97).

JOHN M. ROBSON

Crime in *Our Mutual Friend*

Novelists, like other artists, do not create to make life easy for critics; they have their own goals and their own pots to boil. In choosing examples, we distort our sources, and if we distort them overmuch, the activity is less scholarship than butchery. A resulting shambles is particularly likely when dismembering artists like Dickens whose infinite variety invites dis-articulators and deconstructors of many persuasions. But there can be no doubt that crime figures prominently in his novels, and so long as we are careful to remember that he was not writing what we think of as 'crime novels' in a narrow sense, the risk of misreading is acceptably small. In fact, one of the most respected of Dickens' scholars, Philip Collins, has published a book called *Dickens and Crime* without being accused of larceny, fraud, or dismemberment.[1] Still, my first caveat is that Dickens was not writing of the lifestyles of the rich and shamus.

My second caveat is equally important. What counts as 'crime'? To discuss only violations of positive law would be to distort both materials and common understanding. In everyday judgments, sin is a crime deserving punishment, and the certainty of punishment is for most people much more important than its source. By bringing in poetic, 'rough' justice, creative literature is able to satisfy the normal desire – or, by frustrating that desire, to induce despair, pathos, and tragedy. Therefore, while dealing with matters relevant to the criminal law, I take my general brief in this paper to be 'crime' in a general and pervasive sense, pertaining to moral as well as 'legal' crimes, and to motives, whether merely perceived or actual.[2] This broader view is essential to my purpose, which is to show some of the ways in which

Dickens, through theme, technique, and characterization, demonstrates Victorian attitudes to crime.

He is a reformer, of course, but that term is not as translucent as one might wish. The main concerns of reformers may be summarized as (a) what is wrong (or evil)?, (b) what made it wrong (or what is the source of evil)?, (c) what is right (or good)?, and (d) how do we get from wrong to right (from evil to good)? This is a very large brief, and few indeed are willing to take it on alone; furthermore, anyone's attitudes are likely to change over time, especially with reference to the ways of getting from evil to good. And, as suggested above, fictional representations are apt to lead by misleading. It is not surprising that Dickens spends much time on what is wrong – that is a constant activity for human beings – or that he is less than satisfactory in stating except in anodyne terms what is right – that is a constant failing of moral guides. As to the source (or sources) of evil, the debate is endless, with the proponents of breeding and feeding never quiet or easy with one another, and the supernaturalists and naturalists at permanent odds.

Taking all into account, including the fact that *Our Mutual Friend* is a 'late' novel, one of those thought of as dark and foreboding, one must not see Dickens as the 'compleat reformer.' Philip Collins suggests, with an intention close to mine, that 'students of criminology may ... learn something from a novelist so enormously talented and yet so close in outlook to the ordinary man.'[3] In looking both at his enormous talent and normal Victorian experience, I shall not be establishing new generalizations about his reforming beliefs and activities, but shall attempt to demonstrate how talent and experience come together to suggest that effective and prompt criminal and legal reform is for Dickens, as for most of us, equally urgent and impossible.

Of all the writers in English literature – except God, as Northrop Frye shows – Dickens is probably the most obvious choice for this theme. As Mrs Gamp says in *Martin Chuzzlewit* of Young Bailey, 'There's nothin' he don't know; that's my opinion ... All the wickedness of the world is Print to him.'[4] Some of the reasons are historical. Beth Kalikoff comments: 'Sensational crimes have riveted readers and playgoers for centuries, and surely homicides were not more grotesquely or frequently committed in the Victorian period than at any other time in history. Yet there was a "sustained enthusiasm for murder" all through the nineteenth century and a corresponding emphasis on homicide in a variety of popular genres.'[5] And, as Philip Collins points out, Dickens' lifetime 'spanned a period of remarkable developments in the criminal law and its administration, in the scale and spirit of punishment, in police organisation and techniques, in the study of the causes of crime, and in attempts to remove or reduce these causes.'[6] He saw, as a young man, the founding in the late 1820s of the metropolitan police force, and the establishment of the detective force in the early 1840s; he took part in the severe criticism that led to the reform of the courts and processes of law; equally important is his witnessing the growth of London, on which most of his work centres, a growth that led to greater separation between the West and East ends, the deterioration of some neighbourhoods and the improvement of others, and more sense of foreboding mystery about the dark and winding streets. While the primordial passions still led (as they still lead) to criminal behaviour everywhere, 'urban crime,' as we understand it, seemed almost a new phenomenon in London, 'the Great Wen' as William Cobbett called it. In these years also the heart of the metropolis, the City of London, reached its height as a commercial centre, full of opportunities for swindling as well as honest profit, years in which the lists of bankruptcies in the *Times* became swollen, and bills of hand were likely to be as 'queer' as Jenny Wren's legs.

Many other nineteenth-century novelists dwelt on these matters: there was a popular genre of so-called 'Newgate Novels,' based often on the semi-factual *Newgate Chronicles* recording the lives, crimes, and deaths of notorious criminals, and a later similarly popular genre of 'Sensation Novels,' combining extravagant detail and violent emotion with realistic reports, and moving the scene of threat from the underworld to the middle- and upper-class domestic hearth, and from a small group of the innately criminal to a universal population of innate sinners.[7] The complicated laws of inheritance and property fostered plots turning on wills and legal chicanery; and the mystery novel featuring police detectives was born. Moreover, street literature, melodrama, and the new cheap newspapers, all having great attraction for the lower classes, were saturated with criminal detail.

Dickens, the greatest artist of his period who dwelt on these subjects, was influenced though not contained by these genres; indeed, he was not only intimately acquainted with but compulsively fascinated by the literary as well as the social trends. Leaving aside his genius, one can look to evidence showing his reliability as a presenter of attitudes to crime: he was a native of London who became a shorthand reporter in a law court, in parliament, and for a newspaper. He knew London topography extremely well, and used his knowledge in ways amenable to portrayal of criminal scenes and characters. Further, he founded and closely edited journals that kept track of the materials of social history, the details that make up daily life and reveal attitudes toward the immediate mundane environment. Also, he was fascinated by the new detective force, following not just the career but the footsteps of Inspector Field of the CID. In the words of one of his young colleagues, George Sala, he had 'a curious and almost morbid partiality for communing with and entertaining police officers ... He seemed always at his ease with these personages, and never tired of questioning them.'[8] Finally, he was fascinated also by crimes of violence (in this he is far from singular), by inquests and morgues (here one thinks with fewer fellow addicts, until one recalls the popularity of P.D. James and of *Quincy*).[9]

Many of Dickens' novels could be chosen to demonstrate these generalizations. *Bleak House* is an obvious choice, and other strong candidates would be the unfinished *Edwin Drood, Oliver Twist,* and *Little Dorrit*, and so on. But apart from personal predilection, the choice of *Our Mutual Friend* is certainly justifiable. Criminal activities entwine throughout it: the central plot turns on a murder in which the wrong man is killed and the intended victim's acquiescence in the supposition that he is dead leads to other crimes through deception and confusion. There is a brutal assault with intent to murder, a murder-suicide, assault (aggravated by pepper), extortion and blackmail,[10] robbery, bribery, false witness, and interference with the due (or undue) process of law.

Equally pervasive are violent symbolic acts (both Gaffer Hexam and Bradley Headstone are given to striking down with the fist) and weird threats, sometimes coming from such surprising sources as Jenny Wren, whose unfilial wishes for her father include the desire that he be 'poked into cells and black holes, and run over by rats and spiders and beetles,' and the more probable promise, 'I'll give you in charge to the police, and have you fined five shillings when you can't pay, and then I won't pay the money for you, and you'll be transported for life' (292).

Perhaps the most tainting evidence of endemic – even epidemic – criminality comes in passages of self-examination and self-revelation. Harmon/Rokesmith's introspections, including his fear (in fact realized) that he will be accused of his own murder, and Headstone's tormented thoughts are leading instances, but even Eugene is caught by the malaise, when, hiding under the boat on the lookout for Gaffer, he confides to Mortimer: 'Mentally, I have now committed a burglary under the meanest circumstances, and the myrmidons of justice are at my heels'; later he adds, 'Two burglaries now, and a forgery!'; and finally, 'Three burglaries, two forgeries, and a midnight assassination.'[11]

In one of the common parodic parallels found in the work, Pa Wilfer joins in the chorus; when he is sneaking away in the morning to her wedding, Bella asks him how he is feeling. He replies: 'To the best of my judgement, like a housebreaker new to the business, my dear, who can't make himself quite comfortable till he is off the premises' (728). Even the innocent Lizzie has 'a sense of being involved in a murky shade of Murder' (114). Judgments of behaviour by other characters reinforce the mood. Rokesmith's manner is so 'awkward' that Bella says, 'Pa, ... we have got a Murderer for a tenant,' while her sister, Lavinia, opts for an apparently less serious accusation, 'Pa ... we have got a Robber' (83).

Compounding the dread is the presentation of what is threatening as normal and even profitable, especially in the cases of Gaffer and the Inspector. There is no need for speculation, as Eugene asks Hexam about the corpses he finds in the river: 'Do you suppose there has been much violence and robbery, beforehand, among these cases?' Gaffer replies, 'I don't suppose at all about it' (65). His gaze is of 'business-like usage'; Lizzie's 'look of dread or horror' is also 'of usage' (44). And Rogue Riderhood says, enviously, when he sees that Gaffer's boat is again towing a dead body (it is, in fact, Gaffer's own corpse) that Gaffer is 'in luck again' (217).

These are the main criminal themes in the novel, but there is much more about the law. We are presented with various members of the legal profession, are assailed with the wickedness of the Poor Law, are told of the effect of the law concerning the property of married women, and get a glimpse of a coroner's court. The laws of inheritance are vital to the plot, and here too there is parodic echoing. Apart from the central plot, with the inheritance of Harmon's fortune driving the events, Eugene has serious questions about the likelihood of his 'Most Respected Parent' cutting him off; on the river-side level, Gaffer in a rage 'disowns' his son Charlie because he (like Eugene) is abandoning his proper station (120).

And some quite unusual legal questions are raised, as in the scene where Wegg retrieves his amputated leg from Venus, the taxidermist to whom he had sold it:

'Here is your purchase, Mr Wegg,' says Venus, politely handing it over, 'and I am glad to restore it to the source from whence it – flowed.'

'Thankee,' says Wegg. 'Now this affair is concluded, I may mention to you in a friendly way that I've my doubts whether, if I had consulted a lawyer, you could have kept this article back from me. I only throw it out as a legal point.'

'Do you think so, Mr Wegg? I bought you in open contract.'

'You can't buy human flesh and blood in this country, sir; not alive, you can't,' says Wegg, shaking his head. 'Then query, bone?'

'As a legal point?' asks Venus.

'As a legal point.'

'I am not competent to speak upon that, Mr Wegg,' says Venus, reddening and growing something louder; 'but upon a point of fact I think myself competent to speak; and as a point of fact I would have seen you – will you allow me to say, further?'

'I wouldn't say more than further, if I was you,' Mr Wegg suggests, pacifically.

– 'Before I'd have given that packet into your hand without being paid my price for it. I don't pretend to know how the point of law may stand, but I'm thoroughly confident upon the point of fact.' (351)

Where common understanding comes into conflict with law, and reality with fiction,[12] a question is bound to arise about the accuracy of Dickens' portrayal of legal matters. Not that one would wish to go to him, no matter how accurate his presentations, for primary information about the law, even if one repudiates the sneering if learned judgment by Sir James Fitzjames Stephen that Dickens' 'notions of the law ... are precisely those of an attorney's clerk.'[13] What one actually gets in full measure in *Our Mutual Friend* is a Victorian view of crime and the law; the great mass of Victorians who shared or were informed by Dickens' vision were certainly no better informed than attorney's clerks – not, when one thinks about it, a low standard, then or now. A better judgment than Stephen's is that of Sir William Holdsworth, who believed that Dickens gave information about law and lawyers not available elsewhere, 'painted by a man with extraordinary powers of observation, who had first-hand knowledge.'[14]

We do not get law from this source, but we get a rich medley of attitudes that resulted from and then helped to change the law. Consequently it is appropriate, without dwelling on the much-vexed question of literary 'realism,' to provide some indications of what the real world of Dickens was, and in the process say something about his way of portraying it.

In *Our Mutual Friend* 'crime' encompasses all wrong attitudes and actions: whatever is thought to require redress or punishment because it threatens or causes damage; whatever, to use a common nineteenth-century criterion, threatens 'security.' A constant question is, How can we be secure, in person and property?[15] The obvious agencies for answers are the police and the law. But in his novel the former is (surprisingly for Dickens) no help, and the latter (not surprisingly for Dickens) proves woefully inadequate except for chicanery.[16] Human beings and God (characters and author) must therefore do what they can, supplying rough and/or 'poetic' justice. Not that Dickens thinks all claims for security and 'rights' are valid: his fictional society, like our real one, is often litigious to the point of paranoia – think of Wegg and Fledgeby. And Rogue Riderhood, who is hell-bent for justice when a steamer runs down his boat and nearly drowns him, says: 'I'll have the law on her, bust her! and make her pay for it.' As he adds later: 'I ain't a goin' to be drownded and not paid for it!' (508, 613).

How does Dickens portray this world? Obviously by means of theme, plot, and character. Each of these opens avenues to crime through obsessive interest in inheritance, greed, mercenary love, and the search for a 'respectable' personal identity: almost always money or what money will buy moves people to action, and their actions are seen by others as threatening. Much has been made, and properly, of Dickens' use of diction, imagery, and stark contrast to elicit atmosphere and advance the story. What is not so obvious is his narrative skill in the dramatic mode. In fact the case can be made that this ability goes a long way to explain his artistic success; he was enormously popular as a reader of his own works, and was also a formidable amateur actor. *Our Mutual Friend* offers fine illustrations with reference to crime.

Some years ago, the manuscript of T.S. Eliot's *The Waste Land* revealed that his first choice of a title had been 'He do the Police in different voices.' A puzzling hint – but then the whole poem (if it is whole) is meant to be puzzling. The phrase comes from *Our Mutual Friend*, when Betty Higden introduces her mangling helper: 'You mightn't think it, but Sloppy is a beautiful reader of a newspaper. He do the Police in different voices' (246). What she means is that Sloppy gives dramatic readings from the 'Police' columns in newspapers, one of the most abundant elements in those always fascinating sources of Victorian information. We have to take Betty Higden's word for it, because we do not in fact hear Sloppy read the police news (though his vocal antics are displayed, and he is able to fool Wegg by posing as a dust foreman), but we do hear Dickens.

A few passages will demonstrate his skill. First, from the early scene in the police station, where the Inspector sums up the facts. Dickens uses 'free indirect speech' (signalled here by bold-face type); that is, the words are not in quotation marks, but the 'that' normally used to introduce reported speech is lacking. The effect is of condensed reproduction, with the suggestion of actuality given by words taken from the special jargon connected with occupation and status, as well as the speaker's unique idiolect (his or her unique use of language). In addition, Dickens here (and usually when using this device) truncates the syntax, as though giving shorthand notes when 'doing the Police'; it can hardly be doubted that his own experience provided the clue, when one thinks of the effect of reading back such notes. Here then are 'the merits of the case as summed up' by the Inspector:

'A bull's-eye,' said the Night-Inspector, taking up his keys. Which a deferential satellite produced. 'Now gentlemen.'

With one of his keys, he opened a cool grot at the end of the yard, and they all went in. They quickly came out again, no one speaking but Eugene: who remarked to Mortimer, in a whisper, 'Not *much* worse than Lady Tippins.'

So, back to the whitewashed library of the monastery – with that liver still in shrieking requisition, as it had been loudly, while they looked at the silent sight they came to see – and there through the merits of the case as summed up by the Abbot. **No clue to how body came into river. Very often was no clue. Too late to know for certain, whether injuries received before or after death; one excellent surgical opinion said, before; other excellent surgical opinion said, after. Steward of ship in which gentleman came home passenger, had been round to view, and could swear to identity. Likewise could swear to clothes. And then, you see, you had the papers, too. How was it he had totally disappeared on leaving ship, 'till found in river? Well! Probably had been upon some little game. Probably thought it a harmless game, wasn't up to things, and it turned out a fatal game. Inquest to-morrow, and no doubt open verdict.**

'It appears to have knocked your friend over – knocked him completely off his legs,' Mr Inspector remarked, when he had finished his summing up. (67)

It should be noted that Dickens moves back to direct quotation at the end, when the 'summing up' is concluded.

Again, when asked whether the facts suggested that something 'really looked bad here,' the police Inspector, once more called the Abbot of that Monastery, replies, 'with reticence,' and in free indirect speech (in bold-face), with a transition to direct speech by way of a narratorial aside (signalled by underlining):

[The Inspector] **couldn't say. If a murder, anybody might have done it. Burglary or pocket-picking wanted 'prenticeship. Not so, murder. We were all of us up to that. Had seen scores of people come to identify, and never saw one person struck in [the] particular way [that Julius Handford was]. Might, however, have been Stomach and not Mind. If so, rum stomach. But to be sure there were rum everythings. Pity there was not a word of truth in that superstition about bodies bleeding when touched by the hand of the right person; you never got a sign out of bodies. You got row enough out of such as her – she was good for all night now** (referring here to the banging demands for the liver), 'but you got nothing out of bodies if it was ever so.' (69)

Perhaps the best example in *Our Mutual Friend* is the account of the proceedings before the coroner's jury concerning the corpse found in the river, where Dickens parodies the form while using it. Here the passages that echo newspaper style are printed in italic, with one place where indirect speech takes over in bold-face italic:

The case was made interesting to the public, by Mr Mortimer Lightwood's evidence touching the circumstances under which the deceased, Mr John Harmon, had returned to England; exclusive private proprietorship in which circumstances was set up at dinner-tables for several days, by Veneering, Twemlow, Podsnap, and all the Buffers: who all related them irreconcilably with one another, and contradicted themselves. *It was also made interesting by the testimony of Job Potterson, the ship's steward, and one Mr Jacob Kibble, a fellow-passenger,* **that the deceased Mr John Harmon did bring over, in a hand-valise with which he did disembark,** *the sum realized by the forced sale of his little landed property, and that the sum exceeded, in ready money, seven hundred pounds. It was further made interesting, by the remarkable experiences of Jesse Hexam in having rescued from the Thames so many dead bodies,* and for whose behoof a rapturous admirer subscribing himself 'A Friend to Burial' (perhaps an undertaker), sent eighteen postage stamps, and five 'Now Sir's to the editor of the Times. (73-4)

Noteworthy here are the passages where the narrator's voice is heard (in roman type). The first of these is an intervention to keep the satirical portrait of 'Society' before the reader; the second is a typically bravura performance by Dickens that, however, also maintains the journalistic pretence and the contemporary reference.

One more instance, this dealing with legal matters. Mortimer, having just come from attending on the Proctor concerning Boffin's affairs, is met by Boffin's comment that 'they seem to have taken a deal out of you.' With the free indirect summary (preceded by a 'that,' as is appropriate in a newspaper report) indicated in bold-face, the narrative continues:

> Mr Lightwood, without explaining that his weariness was chronic, proceeded with his exposition that, **all forms of law having been at length complied with, will of Harmon deceased having been proved, death of Harmon next inheriting having been proved, &c. and so forth, Court of Chancery having been moved, &c. and so forth, he, Mr Lightwood, had now the gratification, honour, and happiness, again &c. and so forth, of congratulating Mr Boffin on coming into possession as residuary legatee, of upwards of one hundred thousand pounds, standing in the books of the Governor and Company of the Bank of England, again &c. and so forth.**
> 'And what is particularly eligible in the property Mr Boffin, is, that it involves no trouble.' (133)[17]

Again the last sentence only is in quotation marks.

The basis of reality in that last example will be obvious to lawyers; indeed the effect of satire depends on the audience's ability to recognize what is being satirized. The earlier examples, however, are less satirical, and their foundations in the life that surrounded Dickens and his audience is distanced from us. To bring it closer, here are some samples from what passes as real life: crimes from *The Times*.[18] These have been chosen, without anything like a thorough search, from the police news about the time Dickens was working on *Our Mutual Friend*; there is no implication that these stories are actual sources for the novel.[19] They are intended only to demonstrate that there are marked and significant resemblances in the representation of crime in his actual and fictional worlds. The resemblance is in both matter and manner, the newspaper using what is very close to free indirect speech (the third-person reference is maintained) and unmarked transitions of voice, and sometimes even omitting definite articles.

> A seafaring man, dressed only in a shirt, trousers, and slippers, applied to [the magistrate] Mr. Arnold for advice.
>
> He had arrived in the port of London, from Havre, on Thursday afternoon, and determining to take some recreation after his last voyage, went to Drury Lane Theatre. At the conclusion of the performance he made inquiries as to where he could get a respectable lodging for the night, and having met with a woman of creditable appearance she recommended him to a place where he would be well suited. He went to a tavern and had a pint of ale, after taking which he became perfectly unconscious, and he remembered nothing until he awoke yesterday morning. He was very cold and found himself in a miserably furnished room in Old Pye-street, Westminster. When he left the theatre he had his wages, amounting to upwards of £10, in a belt round his body, and was dressed in a respectable suit of clothes, but when he awoke in Old Pye-street he found that everything he possessed was his shirt; his money, his coat, waistcoat, trousers, shoes, and hat had been carried off. A pair of ragged old trousers and slippers were found for him at the house, and in these he had presented himself at the court. He had no friends in London and not a farthing in his pocket to procure necessary food or clothing.
>
> Mr. Arnold inquired whether his object was to discover and bring to justice those who had robbed him, if so, he must apply to the police.
>
> Applicant asked if the magistrate could not afford him some pecuniary assistance.
>
> Mr. Arnold declined to do so until the matter of which he complained had undergone some investigation, and told applicant that in the meantime he must apply to the parish authorities for assistance. (*The Times* 27 February 1864, 11)

Here is the opening of a report on a suspected poisoning:

> Various rumours having been afloat for some time past respecting the death of Jemima, mother of John Garner, grocer, etc., of Moorhouses, in the parish of Mareham-le-Fen, near Horncastle, whose death occurred in December, 1861, the coroner (Dr. Clegg, of Boston) at length issued his warrant for the exhumation of the body. It had been buried in the

churchyard of the adjoining parish of Revesby, and was exhumed on Thursday, the 27th of November last. A *post mortem* examination having been made by Dr. Boulton, of Horncastle, and Mr. George, surgeon, of Revesby, and the body identified by the sexton of the parish and the joiner who made the coffin, the coroner ordered the stomach, etc., to be placed in sealed jars and conveyed by Police-Sergeant Lampton to Professor Taylor, the celebrated analytical chymist, at Guy's Hospital, London, and then adjourned the inquest which was reopened on Tuesday, the 16th of December, at the Red Lion Inn, Revesby, before Dr. Clegg, coroner. The evidence of William Taylor, sexton, and William Weldon, carpenter (taken on the 27th of November), proving the identity of the body exhumed, was read over, and the following additional witnesses called: –

William Lampton. – I am sergeant of police. On the 27th of November I received three jars, sealed, and took them to London. I delivered them to Professor Taylor on the 29th, with the seals unbroken, and he gave me a receipt for them.

Dr. Boulton – On the 27th of November I saw a coffin opened containing the body of a woman, and made a *post mortem* examination. I removed the viscera of the chest and abdomen, some of the blood, and a portion of the spine. The tissues of the spine were deeply tinged and saturated with a bright yellow colouring matter. I placed the whole in jars, which I sealed, and gave them to Sergeant Lampton to convey to Professor Taylor. There was some difficulty in removing the lid of the coffin. There was no earth in the coffin. The outer parts of the body were in an advanced state of decomposition.

And so on and on, including the 'analytical chymist's' detailed account of his analysis, concluding with 'I should say that deceased must have had arsenic in several doses for two days or more prior to death' (*The Times* 6 January 1863, 10). Eventually the body of John Garner's first wife was also exhumed and traces of poisoning were found, and Garner and his second wife were brought to trial on two counts of murder. For more details, and the conclusion, see further numbers of *The Times*.

There is, of course, an 'analytical chemist' in *Our Mutual Friend*, the Veneering's butler, whose announcement that 'Dinner is on the table!' calls forth the narrator's comment: 'Thus the melancholy retainer, as who should say, "Come down and be poisoned, ye unhappy children of men!"' A few lines later we find the analytical chemist 'always seeming to say, after "Chablis, sir?" – "You wouldn't if you knew what it's made of'' (51–2).

My final newspaper example is the opening of a story from the Thames police court, almost contemporaneous with the last account; here one needs Sloppy's (or rather Dickens') talents, for these voices from the 'Police' are quite sufficiently varied:

> Diego Salinas, a Spanish seaman, belonging to the Peruvian man-of-war Arica, lying in the West India Dock, and Serafino Galati, an Italian seaman, were charged with being concerned with another man, not in custody, in attempting to murder Michael Clinton, an Irishman, belonging to the American ship Meridian.
>
> As soon as the magistrate [Mr. Woolrych] had taken his seat on the bench he was informed by Inspector Holloway, of the H division, that the wounded man, Clinton, was in a dying state, and handed to him a certificate, of which the following is a copy:–
>
> London Hospital, Jan. 6, 1863.
>
> 'This is to certify that Michael Clinton was admitted into this Hospital this morning, with a very severe wound in the back. I consider the man is in imminent danger, and advise that his deposition be taken immediately.
>
> James Jackson, House-Surgeon.'
>
> Mr. Woolrych immediately proceeded to the London Hospital. The patient, a young man, appeared to be sinking fast. He said he knew he was dying, and, having been sworn, made the following deposition in presence of the prisoners: –
>
> 'I am a sailor, stopping at the Neptune coffeehouse since Sunday last, when I came into this port. Last night I met some of my shipmates in a dancing house in Ratcliff-highway. I had been drinking, but was quite sober. Five or six persons were with me. They left me. I think Galati and another man were quarrelling about a girl. Two of my party left, and I was going to follow them when somebody came behind and stabbed me in the back. I cannot tell which did it. I expect the fellow in the red shirt was the man. He was nearest to me. Before that Galati caught hold of me by the shoulders. I said I did not want to fight. I believe Salinas was there, but I am not certain. Three of my shipmates were by me when I was stabbed. I ran towards a doctor's shop, bleeding. I became exhausted, and fell insensible. I had not offered to fight any man. Galati was there, and dressed as he is now. There was a short, stout man, with big whiskers,

in a red shirt, there, and I think he stabbed me, but one of my shipmates told me he did not.'

On the return of the magistrate to the police-court, and after hearing the night charges, the prisoners were arraigned in the dock, and the following evidence was taken: –

James Colbert, a seaman, said I belong to the American ship Meridian. She hails from New York. The poor man Clinton is a shipmate of mine. I was at the White Boar dancing-room, in Ratcliff-highway, last night with four shipmates, including Clinton.

Colbert's testimony, which implicated Galati, was interrupted by the latter, who 'said in Italian' (and I assume that Sloppy would render it in what passed for comic accent): 'I have several witnesses to prove I was at home and in bed when this happened. I went to bed at Simpson's lodging-house at 10 o'clock.' More evidence was given by other mates of Clinton and Colbert, and a police officer and a surgeon, and the prisoners were remanded (*The Times* 7 January 1863, 9).

A further indication of Dickens' closeness to contemporary attitudes is seen in a best-selling street ballad that was undoubtedly prominently displayed on Wegg's screen, entitled 'Life of the Mannings,' with subtitle, 'Executed at Horsemonger Lane Gaol on Tuesday, 15 Nov., 1849,' and illustrated with crude woodcuts. It will be recalled that this case caught Dickens' moral and imaginative attention.[20] Here are the first two stanzas, the crucial central one, and the conclusion:

See the scaffold it is mounted,
And the doomed ones do appear,
Seemingly borne wan with sorrow,
Grief and anguish, pain and care.
They cried, the moment is approaching,
When we, together, must leave this life,
And no one has the least compassion
On Frederick Manning and his wife.

Maria Manning came from Sweden,
Brought up respectably, we hear,
And Frederick Manning came from Taunton,
In the county of Somersetshire.
Maria lived with noble ladies,
In ease and splendour and delight,

But on one sad and fatal morning,
She was made Frederick Manning's wife.

...

At length they plann'd their friend to murder,
And for his company did crave,
The dreadful weapons they prepared,
And in the kitchen dug his grave.
And, as they fondly did caress him,
They slew him – what a dreadful sight,
First they mangled, after robbed him,
Frederick Manning and his wife.

...

Old and young, pray take a warning,
Females, lead a virtuous life,
Think upon that fatal morning,
Frederick Manning and his wife.[21]

Yet another link between Dickens' actual and fictional worlds is that invaluable source of information about the underclasses in London, Henry Mayhew's *London Labour and the London Poor*, the first volumes of which appeared at the time of *Our Mutual Friend*.[22] Its illustrations introduce us to some street characters whose mates appear in Dickens: if we don't have a single Silas Wegg, we can add two or three of these street-sellers to get him (without subtracting a leg).

It should be noted in connection with Wegg that many of Dickens' grotesque folk have extraordinary and improbable names. Here he may well be taken simply to follow the literary tradition of describing characters, especially stereotypical characters, by epithetical names: who ever heard in real life of a Wegg, a Venus, a Boffin, a Twemlow, a Headstone? In fact, the answer is, all percipient Victorians. As I have demonstrated elsewhere, Matthew Arnold, for instance, was much offended by names with hard 'g's: Wragg, Higgenbottom, Stiggins, Bugg, all genuine names.[23] And consider some of the actors in the Manning case: Sir Lawrence Palk, who married Anna Eleonora Hartopp, the eldest daughter of Sir Bourchier Wrey (and who employed Maria de Roux, the villainess of the piece). Two of the surgeons in the case were called Lockwood and Odling; police officers including Slow and

Moxey. (Inspector Field, the model for Inspector Bucket in *Bleak House* as well as for the unnamed inspector in *Our Mutual Friend*, also appeared in the Manning case.) Had Dickens still been around for the Pall Mall affair of 1886, he would have welcomed, one is sure, Chief Inspector Cutbush of the Yard.[24]

For many characters in *Our Mutual Friend* the menace of their surroundings is increased by an uncertainty about their identity, which is reflected in their puzzling over names.[25] The leading instance must again be Silas Wegg, who 'doesn't know why Silas,' and doesn't know 'why Wegg.' Rogue Riderhood, who is exasperated by people using his name without, as it were, his permission, as though it were a common 'pump,' has a daughter Pleasant, a cognomen that leads to the comment, 'Why Pleasant?' And, apart from the main male character, who has three names in the novel, his 'real' one (and quotation marks seem appropriate) being hidden almost throughout, nearly everyone in the novel has at least one alias. Eugene Wrayburn (like John Harmon) spends much time quizzing himself, the central issue (expressed in nursery rhymes and jingles) being his identity, as he feels torn between stereotyped unreflecting safety and dangerous individuality. Jenny Wren, whose real name (which few recall) is Fanny Cleaver, has a father referred to as 'Mr Dolls'; Riah is her Fairy Godmother; Fascination (!) Fledgby is 'the Wolf.' Can anyone remember all the names attached to Bella's father, apart from 'Pa'? People are as unsure about their names as Wegg is about his amputated leg: he has more difficulty in connecting it with himself than Venus would have in adding it to his 'human warious.' So pervasive is the practice that the final impression is that there is little settled foundation for most characters; they are creatures of their surroundings, human and artificial.

It should also be noted that names are significant in several legal ways: one may sign an 'Alfred David' as Rogue is anxious to do; one must establish identity to convict or to inherit; in marriage one takes or gives a name. And of course there are the names Dickens gives to persons in the law in other novels: Dodson and Fogg, Guppy, Vholes, Tulkinghorn, Jaggers, Wemmick, Craggs and Snitchey, etc. The final insult is in *Bleak House*, where the drunken parody of the Lord Chancellor is simply 'Krook.'

Mayhew's text suggests much in addition to character; some passages in *London Labour and the London Poor* will sound very familiar to readers of *Our Mutual Friend*.

The dredgerman and his boat may be immediately distinguished from all others; there is nothing similar to them on the river ...

The dredgers ... are the men who find almost all the bodies of persons drowned. If there be a reward offered for the recovery of a body, numbers of the dredgers will at once endeavour to obtain it, while if there be no reward, there is at least the inquest money to be had – beside other chances. What these chances are may be inferred from the well-known fact, that no body recovered by a dredgerman ever happens to have any money about it, when brought to shore. There may, indeed, be a watch in the fob or waistcoat pocket, for that article would be likely to be traced. There may, too, be a purse or pocket-book forthcoming, but somehow it is always empty. The dredgers cannot by any reasoning or argument be made to comprehend that there is anything like dishonesty in emptying the pockets of dead men ...[26]

It may be recalled that Gaffer Hexam has similar views. He repudiates his partner, Riderhood, when the latter is accused of robbery, and is mightily indignant when Rogue retorts that Gaffer might well be accused of robbing the dead. 'You COULDN'T do it,' he says, and explains in a series of questions, mostly rhetorical: 'Has a dead man any use for money? Is it possible for a dead man to have money? What world does a dead man belong to? 'Tother world. What world does money belong to? This world. How can money be a corpse's? Can a corpse own it, want it, spend it, claim it, miss it? Don't try to go confounding the rights and wrongs of things in that way' (47).[27]

Mayhew quotes a dredgerman directly on other related issues: 'I've found a good many bodies. I got many a reward, and a tidy bit of inquest money. There's 5s. 6d. inquest money at Rotherhithe, and on'y a shillin' at Deptford; I can't make out how that is, but that's all they give, I know. I never finds anythink on the bodies. Lor bless you! people don't have anythink in their pockets when they gits drowned, they are not such fools as all that.'[28] Gaffer Hexam sounds remarkably similar when responding to Mortimer's comment that when the body was examined the trousers pockets were 'empty, and turned inside out.' "But that's common. Whether it's the wash of the tide or no, I can't say. Now, here," moving the light to another similar placard, "*his* pockets was found empty, and turned inside out. And here," moving the light to another, "*her* pocket was found empty, and turned inside out. And so was this one's. And so was that one's'" (64).

Mayhew also has a full section, with heaps of statistics, on the profits, the practices, and habits of the dust-contractors and gatherers.[29] 'Dust' (in general, refuse – it is not, as some incautious but eager critics have asserted, human excrement) is of course one of the dominant images in the novel, connected especially with money and the vanity of human wishes. It blows about, is gathered, heaped up, coveted, and then dispersed by sale. It can hide valuables, as Wegg and Venus believe, and as is suggested early on, when one of the unnamed supernumerary diners – surely 'Bar' – guesses that the mystery involves a 'Codicil among the dust?' (59). Ashes to ashes, dust to dust, can be part of a daughter's threat to her father-child, as when Jenny says: 'I'd give the dustman five shillings, to carry you off in the dust cart.' (595). And it appears in disturbing metaphoric guise, when Boffin says he went to the Temple as a place 'where lawyer's dust is contracted for' (136).

Through this dusty land flows a river from which its inhabitants also draw sustenance, though its gifts too are not always the most obvious ones: in providing for Gaffer's family, it yields up coal and dead bodies. Its windings, like the windings of the street, are labyrinthine; they force one to follow, but provide no clear guide as to ends. The central crimes of violence are committed in this environment, where the inhabitants, to say the least, are not disinterested friends to the law: Rogue, seen by himself as the 'honest man,' 'the honest witness,' has been in 'Quod' for stealing, tries to get a reward by bearing false witness, and blackmails Headstone. He, of course, is a consummate villain, but in general, we are told, the inhabitants of Limehouse Hole (for short, 'The Hole') 'held a true witness before Justice to be the next unneighbourly and accursed character to a false one' (406). Pleasant Riderhood is a more plausible witness than her father, but one has to suspect her accuracy in this exchange with the disguised John Harmon:

> 'pray is there much robbing and murdering of seamen about the waterside now?'
>
>   'No,' said Pleasant.
>
>   'Any?'
>
>   'Complaints of that sort are sometimes made, about Ratcliffe and Wapping, and up that way. But who knows how many are true?'
>
>   'To be sure. And it don't seem necessary [to find out].'(410–11)

She, however, objects to his having been drugged before being robbed and left for dead – recall the case in *The Times* – ironically, this crime is exactly what put her father in gaol.

It will have been noticed that these characters are seen in a fog, in dim rooms barely lit, and in streets even more obscure. In fact Dickens takes us on nightmare journeys by land and water through a London geographically real, from Southwark Bridge to Belgravia; one can plot all the places on a map. This plotting is especially impressive when one heeds the names, such as Limehouse Hole, Ratcliff Highway, Maiden Lane at Battle Bridge, Mincing Lane in Cheapside, St Mary Axe, and Leadenhall St (where one finds the burial ground).

Through this world the crimes draw us, as we follow the characters in their attempts to find security and 'securities'. The dominant images reinforce the themes: there is a desperate and constant life-and-death struggle by the 'unders' to get up, and by the 'uppers' to keep from going under. Our attention is constantly called to surfaces and depths (both ironically reversed), to certain death and possible resurrection, to abiding chaos and evanescent order. The human beings are in dire need of vital connections, beyond those supplied by the metonymically occupied Venus, an 'articulator' of bones (who gets some supplies from Boffin's dust-heaps). Who else can connect and so protect?

We come again to the law. Surely it is a corporate guide and protector? Well, though Dickens pays nice compliments to lawyers in letters and speeches, *Our Mutual Friend* is hardly likely to be used as an anthology of legal eulogies. No one would wish to depend on the languid services available from those two unestablished, nearly briefless youths, Mortimer Lightwood and Eugene Wrayburn. In characterizing them, Dickens is employing one of his commonplaces, the bored young man in search of something, anything, to relieve his ennui.[30] Recall the tone of the scene in which Mortimer and Eugene outline their legal careers. It begins as they loll, smoking cigars, in the carriage that is taking them to see the body. Mortimer speaks: 'I have been, Eugene, upon the honourable roll of solicitors of the High Court of Chancery, and attorneys at Common Law, five years; and – except gratuitously taking instructions, on an average once a fortnight, for the will of Lady Tippins who has nothing to leave – I have had no scrap of business but this romantic business.' (Note that he makes light 'romantic business' of what is a matter of life and death.) His friend replies: 'And I ... have been "called" seven years, and have had no business at all, and never shall have any. And if I had, I shouldn't know how to do it.' Later he adds: 'There are four of us, with our names painted on a doorpost in right of one black hole called a set of chambers, ... and each of us has the fourth of a clerk – Cassim Baba, in the robber's cave – and Cassim is the only respectable member of the party.' (Note again the attempt at romantic mutation.) To this Mortimer responds: 'I am one by myself, one ... high up on an awful staircase commanding a burial-ground, and I have a whole clerk to myself, and he has nothing to do but look at the burial-ground ... Whether ... he is always plotting wisdom, or plotting murder; whether he will grow up, after so much solitary brooding, to enlighten his fellow-creatures, or to poison them; is the only speck of interest that presents itself to my professional view. Will you give me a light?' (61–2)[32] But the only light he gets is one to his cigar.

While Eugene never does anything profitable in the legal line, Mortimer, in fact, comes upon a little further solicitor's business: he is hired by Boffin (making 'a very short note ... with a very rusty pen') to offer a reward for apprehension and conviction of the murderer (137). This trivial task pushes on the plot, by making the search doubly profitable, and brings even more business to Mortimer when Rogue seeks him out to claim the reward by swearing his 'Alfred David' about Gaffer's guilt (195ff); indeed this action gives Eugene occupation as 'clerk or notary' in taking down Rogue's evidence as elicited by Mortimer in a question-and-answer session (197).[32] Boffin also employs Mortimer to make a 'short' but 'tight' will leaving all to his wife; Mortimer does not seem able to grasp the meaning of 'tight' in relation to a will, and is surprised to find that Boffin wishes there to be no conditions, with Mrs Boffin to have all his property absolutely (137–8).

Another man of the law appears in a satirical light when Veneering's political career is launched. Here Dickens uses one of the stock characters in Victorian fiction, the election agent, almost always a solicitor, and always engaged in bribery and corruption:

> Britannia, sitting meditating one fine day (perhaps in the attitude in which she is presented on the copper coinage), discovers all of a sudden that she wants Veneering in Parliament. It occurs to her that Veneering is 'a representative man' – which cannot in these times be doubted – and that Her Majesty's faithful Commons are incomplete without him. So, Britannia mentions to a legal gentleman of her acquaintance that if Veneering will 'put down' five thousand pounds, he may write a couple of initial letters [i.e., MP] after his name at the extremely cheap rate of two thousand five hundred per letter. It is clearly understood between Britannia and the legal gentleman that nobody is to take up the five thousand

pounds, but that being put down they will disappear by magical conjuration and enchantment. (295)

Little more need be said about the general attitude toward legal procedures: it is summed up in the exchange between Boffin and his secretary, Rokesmith/Harmon. 'Had he suffered from lawsuits?' asks Boffin in free indirect speech. '"Not more than other men," [is] his short answer' (242). At best, it seems, nonchalant and perfunctory service; normally, mercenary self-service; at worst, damage and damages.

As indicated above, Dickens usually offers to the police the admiration he refuses to the law. But in this novel the ways of the police remain somewhat mysterious and indeed ineffectual. They first appear in the police office that is compared to a monastery, with the Inspector as Abbot, imperturbable, methodical, exercising – indeed emanating – an authority that is never questioned.[33] The quiet efficiency of the police and their ready if unobtrusive availability is demonstrated when Rogue's apparently drowned body is brought into the Seven Jolly Fellowship Porters (502). Their behaviour and habits are not without sombre overtones: when Mr Dolls died, 'He was taken on the shoulders of half a dozen blossom-faced men, who shuffled with him to the churchyard, and who were preceded by another blossomed-faced man, affecting a stately stalk, as if he were a Policeman of the D(eath) division ...' (803). And their 'coming down on one' can be sudden and threatening: Bella and John were sitting contentedly together as dusk fell,

> until a strange voice in the room startled them both. The room being by that time dark, the voice said, 'Don't let the lady be alarmed by my striking a light,' and immediately a match rattled, and glimmered in a hand. The hand and the match and the voice were then seen by John Rokesmith to belong to Mr Inspector, once meditatively active in this chronicle.
> 'I take the liberty,' said Mr Inspector, in a business-like manner ... (830)

But there is something rather peculiar about *Our Mutual Friend* if viewed as a typical police procedural or even as a typical murder mystery. Not only do we not see much of the procedure, but the police are as confused as anyone else. Note particularly that the Inspector is 'considerably astonished' when he hears from John Harmon the true tale, of which he had no inkling (832). And the relation between reward money and endeavour must at least qualify our – though it may not qualify Dickens' – admiration. Near the close of the novel it is said that the Inspector was not a loser by his 'having been trepanned into an industrious hunt on a false scent. It may be remarked, in connexion with that worthy officer, that a rumour shortly afterwards pervaded the Force, to the effect that he had confided to Miss Abbey Potterson, over a jug of mellow flip in the bar of the Six Jolly Fellowship Porters, that he "didn't stand to lose a farthing," through Mr Harmon's coming to life, but was quite as well satisfied as if that gentleman had been barbarously murdered, and he (Mr. Inspector) had pocketed the government reward' (875). He presumably does not benefit from the reward offered by Boffin.

Whatever the character of the Inspector, one should not overlook a more serious failure. Though curiously few readers seem to note this strange fact, the persons or person who perpetrated the central crime, the drugging, robbery, and murder (of the wrong person), are not apprehended! It is hinted, of course, that Rogue Riderhood is the villain, but no proof is offered, and his death is unconnected with that crime.

Finally, then, in *Our Mutual Friend* no institution offers a reliable version of 'To Serve and Protect.' Perhaps we can comfort ourselves by saying it is, after all, a novel, even if we do not say 'merely a novel.' The practical inference is that we are in the hands of the author. His view could not be called unrelievedly optimistic (though most readers miss the implication of the final word, as Mortimer sets out for 'the Temple' – here there seems no irony – 'gaily'). Looking only at the major crimes, at least rough justice is done. Rogue, the deepest-dyed villain, ends deepest dead, with Headstone, who attempted murder. As to George Radfoot, whose villainy led to his becoming the corpse on which the investigation turns, when Pleasant asks John Harmon about the drugging and robbery, 'Did you get the parties punished?' he replies: 'A tremendous punishment followed, ... but it was not of my bringing about' (411). Gaffer, whatever the extent of his criminality, dies as he lived, by a line in the river. The 'white-collar' criminals, Veneering and Lammle, go down and down, the latter slightly redeeming himself by acting as an agent of poetic justice in assaulting Fledgeby, who certainly deserves even the pepper with which Jenny Wren salts his wounds. The apparently wicked, guilty prima facie at least of crimes of the heart, from John Harmon and Eugene Wrayburn through Bella to Noddy Boffin, are healed or revealed as attaining the innocence of experience. One criminal remains unpunished and apparently unpunishable: 'Society.' Dickens seems to be saying that from some evils one simply walks away, in the belief that the father of crime, as of sin, can be put behind one. It is not surprising that some readers come away, unlike Mortimer Lightwood, convinced that menaces of this magnitude are likely to continue to breed crime.

Notes

John M. Robson received his PHD from the University of Toronto in 1956. For over thirty years he has been publishing, inter alia, works on John Stuart Mill and serving as the textual and general editor of the now complete *Collected Works of John Stuart Mill*, published by University of Toronto Press. He is now at work on a biography of Mill.

1 Philip Collins' *Dickens and Crime* (London: Macmillan 1962) is vol 17 of the Cambridge Studies in Criminology ed L. Radzinowicz. Collins also has published *Dickens and Education*; any number of titles based on that formula by other scholars are in print and preparation.

2 Collins' excellent work, full of detail here not repeated, focuses on criminal law, but touches on moral issues. I also omit consideration of criminal psychology, much discussed in the critical literature, as it should be given Dickens' fascination with the subject, which is evident in *Our Mutual Friend* in such passages as this: 'If great criminals told the truth – which, being great criminals, they do not – they would very rarely tell of their struggles against the crime. Their struggles are towards it. They buffet with opposing waves, to gain the bloody shore, not to recede from it' (609). All references to this novel are to the Penguin edition (Harmondsworth 1971, with subsequent reprintings).

3 Collins *Dickens and Crime* xi

4 Dickens *The Life and Adventures of Martin Chuzzlewit* (Harmondsworth: Penguin 1986) 491

5 Beth Kalikoff *Murder and Moral Decay in Victorian Popular Literature* (Ann Arbor: UMI Research Press 1986) 1, quoting Richard Altick *Victorian Studies in Scarlet* (New York: Norton 1970) 9

6 Collins *Dickens and Crime* 10

7 Cf Kalikoff *Murder and Moral Decay* 169.

8 Quoted by Collins *Dickens and Crime* 196. Collins devotes a valuable chapter to Dickens and the police.

9   The vast literature on Dickens bears out these generalizations in ways I
     need not demonstrate here. I may mention, however, two recent works
     where his novels quite properly supply relevant instances. For instance,
     in *Murder and Moral Decay in Victorian Popular Literature*, Beth Kalikoff
     analyses *Oliver Twist* and *Bleak House*. More closely tied to my approach
     is a book by Albert Borowitz, *The Woman Who Murdered Black Satin*
     (Columbus: Ohio State University Press 1981), which dwells on the
     notorious murder by the Mannings in 1849, a case that much interested
     Dickens, and made him an opponent of public hangings (but not of
     capital punishment). Borowitz heads each chapter with a quotation
     from Dickens that sets the tone properly. One interesting example is
     taken from *Our Mutual Friend*: as an epigraph for chapter 7, 'Inquest at
     the Tavern,' he chooses this exchange:
     'You expected to identify, I am told, sir?'
     'Yes.'
     '*Have* you identified?'
     'No. It's a horrible sight. O! a horrible, horrible sight!' (68)
10   Parenthetically it may be remarked that blackmail, as we understand
     the term, seems to have come to have its modern meaning only about
     1840, but soon became a staple of the Victorian novel.
11   Pp 212, 214, and 216. For Harmon's fear, see 443 and 829; for
     Headstone's torments, 609, 776, and 863.
12   Though the question does not arise significantly in *Our Mutual Friend*,
     it should be mentioned that Dickens was much intrigued by the notion
     of 'legal fictions.' Marjorie Stone has shown that, if Dickens does not
     owe a direct debt to Jeremy Bentham's assault on their use, he
     certainly reveals, especially in his early fiction, an awareness of the bad
     effects of dependence on them. She also explores skilfully the relation
     between 'legal fictions' and other kinds of 'fictions.' See her 'Dickens,
     Bentham, and the Fictions of the Law: A Victorian Controversy and Its
     Consequences' *Victorian Studies* 29 (Autumn 1985) 125–54, and her
     unpublished PHD thesis 'Charles Dickens and the Description of
     Fictions: Fictions of Art, Fictions of Law, and the "Extraordinary
     Fictions" of Everyday Life' (University of Toronto 1981).
13   'The Licence of Modern Novelists' *Edinburgh Review* 106 (1857) 128
14   Sir William Holdsworth *Charles Dickens as a Legal Historian* (New
     Haven: Yale University Press 1957) 43. Cf Collins 175.
15   How can we secure our 'Securities'? In another context it would be
     appropriate to look at Dickens' and the nineteenth century's views of
     the goals of punishment; here it is appropriate only to say that

retaliation had a supernatural sanction now generally lacking in Western societies; reformation was seen as an ideal based more on sticks and reason than on carrots and sentiment; and deterrence was taking on new meaning as transportation was phased out and the death penalty came under more and more criticism. What needs to be added is that protection was not, as I read the evidence, completely subsumed under deterrence. At the very least, the difference lies in looking primarily at the ordinary members of society rather than at the dangerous.

16 One could credit Dickens with the archetypical legal joke: a junior partner telephones the office from the court, saying 'Justice has triumphed!' The senior partner immediately responds, 'Appeal!!' Dickens' sardonic tone is perhaps best caught in a passage in *The Battle of Life* (1846), which features the firm of Snitchley and Craggs. The former puts a question:

'What do you call law?'

'A joke,' replied the Doctor [Jeddler].

'Did you ever go to law?' asked Mr. Snitchley, looking out of the blue bag.

'Never,' returned the Doctor.

'If you ever do,' said Mr. Snitchley, 'perhaps you'll alter that opinion.' (In *The Christmas Books* ed Michael Slater [Harmondsworth: Penguin 1971] 2: 147)

17 Incidentally, and to indicate that many other approaches to this novel are possible and rewarding, I should make it clear that Dickens uses varied voices of different kinds elsewhere, not least in giving the report of the Lammles' wedding that Veneering prepares 'for the trumpets of fashion,' ie, the newspapers (163).

18 Dickens is not a full member of the 'sensational' novelist school, and *Our Mutual Friend* lacks their obsessive concentration on themes of betrayed and betraying women, bigamy, and madness. Still, the similarity of some of his material to that in newspapers marks a close resemblance between him and such practitioners of the genre as Wilkie Collins, Charles Reade, and Mary Elizabeth Braddon. Reade is the main exemplar: he based his novels in large measure on his collection of newspaper clippings, and replied to a negative review in *The Times* by saying in a letter to the editor, 'For 18 years at least, the journal you conduct so ably has been my preceptor, and the main source of my works' (quoted in Patrick Brantlinger 'What is "Sensational" about the "Sensation Novel"?' *Nineteenth-Century Fiction* 37 [1982] 10). Of Braddon's

best-selling *Lady Audley's Secret*, Henry James said: 'Modern England – the England of to-day's newspaper – crops up at every step' ('Miss Braddon' *The Nation* 9 November 1865, 593–4). I am grateful to Lisa Surridge for these two quotations and the next reference.

19 So prevalent was the practice among other novelists that *Punch* proposed a new periodical, the *Sensation Times*, which would be devoted to 'Harrowing the Mind, Making the Flesh Creep, Causing the Hair to Stand on End, Giving Shocks to the Nervous System, Destroying Conventional Moralities, and generally Unfitting the Public for the Prosaic Avocations of Life.' The journal would include 'Horrors of every kind,' 'Murder,' 'the most graphic accounts of all Crimes with Violence, merciless Corporal Punishments (especially in the case of children) Revolting Cruelties to Animals, and other interesting matters' ('Prospectus of a New Journal' *Punch* 9 May 1863, 193).

20 See note 9 above.

21 Quoted from Borowitz 278–80

22 Mayhew's text first appeared in a newspaper, the *Morning Chronicle*, at the end of the 1840s, but attracted much attention when it was published in revised and illustrated book form.

23 See John M. Robson 'Surnames and Status in Victorian England' *Queen's Quarterly* 95 (Autumn 1988) 642–61.

24 See Donald C. Richter *Riotous Victorians* (Athens, Ohio: Ohio University Press 1981) 105.

25 For an examination of this question, see John M. Robson 'Our Mutual Friend: A Rhetorical Approach to the First Number' in Wendell Stacy Johnson ed *Charles Dickens: New Perspectives* (Englewood Cliffs, NJ: Prentice-Hall 1982) 159–83.

26 Mayhew *London Labour and the London Poor* 2 (London: n.p. 1864) 167

27 Cf Wegg's rather complacently self-serving views of the rights and wrongs of 'finders-keepers' (356–7).

28 Mayhew 2:168, where the text actually reads 'a many reward'.

29 Vol 1:177ff

30 A memorable instance is in *Hard Times* where James Harthouse, having vainly thought of 'going in for Blue Books' (bk II, ch ii), decides to 'go in for camels' (bk III, ch ii).

31 For more on Mortimer's clerk, 'Young Blight,' see his interrogation by Boffin, followed by a scene with Mortimer and Lightwood (132ff).

32 No one is safe from Dickens. Not only lawyers live by interrogation, but also teachers. The 'habit of questioning and being questioned had

given [Headstone] a suspicious manner, or a manner that would be
better described as one of lying in wait' (267).

33 These qualities are repeatedly reinforced whenever he appears; see, eg,
203, 205–7, 222–3, and 835.

J. E. CHAMBERLIN

Oscar Wilde

It was in the 1890s that Oscar Wilde became both an extraordinarily prominent figure in English life and letters, and a criminal. His particular notoriety coincided with a general fascination with the nature of crime and criminality, and with substantial changes in the way people thought about both crime and punishment (and especially its most important instrument, the prison system.)[1] Merely being Irish, of course, gave Wilde a good beginning in crime, at least from an English perspective. The political agitation for Home Rule had created two generations of Irish activists who were in and out of court and of jail. Wilde's father, in his erratic way, was very much an Irish nationalist, though his most energetic irregularity was fathering illegitimate children; and his mother had been directly involved in the Irish revolutionary patriotism of the late 1840s. Under the pen name of 'Speranza' she wrote some seditious verse and prose in *The Nation*, a weekly published by the Young Ireland Party. One of her articles, a call to arms to the young men of Ireland, contributed to the suppression of *The Nation* in 1848 and to the prosecution of its editor Charles Gavan Duffy; at the trial, she confused the jury sufficiently to procure Duffy's acquittal when she cried out in court that she was responsible, not he. By the end of the century, there was a long catalogue of Irish patriots who had been in British jails; and a succession of English laws – from the Vagrancy Act of 1824 which made a criminal of 'every suspect person or reported thief' who frequented dockside areas in England, to the various licensing and education acts – criminalized behaviour that was predominantly characteristic of Irish emigrants to Great Britain.[2] Wilde was very conscious of the political dimensions of what was called crime; and, of course, of punishment, its grim counterpart. Indeed, Wilde was inclined to perceive all crime – at least, all interesting crime – as essentially political.

Throughout the late 1880s, Wilde had been perfecting his pose as the apostle of beauty, and trying to pay the bills that went along both with this kind of life, and with the responsibilities of a new family (he married in 1884, and by 1886 had two children. His comment that 'it is only by not paying one's bills that one can hope to live in the memory of the commercial classes'[3] has an appropriate ring of experience about it). He lectured, wrote poems and plays and essays and reviews and children's stories (collected together in 1888 in *The Happy Prince and Other Tales*), edited a magazine (*The Woman's World*), and then in 1890 he published a novel, *The Picture of Dorian Gray*, a novel very much about crime, and in fact begun after a dinner party with Arthur Conan Doyle in which both agreed to produce novels for *Lippincott's Magazine*: Conan Doyle's contribution was *The Sign of Four*. 'Lord Arthur Savile's Crime' appeared in 1891 in a second collection of Wilde's short stories; and in the same year Wilde published a new piece of social commentary called 'The Soul of Man Under Socialism,' and a volume of essays entitled *Intentions*, which included not only important essays of literary criticism such as 'The Decay of Lying' and 'The Critic as Artist', but also 'Pen, Pencil and Poison,' about the murderer Thomas Griffiths Wainwright. Wilde introduced Wainwright as a corrective to the view 'that artists and men of letters are lacking in wholeness and com-pleteness of nature.' Not so Wainwright, who in Wilde's words 'fol-lowed many masters other than art, being not merely a poet and a painter, an art-critic, an antiquarian, and a writer of prose, an amateur of beautiful things and a dilettante of things delightful, but also a forger of no mean or ordinary capabilities, and as a subtle and secret poisoner almost without rival in this or any age.'[4] Here, presumably, is genuine wholeness and completeness of nature.

By this time – the early 1890s – Wilde's career as a playwright had begun to take shape, with the production of *Lady Windermere's Fan* in 1892, followed about a year later by *A Woman of No Importance*. Also in 1892, *Salome*, written in French, went into rehearsal in London, with Sarah Bernhardt and an all-French cast. But then in June, the Lord Chamberlain's Office – the censor board – refused to licence the play for public performance on the grounds that it portrayed Biblical char-acters, whose representation on stage was forbidden by a law dating back to Reformation times, enacted for the suppression of Catholic mystery plays. The play was published in French the next year – the

Lord Chamberlain could not do anything about that – and then in English (translated by Alfred Douglas, with 'schoolboy faults' later corrected by Wilde) with illustrations by Aubrey Beardsley, in 1894.

For Wilde, 1895 was a particularly unforgettable year. First of all, he had two new plays opening on the London stage, to confirm his already impressive stature as a popular playwright. Although *Salome* had been banned from the stage, its notoriety enhanced his growing reputation. *An Ideal Husband*, the third of Wilde's social comedies, opened to an enthusiastic audience at the Haymarket Theatre on 3 January 1895. The Prince of Wales was in the royal box, and congratulated Wilde after the performance, appealing to him to cut 'not a single word' when Oscar lamented that it was overly long. A couple of nights later, Henry James went to see the play, just as his own *Guy Domville* was opening at the St James Theatre. Wilde had written elsewhere of James that he 'writes fiction as if it were a painful duty,'[5] so perhaps it was inevitable for James to find Wilde's play 'helpless, crude, clumsy, feeble and vulgar.' At the same time he was struck by its obvious appeal to its audience, and wondered 'how *can* my piece do anything with a public with whom *that* is a success.'[6] It could not; and James's play was an immediate failure. Accordingly – and with relentless irony – James's piece made way, within several weeks, for the opening on 14 February 1895 at the St James Theatre of Wilde's second success of the year, and his best-known play, *The Importance of Being Earnest*. Allan Aynesworth, who played the role of Algernon Moncrieff in the first production, remarked years later that 'in my fifty-three years of acting, I never remember a greater triumph than the first night of *The Importance of Being Earnest* ... The audience rose in their seats and cheered and cheered again.'[7]

One of those who was not there to cheer, however, was the Marquis of Queensberry, the father of Wilde's young friend and sometime lover Alfred Douglas. A slightly mad, erratically dangerous, habitually vicious man, the Marquis of Queensberry had become obsessed with the notion that Wilde was the seducer of his son into the rather unspecifically perverse ways with which Wilde was by this time generally associated. On hearing that Queensberry has booked a seat for the opening night and intended to cause a scene of his own, Wilde arranged with the business manager of the theatre for his money to be returned with a note that the seat had already been sold. Queensberry arrived at the theatre anyway, but twenty specifically assigned policemen ensured that he could not gain admission, even to the gallery or through the stage door, with the bouquet of carrots and turnips that he intended to throw at Wilde when he took his author's call at the end of the play.

A few days later, Queensberry went to Wilde's Club, the Albemarle, and left his card, on which he had written 'To Oscar Wilde posing as a somdomite' (his spelling was as bad as his personality). When Wilde went to the club, he was handed the card – and in catastrophically short order he sued the Scarlet Marquis, as he called him, for criminal libel; lost the suit; and was himself arrested on criminal charges relating to alleged homosexual offences with minors (the evidence for which Queensberry had scurrilously rounded up and turned over to the prosecution). After one hung jury, Wilde was convicted and sentenced on 25 May to two years' hard labour. He was convicted under the Criminal Law Amendment Act of 1885, a piece of legislation passed primarily to prevent the spread of organized crime, in particular what was popularly termed the 'white slave trade' in young girls. The inclusion of homosexual acts into the legislation, and especially its vague wording, was widely criticized between 1885 and 1895, but that did not help Wilde. The year that had begun so well ended very badly indeed. As though to complete the scheme, when *The Importance of Being Earnest* was finally taken off the stage of the St James Theatre on 8 May (Wilde's name having been removed from the playbills a month earlier), it was replaced by Henry Jones's *Triumph of the Philistines*.

The public with whom Wilde's plays were such a success was also, with some exceptions, the public which relished his trial and disgrace; and this may say something about the nature of the plays as well as their public. Wilde's instincts were in this at least remarkably sure, that he knew his public well, even or perhaps especially when he deliberately bewildered and offended their middle-class sensibilities. He had long been a public figure, ever since his days at Oxford in the 1870s, and more significantly since Gilbert and Sullivan's *Patience* brought him notoriety (and a publicity trip in 1882 to the United States and Canada sponsored by Richard D'Oyly Carte) as a representative – soon as *the* representative – of the 'perfectly precious' young aesthetes who were satirized in the comic opera. His career in the 1880s as an apostle of beauty was a genially mixed one, and it was not until the 1890s that he established his reputation as a novelist, critic, and playwright; and eventually as a public figure of considerable importance and even more considerable controversy, one of the last, certainly the most irreverent, and probably in the long run the most influential, of the formidable Victorian sages. By the time *The Importance of Being Earnest* was produced, Wilde was a significant, albeit sometimes scandalous, presence in English public as well as playgoing life. When he was on his way down and out a few months later, the critic William Archer lamented in a letter to his brother that 'really the luck is against the poor British drama – the man who has more brains in his little finger than all the rest of them in their whole body goes and commits worse than suicide in this way.'[8]

It was Wilde's intimate and ostentatious association with Lord Alfred Douglas (whom he met in 1891), along with his flagrant disregard for the decorums of late Victorian society, that precipitated his public disgrace. But it was Wilde's (un)discriminating purchase of boys with beautiful profiles that brought him two years with hard labour. This distinction haunted Wilde as he languished in prison, thinking about his fate, and it complicated contemporary responses to his crime and his punishment. Certainly, Wilde's love for Douglas led him to court, for it was this that infuriated Douglas' father, and provoked him into what Wilde charged was a libellous statement. Queensberry was a brutal and somewhat unbalanced man who had wrecked his own household long before; but his hatred of Wilde, who was sixteen years older than his son, was probably not so very much different in *some* respects from what any unsympathetic parent might have felt, considering especially his son's infuriating insults to him (which included sending him a telegram with the message 'what a funny little man you are'),[9] and given the public way in which Oscar and Bosie flaunted their relationship. (After all, one Rvd Miles – who was not, like Queensberry, a malicious fool, and was for a period quite friendly with Wilde – had exercised his righteous indignation about the possible influence of a book of Wilde's poems [and the kind of character responsible for them] on his son, who was two years older than Oscar, and with whom he lived when he came down from Oxford to London. The difference in Queensberry's case was that he detested his *son*, as well as his son's companion.)

In any event, Wilde's relationship with Douglas brought him to court, first of all as the accuser in a libel suit. His naïvete – some would say his suicidal arrogance – in initiating this action did not make him unique among his contemporaries. Libel suits were fashionable, and often unexpectedly disastrous. Wilde's sometime friend, the painter James McNeill Whistler, who actually won his costly libel suit in 1878 against John Ruskin, was awarded a farthing in damages, and went bankrupt.

But the vagaries of libel actions aside, it was Wilde's relationship with numerous young boys who were procured for him by various people for quite specific and, in the law of the land, illegal homosexual purposes that put him on the defensive and brought him to prison, after Queensberry's paid muck-rakers had discovered enough to turn the legal tables on him and transform a civil into a criminal trial. There is nothing particularly heroic or enlightening about this aspect of Wilde's behaviour. He chose, quite simply, to enter the market in a pitiful and sometimes brutal trade; though it is of course arguable that he was forced to do so by a society that would not explicitly countenance any homosexual attachments. And he paid a pitiful, brutal price.

But still, the broader issue of personal freedom, sexual or otherwise, keeps returning to the foreground, as indeed it should. Wilde's love for Douglas was genuine, though like lots of love affairs it may have seemed odd and inexplicable to others; and Wilde defended it with dignity:

> The 'love that dare not speak its name' in this century is such a great affection of an elder for a younger man as there was between David and Jonathan, such as Plato made the very basis of his philosophy, and such as you find in the sonnets of Michelangelo and Shakespeare. It is that deep, spiritual affection that is as pure as it is perfect. It dictates and pervades great works of art like those of Shakespeare and Michelangelo ... It is in this century misunderstood, so much misunderstood that it may be described as 'the love that dare not speak its name,' and on account of it I am placed where I am now. It is beautiful, it is fine, it is the noblest form of affection. There is nothing unnatural about it. It is intellectual, and it repeatedly exists between an elder and a younger man, where the elder has intellect and the younger man has all the joy, hope, and glamour of life before him. That it should be so, the world does not understand. The world mocks at it and sometimes puts one in the pillory for it.[10]

Wilde's eloquent speech, delivered in response to cross-examination at the Old Bailey after he had been held in prison without bail for a month, ignores the fact that it was not his affection, however noble, for Alfred Douglas that placed him there, but his resorting to telegraph boys and grooms.

One of the more appalling aspects of the appalling trials that led to Wilde's conviction was the extent to which the judicial system displayed its willingness to view the actions and evidence of the various people involved in a different manner according to their station in society. The lower classes were assumed to live sordid lives; the upper classes were expected to be above that, and their transgressions judged accordingly. So, on the whole, were their words on the witness stand. The courts were not inclined to credit the words of London's low life. And yet at the same time, for all of their hideousness there was something disturbingly egalitarian about Wilde's trials; one can understand the mob dancing in the street when the final verdict was given. Wilde had been brought down to their level, the level of those from whom he had bought sex, the level of those – and some would say that this included most people in late nineteenth-century England – whose lives had become commodities. Wilde's punishment was wretchedly inappropriate and murderously vengeful, but it had, in the end, very little to do directly with his love for Douglas.

Yet, of course, it had everything to do with it as well. It is not easy to separate Wilde's life from his art, a fact which always delighted Wilde – at least until his conviction. It was not simply that he had fallen victim to the zealously cultivated moral outrage of the period, which caught not only moral and legal but also social transgressions (such as the philandering of the great Irish politician Charles Stewart Parnell) in its net. What first came to Wilde's mind as he sat in jail was the feeling that his crime was not his *fault* (in the important sense that he could be said to be the victim of his own degenerate self, a sick man rather than a sinner). What he also sensed was that what he was defending in those parts of the court proceedings that centred on his writings – put simply, the absolute authority of the creative imagination, and the autonomy of works of art – had essentially nothing to do with the sordid events that led to his prosecution (though of course it did, within a logic that identified the source of so-called decadence of art in the degeneracy of those who produced it).

What troubled Wilde as he thought about the devastation that had come upon him was not that he had indulged in some illegal acts, but that he had been acted upon by his own desires. And so, in a way that was entirely consistent with the tenor of the times, though very much out of character with his public style to that point, he submitted a petition to the Home Office, stating that he did 'not desire to attempt to palliate in any way the terrible offences of which he was rightly found guilty, but to point out that such offences are forms of sexual madness and are recognized as such not merely by modern pathological science but by much modern legislation, notably in France, Austria and Italy, where the laws affecting these misdemeanours have been repealed, on the ground that they are diseases to be cured by a physician, rather than crimes to be punished by a judge.'[11]

In his petition, Wilde referred specifically to the work of the Italian criminal anthropologist, Cesare Lombroso, who in a series of widely read (and widely translated) books provided a typology of criminal behaviour, linking it both to atavism (a reversion or throw-back to an earlier biological form, a savage in modern times) and to arrested development. Either way, it was an inherent and perhaps inherited characteristic, evidence of what was commonly referred to as degeneration, and recognizable by various stigmata – signs and symptoms which would indicate the condition to the careful observer.[12] As a celebrated example, there was the case of Charles J. Guiteau, who assassinated James A. Garfield, the president of the United States, in 1881. As Eric Carlson notes in an essay on 'Medicine and Degeneration,'

> In spite of what would be considered obvious insanity today, [Guiteau] was brought to trial, found guilty, and executed. Much about Guiteau appealed to the degenerationists. His appearance was enough to convert a disbeliever – strangely misshapen and asymmetrical, he quickly became a gold mine for the searcher of stigmata. His strange ideas and behaviour made many people have second thoughts about his sanity, once they experienced the relief of his execution. One writer concluded that Guiteau was 'a degenerate of the regicidal class'. D. Hack Tuke, writing in 1885 about the problem of criminals from the preconception of atavism, queried: 'What is to be done with the man who, from no fault of his own, is born in the nineteenth instead of a long-past century? Are we to punish him for his involuntary anachronism?' His article dealt with moral insanity.[13]

There were many others preoccupied with the nature of crime and criminality during this period, motivated in part by a spirit of reform which assumed that a theory of criminal motivation was necessary for practical improvements in the prison system. Some of these theories were politically radical, and admired by Wilde. Edward Carpenter, for example, proposed that in capitalist society, where 'function' is privileged over 'desire,' those who follow their desires may well appear like criminals ... or like children. And the anarchist Peter Kropotkin, whose work was praised by Wilde, went to the root of the problem of penal reform by asking how society can claim a moral right to punish criminals which it admits having produced.[14]

But there was another dimension. It was not simply that degenerates, to use the popular term, were sick people, needing help. In the minds of some chroniclers and critics of life and art during the 1880s and 1890s, the kind of insanity or moral imbecility or dementia which produced aberrant sexual and social behaviour was continuous with the kind of strangeness and perversity that produced artists and writers. The connection was routinely made, most vociferously by the German critic Max Nordau in a book called *Degeneration*, which came out in English the month of Wilde's trial.[15] In his petition, Wilde referred to Lombroso's and Nordau's insistence on 'the intimate connection between madness and the literary and artistic temperament,' adding that Nordau 'had devoted an entire chapter of his book [originally written in 1893] to the petitioner as a specially typical example of this fatal law.'[16]

To a nineteenth-century mind, all natural laws were fatal, in the sense that natural forces operating both inside and outside the individual defined his or her unavoidable fate. There was a continuing argument over the relationship between environment and heredity, or nurture and nature, but through it all came a conviction that life is determined in powerful ways by forces which are ultimately beyond our control, at least by the time we realize their authority.

It was precisely against this kind of debilitating determinism that Wilde and others affirmed the authority of the creative imagination and the autonomy of art. Walter Pater, who gave the term 'art for art's sake' prominence in English,[17] argued that the imagination provides a defence for the beleaguered spirit, and that art is a noble refuge, a haven from vulgarity. It was the tawdriness as much as the terrors of nineteenth-century life that troubled these artists and writers, not only out of a fashionable preciousness but also from a profound sense that in circumstances where mere utility and sordid convenience prevail, and where beauty and grace are therefore absent, the human spirit ultimately withers and dies – and that this degeneration of the spirit signals the death that *really* matters. Their response, naturally enough, was to celebrate all the beauty and grace and style which their imaginations could discover and invent. From this came Wilde's celebrated assertion – which was really a desperate hope – that life imitates art far more than art imitates life, and his embrace of all that is neither socially useful nor superficially good. 'One should so live that one becomes a form of fiction,' he advised. 'To be a fact is to be a failure.' Writing of the eighteenth-century poet Thomas Chatterton, Wilde noted that 'he did not have the moral conscience, which is truth to fact [he was a forger, among other things], but had the artistic conscience which is truth to beauty.'[18] And Wilde would not let that paradox rest, insisting that even in life 'being natural is simply a pose, and one of the most irritating poses I know.'

And so Wilde and his circle raised the stakes, as it were. Against the authority of the natural, they celebrated not only the artificial, but also the unnatural. Concerned about the life of the spirit, and told that the self-satisfied mediocrity and pernicious puritanism all around were manifestations of health, they courted disease as the only salvation for the spirit. Wilde's version of this logic was to assert that not goodness but sin is the essential element of progress.

This conclusion takes us, as it took Wilde, directly to a view of crime as demonstrating independence, an act not so much of rebellion as of imagination. Only *certain kinds* of crime have this character, to be sure; for Wilde felt deeply that there was nothing noble about the crime that is the product of starvation, say, unless and until it becomes an act of resistance. This is the subversive logic of Wilde's essay 'The Soul of Man Under Socialism':

Disobedience, in the eyes of any one who has read history, is man's original virtue. It is through disobedience that progress has been made, through disobedience and through rebellion. Sometimes the poor are praised for being thrifty. But to recommend thrift to the poor is both grotesque and insulting. It is like advising a man who is starving to eat less. For a town or country labourer to practice thrift would be absolutely immoral. Man should not be ready to show that he can live like a badly fed animal. He should decline to live like that, and should either steal or go on the rates, which is considered by many to be a form of stealing. As for begging, it is safer to beg than to take, but it is finer to take than to beg. No: a poor man who is ungrateful, unthrifty, discontented, and rebellious, is probably a real personality, and has much in him. He is at any rate a healthy protest. As for the virtuous poor, one can pity them, of course, but one cannot possibly admire them. They have made private terms with the enemy, and sold their birthright for very bad pottage. They must also be extraordinarily stupid. I can quite understand a man accepting laws that protect private property, and admit of its accumulation, as long as he himself is able under those conditions to realize some form of beautiful and intellectual life. But it is almost incredible to me how a man whose life is marred and made hideous by such laws can possibly acquiesce in their continuance.[19]

The nobility of this kind of protest is matched by another, even nobler and much more deliberate, assertion of individualism and of rebellion. For Wilde, this was routinely expressed in images of creativity, one with a negative cast and the other positive. The negative image is an old trope, revitalized by the Romantic poets, of the poet as a prisoner, and of the prisoner as a great dreamer. Prisons affirm the power of society, but also the corresponding power of the meditative self; in this figuration, the prisoner's cell and the monastic cell look alike, and the paradoxical freedom of the prisoner and the poet is the freedom of the mind and spirit, available only through some form of separation from the world. Something of this was expressed by the American Jesuit Daniel Berrigan, no stranger to prisons himself, during a visit to Northern Ireland when he remarked that if you want to understand a society you begin by visiting its prisons and reading its poets, and by recognizing the ways in which the deviance or dissent of the poet and the prisoner are images of liberation rather than incarceration.[20]

The positive image affirming individualism and rebellion brought crime and creativity together as acts of imaginative expression, deliberate, defiant, and perhaps also inherently tragic. The key to the identification is what Wilde called a sense of style, by which he meant something far beyond the merely fashionable. Style, for Wilde, was the signature not only of a particular personality but of the general condition of human beings as creators of the world they live in. Style exemplifies a certain independence of mind and spirit, a resistance to the debilitating sameness of everyday life, and a disengagement both from bourgeois materialism and from our distressing and shabby natures. Style generates belief ... and belief sustains the spirit. 'In all unimportant matters, style, not sincerity, is the essential,' says Wilde, baiting the hook. 'In all important matters, style, not sincerity, is the essential,' he continues in one of the 'Phrases and Philosophies for the Use of the Young' that were published in *The Chameleon* in 1894 (and brought in as evidence against Wilde during the trials). Another of those phrases puts the case more directly: 'The first duty of life is to be as artificial as possible. What the second duty is no one has as yet discovered.' Or even more dangerously, Wilde remarked elsewhere that 'aesthetics are higher than ethics. They belong to a more spiritual sphere. To discern the beauty of a thing is the finest point to which we can arrive. Even a colour-sense is more important, in the development of an individual, than a sense of right and wrong.'[21]

It is in this context that Wilde subtitles 'Lord Arthur Savile's Crime' 'A Study of Duty,' with its complementary commitments to a sense of style (the terrorist Heir Winkelkopf, to whom Lord Arthur Savile goes for the dynamited clock, says 'I do not work for money; I live entirely for my art'),[22] and to the necessary uselessness of truly imaginative acts. 'All art is quite useless,' said Wilde in the final aphorism of his preface to *The Picture of Dorian Gray*.[23]

Here, art and nature converge in the kind of determinism that gives to life something of the inevitability usually associated by Victorians with either the conventional imperatives of race and gender and class, or with the equally conventional imperatives of literary genres. This is where Wilde's plays are both original and subversive, in that they intensify this determinism along lines typical of Victorian melodrama, while at the same time showing that the escape from determinism lies in engaging rather than ignoring the ruthless inevitabilities of late nineteenth-century social and economic life.

In another part of this agenda, crimes became much more individual than the criminals themselves, since criminals all too often were perceived as 'types.' This heightened consciousness of the individuality of certain crimes led to the enormous popularity of detective fiction, and especially of the Sherlock Holmes stories, where the creative imagination of Holmes becomes different in kind as well as in degree from that of normal folk such as the good Doctor Watson, and similar in kind to the very few great criminal minds of Conan Doyle's fictional world.

But in Wilde there is a final disturbing element, represented by his characteristic juxtaposition of the trivial and the serious. Speaking of Thomas Griffiths Wainwright, Wilde brings together his career as a forger and murderer on the one hand, and what he calls 'his fatal influence on the prose of modern journalism on the other.' In plays such as *The Importance of Being Earnest*, he routinely has his characters confusing categories of experience, as when Lady Bracknell comments that:

To be born, or at any rate bred, in a hand-bag, whether it had handles or not, seems to me to display a contempt for the ordinary decencies of family life that remind one of the worst excesses of the French Revolution. And I presume you know what that unfortunate movement led to? ... I would strongly advise you, Mr. Worthing, to try and acquire some relations as soon as possible, and to make a definite effort to produce at any rate one parent, of either sex, before the season is quite over.[24]

One of the purposes of this kind of juxtaposition is to intensify our sense of the difference between what is serious and what is trivial. This is how irony works, and Wilde's humour is splendidly ironic. But another purpose is to suggest not the difference between the two but their identity, the way metaphoric statements – such as my love is like a red, red rose – create a sense both of difference and identity. Just as when we take a metaphor seriously, or religious paradoxes such as 'service being perfect freedom' or 'losing our lives to find them,' this kind of reading brings us face to face with the kinds of profound questions that, for Wilde, were at the heart of the matter.

This is the most subversive of the acts of language, when by saying A is B it subverts its own ability to discriminate between what is true and what is false, or right and wrong, or fact and fiction; between what is important and what is not. This is ultimately what Wilde's work was about, this kind of subversion, a deconstruction of language and the categories which language creates. Wilde was constantly using the structures of paradox to generate the most disturbing of possibilities. At the end of *The Ballad of Reading Gaol*, a poem that hovers between the prerogatives of realism and romanticism, he wrote the lines:

The man had killed the thing he loved,
And so he had to die.

And all men kill the thing they love,
By all let this be heard,
Some do it with a bitter look,
Some with a flattering word,
The coward does it with a kiss,
The brave man with a sword![25]

It will not do to say that this is only a figure of speech. It is that, to be sure; but if we take language seriously, as Wilde did, then we must also accept that it means what it says. And what it says is that the most terrible of crimes and the most touching of human relationships are, somehow, one.

When Wilde was released from Reading Gaol, he went immediately to France, where he took the name Sebastian Melmoth. Sebastian was a martyr; Melmoth the name of the outcast wandering hero of a novel by the Irish novelist Charles Maturin, Wilde's distant relative. In the novel, Melmoth is described as a figure to whom 'crime gave a kind of heroic immunity,' the more heroic because the crime was the more terrible, in fact a crime against God; he displayed what the narrator calls the 'simplicity of profound corruption.'[26] There was also in this choice of names and associations an instinct that Wilde had been conscious of for some time – that the marriage of heaven and hell is a convincing metaphor for the mortal as well as the immortal condition; that love and hate are like warp and woof, and the fabric that is woven is the fabric of life; that beauty and goodness and truth are aspects of ugliness and evil and lying, and the true artist is the one who recognizes all aspects. 'The criminal classes are so close to us that even the policeman can see them,' concluded Wilde in 'A Few Maxims for the Instruction of the Over-Educated.' 'They are so far away from us that only the poet can understand them.'[27]

Notes

J.E. Chamberlin received his PHD from the University of Toronto in 1969. His publications include *Ripe was the Drowsy Hour: The Age of Oscar Wilde*; *Degeneration: The Dark Side of Progress*; and *Oscar Wilde's London*.

1 For a thoughtful and lively discussion of these changes, see John Stokes *In the Nineties* (Hertfordshire: Harvester Wheatsheaf 1989), in particular chapter 4 'Our Dark Places' 95–113.
2 In a recent essay on the social and political construction of Ireland and Irishness called *Civilians and Barbarians* (1983), Seamus Deane analysed this pattern of English attitudes and actions towards the Irish. Deane's monograph is one of a series published by the Field Day theatre company in Derry, Northern Ireland, which recently staged and published a play by the literary critic Terry Eagleton entitled *Saint Oscar* (Derry: Field Day Theatre Company 1989).
3 Wilde 'Phrases and Philosophies for the Use of the Young' *The Chameleon* December 1894

4 *Complete Works of Oscar Wilde* 6 (London: Methuen 1908) 61–2. The best selection of his work is *Oscar Wilde: Plays, Prose Writings, and Poems* ed Isobel Murray (London: J.M. Dent 1975).

5 Wilde 'The Decay of Lying,' *Complete Works* 6:11

6 *The Complete Plays of Henry James* ed Leon Edel (New York: J.B. Lippincott 1949) 476

7 Hesketh Pearson *Oscar Wilde: His Life and Wit* (London: Harper and Brothers 1946) 228

8 Charles Archer *William Archer: Life, Work and Friendships* (London: George Allen and Unwin 1931) 215

9 *The Letters of Oscar Wilde* ed Rupert Hart-Davis (London: Rupert Hart-Davis 1962) 446

10 H. Montgomery Hyde *Oscar Wilde* (New York: Farrar, Straus and Giroux 1975) 257–8

11 Wilde *Letters* 401–2

12 For an extended discussion of the idea of degeneration in the nineteenth century, see *Degeneration: The Dark Side of Progress* ed J.E. Chamberlin and S.L. Gilman (New York: Columbia University Press 1985).

13 Eric Carlson 'Medicine and Degeneration: Theory and Praxis' in *Degeneration: The Dark Side of Progress* 135

14 See John Stokes *In the Nineties* 102–4.

15 The first German version had been published in 1892. There were several 'replies' to Nordau, the most notable being George Bernard Shaw's 'A Degenerate's View of Nordau' (which first appeared in the American anarchist periodical *Liberty* in July 1895 and was reprinted in *The Sanity of Art*) and A.E. Hake's *Regeneration: A Reply to Max Nordau*. Hake, the author of a book on *Free Trade in Capital* (1891), had invented a system of banking which Wilde found entertaining.

16 Wilde *Letters* 402

17 In the 'Conclusion' to his *Studies in the History of the Renaissance* (1873)

18 Notes for a lecture on Thomas Chatterton, March 1888. Manuscript in William Andrews Clark Memorial Library, Los Angeles, California.

19 Wilde *Complete Works* 6:279–80

20 Richard Kearney *Myth and Motherland* (Derry: Field Day Theatre Company 1984) 5

21 Richard Ellmann *Oscar Wilde* (London: Penguin 1987) 288

22 Wilde *Complete Works* 8:48

23 Wilde *The Picture of Dorian Gray* ed Isobel Murray (London: Oxford University Press 1974) xxxiv

24 Wilde *Complete Works* 5:47–8
25 Wilde *Complete Works* 11:345
26 *Melmoth the Wanderer* (Lincoln: University of Nebraska Press 1961; first published in 1820) 86
27 Wilde *Letters* 870

MICHAEL MILLGATE

Undue Process: William Faulkner's *Sanctuary*

William Faulkner (1897–1962) was no stranger to courtrooms or to members of the legal profession. Although he never received any formal training in the law – or in anything much else, for that matter – he seems to have possessed a considerably better knowledge of it than the average layman, especially of statutes specific to his native state of Mississippi. He was, as an article by a law professor in the *Mississippi College Law Review* puts it, 'an excellent "curbstone lawyer,"'[1] what might in other contexts be called a sea or barrackroom lawyer or, in Faulkner's own corner of the world, a sawmill advocate. There were several lawyers in his family – a great-grandfather, a grandfather, an uncle, and a first cousin – and during his teens and twenties he spent a good deal of time in the Oxford, Mississippi, law office of Phil Stone, the closest of his friends at that period and the strongest of his admirers. It is impossible to determine the sources of any given aspect of his legal knowledge. We simply do not know how much reading he did of the law books in Stone's office, how many legal anecdotes he heard from Stone or from his own relatives, how many cases he attended in the Lafayette County court-house, or how aware of local property law he became during the course of his own land purchases in the Oxford area. But lawyers, legal questions, and actual trial situations certainly appear again and again in his fiction, and the article in the *Mississippi College Law Review* is concerned to demonstrate that his legal references of every sort tend to be more accurate than otherwise.

For lawyers, however, such assurances turn out to be somewhat less than reassuring. In Faulkner's work the persistent failure and even perversion of the legal system serves again and again as both symptom and symbol of a profounder malaise within society at large. The arguments of lawyers and the decisions of judges rarely address the needs, the desires, or even the basic social and economic situations of those seeking justice at their hands. Those with responsibility tend to be corrupted by money or fear or, at the very least, by instinctive identification with the interests of the social or racial group to which they themselves belong or aspire. Legal sophistication is not much in evidence in rural Mississippi – or at any rate in that fictional county Faulkner called Yoknapatawpha – and even when local justices are well-meaning and fundamentally sympathetic to those seeking redress, they are likely to be terrified by the complexity of the issues demanding resolution, dismayed by their own ignorance of the applicable law, and driven to take refuge in narrow and excessively literal interpretations that have the effect of exalting property rights over human rights, or at least over humane considerations. Petitioners, therefore, rarely if ever receive redress. Justice is seen to have been flagrantly not done. Lawyers, attorneys, and judges have for the most part surrendered long ago to a comfortable, self-protective cynicism, only occasional individuals continuing to cherish an idealism that in practice – certainly in their own practices – proves unsustainable, self-defeating, and even actively destructive.

The principal exhibit here must surely be *Sanctuary*, published, in 1931, at a moment when Faulkner was at the height of his creative powers. After *The Sound and the Fury* (1929), the first of the indisputably major texts, came the brilliant short novel *As I Lay Dying* (1930), and after *As I Lay Dying* came *Sanctuary*, to be followed in its turn by *Light in August* (1932), another of the acknowledged Faulknerian peaks. The sequence of publication at this point in Faulkner's career is somewhat misleading, however, in that *Sanctuary* was not only finished but submitted to the publisher *ahead* of *As I Lay Dying* and may have existed in some preliminary form even before the writing of *The Sound and the Fury*. Just why *Sanctuary* was not published when first submitted is by no means clear, although it is possible and indeed tempting to speculate that the publisher may have been somewhat daunted by the violence contained in the book and especially by the directness and specificity with which that violence was presented. What is known is that, when the galley proofs eventually came into Faulkner's hands, he decided that the book was unsatisfactory as it stood and embarked upon a thorough revision of the entire text, one that involved a good deal of rewriting and structural reorganization. The consequent resetting of type also cost him money that he could at that time ill afford, although once *Sanctuary* was finally published he more than recovered his losses in terms both of strong sales and of the Hollywood assignments that came his way as a result of the mildly scandalous publicity the novel attracted.

Sanctuary can be summarized – for the purposes of this present discussion – as the story of the brutal rape and abduction of a Southern 'belle,' Temple Drake, by a gangster known as Popeye, one of Faulkner's most chilling characters. Popeye also kills a man called Tommy who happens to be in the way, but the person brought to trial for the murder is Lee Goodwin, at whose bootlegging hide-out these events occur. Ineptly defended by Horace Benbow, a vacuously idealistic lawyer, Goodwin is eventually lynched by an angry mob after being additionally – and luridly – accused of Temple's rape, leaving Popeye, in a grotesque finale, to be executed for a different murder which he could not have committed because he was murdering yet someone else at the time.

The novel as Faulkner first wrote it[2] began with a scene closely corresponding to the beginning of chapter 16 of the published book[3] – with Horace Benbow visiting Goodwin in jail and beginning his attempt to reconstruct the events leading up to Tommy's murder. Many of the other crucial narrative events have already occurred by this point in the book's chronology, and the prospective reader of the original version was to have been introduced to them retrospectively, sometimes in quite cumbersome ways. The technique, probably originating in Faulkner's reading of Joseph Conrad, was one that he used with great success on other occasions (in *Light in August*, for example), but in this instance he did not handle it especially well. Apparently recognizing this when the proofs arrived, he tore the book apart and then put it together again in more or less chronological order, using as his new opening the brilliantly conceived scene of Benbow and Popeye at the spring that had formerly been located in the second chapter.

The famous – or perhaps infamous – introduction which Faulkner wrote for the Modern Library issue of *Sanctuary* in 1932 gives the impression that the revision process also diminished the violence of a story which he claimed to have written out of the crudest of economic motives: 'To me [he said] it is a cheap idea, because it was deliberately conceived to make money. ... I took a little time out, and speculated what a person in Mississippi would believe to be current trends, chose what I thought was the right answer, and invented the most horrific tale I could imagine ...'⁴ But that introduction was intended to be tongue-in-cheek, though it has rarely been read that way, and comparison of the original and final versions of the novel shows a very different situation. Not only is the original *Sanctuary* a thoroughly serious piece of writing but all the scenes that made the book notorious when it was first published and that led an influential reviewer to categorize Faulkner as a member of the 'cruel school' of American literature, a 'prime example of American sadism'⁵ – all the episodes of the rape and its aftermath, the scene of Red's funeral and all those in the brothel – were in fact carry-overs from that first version, with little or no alteration. Indeed, the violence of the second version was actually increased by the greater directness with which the lynching of Goodwin was presented and by the addition of the bizarre flashback into Popeye's childhood.

Clearly, the violence in the novel was not simply a gimmick for increasing sales but, as Faulkner so often said in later years, a novelistic tool, a means towards a larger end, a fundamental element in his overall conception of the world he wanted to portray. It seems equally clear that, while Faulkner was primarily offering in the novel a radical criticism of his own Mississippi society and what Horace Benbow at one point sourly refers to as its 'free Democratico-Protestant atmosphere' (151), he was at the same time using the linked, abstractable themes of violence and injustice as a means of pointing to a kind of corruption and cynicism that he saw as pervasive of American society as a whole. The novel is, after all, absolutely contemporary in its setting, and it speaks, as such, to a moment in American history characterized by economic depression, by prohibition laws whose unpopularity and unenforceability brought the entire legal system into contempt, and by the spectacular gangsterism which prohibition did so much to promote and sustain. It seems entirely relevant that Memphis should be a big city beyond (if only just beyond) the actual boundaries of Mississippi, as well as beyond the notional boundaries of Yoknapatawpha County, and that Popeye should be based quite closely on a well-known Memphis underworld figure, Neil Karens 'Popeye' Pumphrey, who avoided conviction for the various murders of which he was from time to time accused and then died, apparently by his own hand, in October 1931, just a few months before *Sanctuary* first appeared. Faulkner got the story of rape and abduction from a woman encountered in a Memphis bar who had been Pumphrey's victim in real life,[6] and it could conceivably have been the fear of a response from Pumphrey, in the form of a libel action, or worse, that caused the book's publication to be held up.

Although the action of the novel is thus in many respects time-specific, it undoubtedly raises, often in profoundly ironic terms, a number of persistently relevant questions about the judicial process, about crime and punishment, and about responsibility and guilt. What are readers to think and feel, for example, about Popeye's dodging so many penalties that might be thought of as 'just' only to suffer at the end of the novel a form of judicial murder for a crime he did not in fact commit? And how are responses to the manner of his death modified or complicated by the suspicion that it represents for Popeye himself a form of tidy suicide? '''Fix my hair, Jack,''' he says as the trap is sprung (378) – an episode, incidentally, that appears in the original text and could not, therefore, have been added after the 'real-life' Pumphrey suicide. To what extent, again, is the sense of Popeye's responsibility for his crimes, including his crimes against Temple, affected by that late revelation of his childhood history which Faulkner added to the final chapter of the published version? Given the predominantly comic manner of its telling, can that flashback even be taken seriously as a case history?

Where, in particular, does the primary responsibility lie for what happens to Temple? Is Popeye really the villain? What about Gowan Steven's responsibility for so messily bringing the whole situation into being in the first place? Or does much of the blame lie with Temple herself, arrogant as she is in her sense of middle-class superiority and security ('''My father's a judge''' [60]) and provocative in her empty automatic coquettishness? How, indeed, should Temple be regarded throughout the whole sequence of her experiences? Is she to be condemned, as she was by many early critics, for displaying a total lack of discretion and an actual affinity for evil, or should she rather be seen as so crippled by her patriarchal background and so traumatized by the rape and by everything that follows that she is effectively deprived of all responsibility for her actions? Does Faulkner's presentation of her not confront the reader, in fact, with many of the dilemmas more recently associated with such a figure as Patty Hearst?

There are also a number of more specifically legal or lawyerly issues that seem to arise from the book. At one level, of course, it can simply be said that the entire system of justice, of law and order, is inextricably implicated in the social and moral corruption that comprehensively riddles the novel's entire presented world. Judges use their power and influence to circumvent due process. District attorneys seek convictions on any terms and for purely personal ends. Lawyers, purchasable either by money or by sex, operate by secret manipulation rather than by courtroom argument and are often as corrupt as the clients they serve. (Horace's assertion that there is an inevitable corruption involved in trafficking with evil would seem, if valid, to cast a doubtful shadow over criminal lawyers in general). Along with police chiefs and detectives, lawyers seem also to provide Miss Reba's brothel with some of its best and most regular customers – among them 'the biggest lawyer in Memphis' who earns his superlative not only by being a millionaire but by weighing 'two hundred and eighty pounds' and having his own special bed installed (252). Horace's assurance to Goodwin that he can count on the protection of '"law, justice, civilization"' (156) turns out in practice to be disastrously and culpably naïve, as does almost everything else said and done by the novel's one example of a well-meaning man of law.

Horace's pampered and self-pitying ineffectuality – so sharply contrasted to Ruby's resourceful coping with hardship – is brought out in the early scenes of his talking and drinking too much while at the Old Frenchman place. Ruby's assessment of him at that time is much shrewder than his assessment of her, whom he tends to see as a damsel in distress, a cause to fight for, an occasion to set out on a knightly quest for justice and truth. But strong as he may be on the ethics of his profession, Horace is altogether shakier when it comes to matters of actual practice. Indeed, practising law is what he appears to have done very little of: nothing seems to prevent his simply walking away from either home or office in Kinston, and although Miss Jenny says that even Horace must have some business back there (128), it is not at all clear that he does. It is also Miss Jenny who has to remind him of the need to observe basic professional proprieties in his relations with Ruby. As the novel proceeds Horace has occasion to measure the gulf that divides his limp idealism from the harsh realities of a society whose moral elevation can be measured in terms of its election and toleration of a state senator such as Clarence Snopes. At Goodwin's trial he finds himself standing helplessly and almost wordlessly by while events are grossly manipulated by Eustace Graham and then grotesquely sanctioned by that dignified representative of the legal profession Judge Drake – supported, of course, by his phalanx of sons, at least two of whom are lawyers themselves.[7]

While much in the trial scene remains obscure, to the point that it becomes difficult to determine what, if any, prescribed procedures are in fact being followed, it is at least crystal clear that Horace proves himself hopelessly incompetent as a defence lawyer. It has to be said for Horace that he has arrayed against him a series of forces at once more numerous and more formidable than he could ever have hoped to contend with: Popeye, of course, who has shot Red just a few days earlier, of whom Temple is presumably afraid, and for whom the Memphis lawyer is evidently working; Eustace Graham, seeking a conviction at any cost, secretly abetted by Horace's own sister and perhaps by the Memphis lawyer; and Temple's family, headed by Judge Drake, superficially the very type of Southern judgeship and gentlemanliness but in practice concerned only to defend his family's name. It is Horace, however, who refuses to allow Goodwin to make the guilty plea that the latter believes (rightly, as it turns out) would save his life, who allows Ruby on the first day of the trial to mention Temple as part of her evidence, and who calls Temple as a witness for the defence – only to be stunned into impotence and silence when she perjures herself in such absolute terms.

It appears from the reference to her 'parrotlike answers' and to Graham's concern with 'holding her eyes' (343) that Temple has been 'got at' by the prosecution and drilled to give a series of prepared answers designed to get an easy conviction – and simultaneously protect Popeye – by throwing on Goodwin the blame not only for Tommy's murder but for the rape as well; those same answers also serve to minimize her own, hence her family's public shame by avoiding all reference to Miss Reba's and the life she had led there. Some commentators think that when Temple is asked where she has been living she supplies Miss Reba's address, but it seems more likely, especially in light of her earlier reference to Memphis as her present 'home' (342) and of Graham's use of the term 'in hiding' (343), that she would have given instead either a fictitious address or the actual address to which she was taken following Popeye's shooting of Red on 17 June (361) – evidently the event to which Miss Reba refers when Horace telephones to check on Temple's whereabouts immediately before the opening of the trial (on 20 June) and she asks him, ' "Dont you read no papers?" ' (322).

Horace's collapse at the moment of crisis is generally read as a failure of character, an almost inevitable consequence of his fundamental ineffectuality and of a set of professional and class assumptions and attitudes towards women that prevent him from ever imagining that other representatives of law and justice could behave in so corrupt and ungentlemanly a fashion or that so signal a representative of Southern Womanhood as Temple Drake could prove so dishonest in the witness-box. An American critic, Joseph R. Urgo, has recently argued[8] that the question of Temple's perjury is less straightforward than normally assumed, and although he fails to acknowledge the occasions when she does lie outright – for example, in her direct, deliberate, and unqualified statement that Goodwin shot Tommy (345) – Urgo is certainly correct in insisting that when Temple says at the trial that it was Goodwin from whom she was hiding in the corn-crib (344), she is stating no more than the truth. Goodwin, as Ruby immediately recognized, was as aware of Temple's attraction as any of the other men at the Old Frenchman place, and although it is unclear whether Tommy is speaking on his own or on Goodwin's behalf (or on behalf of them both) when he offers Temple the dubious reassurance that '"Lee says hit wont hurt you none. All you got to do is lay down ..."' (118) the very quotation of these words as originating with Goodwin lends support to Urgo's basic arguments that Temple was already thoroughly terrorized before the actual rape occurred, that Goodwin had participated in that terrorization (even though, as the dominating presence at the Old Frenchman place, he could have protected Temple had he chosen to do so), that the guilt for Temple's violation was thus by no means confined to Popeye himself, and that Goodwin specifically, while technically innocent of the rape, certainly bore a portion of the responsibility for the overall sequence of events. Urgo also hints, though he does not quite say, that there may have been an element of revenge in Temple's courtroom performance – that, given an opportunity to exact retribution from at least one of her terrorizers, she does not hesitate to seize it.

In a sense, of course, these arguments are rather beside the legal, or at any rate the courtroom, point. Goodwin is formally on trial for the murder of Tommy, and on that issue Temple clearly does perjure herself – always assuming, of course, that she retains any clear memory of the whole disastrous train of events: the final scene in the Luxembourg Gardens, often read as emblematic of Temple's immunity from the consequences of the novel's action, can no less plausibly be viewed as indicative of long-term traumatization. The whole character and direction of Goodwin's trial – even, it could be said, its entire claim to be considered a legal proceeding – is distorted and subverted in a moment by the introduction of the rape element, and especially of the blood-stained corn-cob said to have been used in the assault, and it is possible to have some sympathy for Horace's predicament if one assumes that he was indeed taken entirely by surprise by a deliberate and cynical prosecution tactic, presumably prompted by Narcissa's tip-off to Eustace Graham and obviously calculated to arouse the jury's emotions to the point of obscuring the lack of evidence relevant to the murder itself. Whether Horace *ought* to have been taken by surprise after his own interview with Temple is quite another matter – it can be argued[9] that he was in any case disabled by rape-fantasies of his own in which the image of Temple merged with that of his obsessively desired step-daughter Little Belle. The fact apparently remains (once again there is no direct textual evidence) that he immediately realizes that the corn-cob tactic will work – that in a society dedicated to the sanctification of Southern Womanhood it cannot fail to work – and therefore, without speaking another word, lets what he recognizes as an inevitable process take its headlong and ultimately violent course.

Faulkner perhaps counted upon his readers also recognizing what would happen once the corn-cob had been introduced into evidence, and he would not have wanted to blur the issue by narrating stages in the trial that lacked emotional or even thematic significance. What he needed to dramatize – without too much disturbing the crisp narrative pace maintained in the book as a whole – was simply the corrupt alliance of the properly constituted legal guardians of Yoknapatawpha County against Horace's well-meaning but culpable and, for Goodwin, fatal incompetence. The handling of the trial does, even so, seem remarkably scanty and inexpressive, although the fact that the original text of the novel is no clearer at these points seems to leave open the possibility that Faulkner thought he was offering a not excessively caricatured representation of how such a trial might indeed have proceeded in a Mississippi courtroom of that date – a date, certainly, at which lynchings (if almost always of blacks) were by no means unknown in the deep South.

Sanctuary is perhaps a special case among Faulkner's novels, insofar as it seems to have been written almost as a deliberate exercise, at once horrific and subversively comic, in the grotesquerie of violence and judicial corruption. But there is no shortage of other novels and stories by Faulkner in which lawyers, judges, or justices of the peace play significant roles. Although Horace Benbow did not appear again in later novels,[10] he was replaced in Faulkner's battery of recurrent characters by another lawyer, Gavin Stevens, who combined much of Horace's romantic idealism with considerably greater legal and especially courtroom competence. Stevens appears in several of Faulkner's books. *Light in August*, the earliest of these, is profoundly concerned with crime and punishment, but not especially with legal process, and Stevens remains a minor character. He similarly appears in only the final section of *Go Down, Moses* (1942), although that novel again touches upon many issues – most of them relating to the practical and moral implications of inheritance – which the law attempts to address. In *Intruder in the Dust* (1948), however, a somewhat polemical novel about a black man unjustly charged with murder, Stevens is centrally important as the lawyer who proceeds on the assumption of his client's guilt until a small boy proves him wrong. In *Knight's Gambit* (1949) Stevens plays, more or less honourably, the central investigatory role in a series of detective stories, characteristically proving his point in highly manipulated courtroom situations. And in two of the novels of the 'Snopes' trilogy, which touches throughout upon practical and sometimes technical questions of local property law, Stevens appears in modified Benbovian guise as an idealist who repeatedly renders himself ineffective – both as man and as lawyer – by his failure to take sufficiently into account either the complexities of human nature or the practical realities of the society in which he lives. In the later of these novels, *The Mansion* (1959), his idealism itself is called into question by his participation in securing, on compassionate grounds, the release from prison of an elderly murderer who will inevitably seek to kill the man he believes responsible for his forty years' incarceration – the very man whom Stevens himself has for an even longer period regarded with profound personal contempt and extravagant social terror.

Most interesting in relation to *Sanctuary* is *Requiem for a Nun* (1951), in which some of the events and moral issues of *Sanctuary* are revisited from the narrative perspective of some eight years later. The core of *Requiem* consists of a series of scenes in which Stevens, although not in an actual courtroom, persistently and often brutally cross-examines Temple (now married to Gowan Stevens) as to her response to her experiences in Miss Reba's brothel and her degree of responsibility for the violent events that occurred at that time and, more especially, since. Although it may sound from this account that Stevens in effect avails himself of the opportunity that his predecessor, Horace Benbow, so signally failed to grasp, there are too many differences between the two novels – written some twenty years apart – for the one to be read at all straightforwardly as a commentary on the other. What does, however, seem of some significance for a reading of *Sanctuary* is the fact that the Stevens of *Requiem for a Nun* is by no means a wholly positive figure. Interpretations of the novel have varied widely, and many Faulkner commentators, indeed, have shrewdly dodged confronting it at all. But recent criticism[11] has tended to the view that it is Temple who emerges the more sympathetically from the later novel precisely because she does not, like Stevens, brood obsessively on the past but makes a genuine attempt – late and desperate though it may be, and possibly doomed – to escape from that burden and make for herself and those close to her the best life she can. Stevens' insistence in *Requiem* on, so to speak, the letter of the moral law is reminiscent of the self-defeating rigidity of Benbow's specifically legal assumptions in *Sanctuary* itself, and both attitudes seem consistent with Faulkner's persistent representation of lawyers and the law as insufficiently related to life either as it is or as it should be.[12]

Faulkner, an essentially conservative thinker, certainly saw the law as crucial to the maintenance of social order and was in no sense concerned to challenge or subvert either its functions or its enshrined values. He probably did not even entertain any special hostility towards judges and lawyers as a group: nobody else in his novels and stories does much better – apart, perhaps, from the truly innocent, a category from which many more than lawyers must be considered automatically disbarred. But to be thus committed to the law was to become the more sensitive to its abuse, and Faulkner seized almost inevitably upon the unique reticulations of the legal system – its constant institutionalized interactions between the powerful and the powerless, the socially gracious and the socially disgraced – as providing narrative materials and sources of symbolic reference precisely suited to writing about the sickness of specific societies or about the universal experience of human mischancing, the failure of things to be or to turn out as they should. If, in *Sanctuary* and elsewhere, Faulkner's world seems structured upon the relationship – at once intimate and distant – between the panoply of the court-house and the squalor of the jail, that is perhaps only another element in his fundamental recognition of the necessary co-existence and countervailing polarity of human (and especially societal) aspiration and human (and especially individual) defeat.

Notes

Michael Millgate's many publications include *William Faulkner* and *The Achievement of William Faulkner*, and he has edited Faulkner manuscripts for Garland Publishing. He is also the author of *Thomas Hardy: A Biography* and co-editor of the seven-volume Clarendon Press edition of Hardy's letters.

1 Morris Wolff 'Faulkner's Knowledge of the Law' *Mississippi College Law Review* 5 (Spring 1984) 245. See also the articles by Noel Polk and Thomas L. McHaney in the same issue.

2 It is now conveniently available in *'Sanctuary': The Original Text*, edited by Noel Polk and published by Random House in 1981.

3 William Faulkner, *Sanctuary* (New York: Jonathan Cape & Harrison Smith 1931) 135; subsequent references are supplied within parentheses in the text.

4 *Sanctuary* (New York: Modern Library 1932) v–vi; the introduction is reprinted in William Faulkner *Essays, Speeches & Public Letters* ed James B. Meriwether (New York: Random House 1965) 176–8, and in the Editor's Note to *Sanctuary: The Corrected Text* (New York: Vintage 1987) 337–9.

5 Henry Seidel Canby in the *Saturday Review of Literature* 21 March 1931, quoted in John Bassett ed *William Faulkner: The Critical Heritage* (London: Routledge & Kegan Paul 1975) 109

6 Carvel Collins 'A Note on *Sanctuary*' *Harvard Advocate* November 1951, 16

7 See p 62. The son still at Yale may yet become a lawyer, presumably, given the fact that Phil Stone, Faulkner's early supporter, went there for one of his law degrees.

8 Joseph R. Urgo 'Temple Drake's Truthful Perjury: Rethinking Faulkner's *Sanctuary*' *American Literature* 55 (October 1983) 435–44

9 See, for example, Urgo, 441–2.

10 He had appeared earlier as a major character in the novel published as *Sartoris* (1929) but now available under its original title, and in unabridged form, as *Flags in the Dust* (New York: Random House 1973).

11 Initiated by Noel Polk's *Faulkner's 'Requiem for a Nun': A Critical Study* (Bloomington: Indiana University Press 1981).

12 It is amusing, and characteristically Faulknerian, that in a novel that might almost serve as a temperance tract Popeye is the only non-drinker: '"There ought to be a law,"' he declares (115), meaning a law

against drinking and quite charmingly overlooking not only the fact that such a law notoriously does exist but that he himself, as a bootlegger, is specifically dedicated to its universal evasion. Horace, too, in what functions as a deliberate echo, thinks there should be a law against the disturbing sexuality of summer nights (359).

BARRIE HAYNE

Dreiser's *An American Tragedy*

Theodore Dreiser is the first major American novelist of 'ethnic' background and name (following on the Browns, the Hawthornes, the Jameses, the Clemenses), a member of a deprived minority looking in on a world not hitherto his own. In *An American Tragedy* (1925), his masterpiece, he wrote a novel which was strongly doctrinaire, showing its hero as the victim of that world not his own. He wrote a novel which drew heavily on the contemporary people's (and immigrants') art of the cinema, and then gave that novel, rather less than willingly, back to the cinema. And he wrote a novel which was based in a real crime, committed by a young man, not 'ethnic', but determined to rise above his own more or less predetermined lot. In this clash of deprived and blessed, not having and having, especially as Dreiser dramatized it, was the stuff of crime, and crime of a kind peculiar to a country where rising through class lines was possible, though fraught with danger – a peculiarly *American* tragedy.

The first thing to do with *An American Tragedy*, therefore, is to set it in its literary-historical context, and see it as a naturalistic novel – perhaps the best, the copy-book, example of that genre produced on this side of the Atlantic. While we must, therefore, begin with a working definition of naturalism,[1] we shall pass by here the preference American fiction has always had for the romantic over the real. This is a preference that naturalism itself cultivated; and European naturalism – we will take it for granted – found, when it crossed the Atlantic, a very congenial soil for its growth.

The earliest exponents of naturalism conceived their fictional writings as essentially laboratory examinations: the central character is placed in a controlled environment so that the novelist-scientist may observe and analyse what becomes of him. Coming, moreover, after Darwin, naturalism in fiction assumes that the character – he is generally too commonplace to be called a *hero* – will survive in that environment only so long as he adapts to it; and only the fittest survive. The world in which he struggles is a deterministic world, so deterministic as finally to deny him any freedom of will; and as he adapts he moves from one role to another. A player of pre-ordained parts, he loses himself when he loses his social role. The characters of naturalistic fiction are thus presented *as* their roles rather than as individuals: in Dreiser's first novel, *Sister Carrie* (1900), the heroine is 'the little battler' 'the waif amid forces'; Hurstwood, who steals money lest he lose her, is 'the manager,' and, when at the nadir of his fall he is asked if he is a motorman on strike, he replies, 'No, I'm nothing.' The people of naturalistic fiction are indeed nothing when their adaptations have failed, and their roles are gone.

Yet lest naturalism become even more dreary, dull, and dark than it is, the hero is not uncommonly given a humanistic value, an aspiration which, so long as he does adapt, may leave him undefeated at the end. The relentless determinism is certainly realistic, and grimly so; the aspiration is romantic, and characteristically American, if we allow Howells' famous *obiter* about 'the smiling aspects of life.'[2] One of the leading critical commentators on American naturalism, Charles C. Walcutt, describes the genre as both 'a shaggy apelike monster' and a 'godlike giant.' 'Whereas,' he goes on, 'one authority describes it as an extreme form of romanticism, another counters that it is the rigorous application of scientific method to the novel. When others say it is desperate, pessimistic determinism, they are answered by those who insist that it is an optimistic affirmation of man's freedom and progress.'[3] All are correct, as Walcutt says in summarizing; and Frank Norris, whose novels include such finely balanced treatments of realism and romance as we find in *McTeague* (1899), which became Stroheim's famous film *Greed*, and *The Octopus* (1902), claims Emile Zola as the apostle of that balance. Naturalism represents the transcendent synthesis of the dialectics of romance and realism. Realism, as Norris says, is what happens between lunch and supper; romance takes the whole wide world for range, 'the unplumbed depths of the human heart [with its distinct echo of his compatriot Hawthorne], and the mystery of sex, and the problems of life, and the black, unsearched penetralia of the soul of man.'[4] Since Norris' catalogue does not omit a great deal, we need not be surprised to find him claiming Zola, an accumulator of realistic detail of Dreiserian proportions, as a naturalist – whose naturalism underscores the romantic elements in the school:

> These great, terrible dramas no longer happen among the personnel of a feudal and Renaissance nobility, those who are in the fore-front of the marching world, but among the lower – almost the lowest – classes; those who have been thrust or wrenched from the ranks, who are falling by the roadway. This is not romanticism – this drama of the people, working itself out in blood and ordure. It is not realism. It is a school by itself, unique, sombre, powerful beyond words. It is naturalism.[5]

It is clear that Dreiser's whole *oeuvre* belongs to naturalism, from Sister Carrie, who comes from the provinces to Chicago, and adapts to make her fortune there, to Frank Cowperwood, who becomes, from *The Financier* (1912) to *The Titan* (1914), a millionaire by surviving and thriving in a very Darwinian way. And beneath the relentless beat of factual detail in *An American Tragedy* is a strong strain of romance – Clyde's whole drive towards success is motivated by his dreams (an insistent metaphor in the novel); but those dreams, because of their very romantic, Arabian Nights quality, are doomed to pre-ordained defeat. As the tips pour into the hands of the bellhops at the hotel in Kansas City, 'He could scarcely believe it. It seemed fantastic, Aladdinish, really.'[6] His uncle, before he meets him, 'must be a kind of Croesus living in ease and luxury.' Ultimately, Clyde's dreams of romance come to be centred upon the dream figure of Sondra Finchley. (The dream is also Dreiser's: could anyone real bear such a name?) When his desire for her leads him to plan murder, he is even denied free will itself; and this young man is executed for a crime he did not, technically, commit – for he suffers at the moment of Roberta's drowning a 'palsy of the will.'

If dream is associated with the world of film, the repository of so many individual dreams as well as the collective one, put out by the 'Dream Factory' itself, then we are reminded again of the strength of the connections between Dreiser's novel and the new 'democratic art.' But there are other indications of the affinity, most notably the insistently visual quality of *An American Tragedy*.

The whole story is enclosed within the dusks of two summer nights, vividly brought before our eyes, with the tall walls of the two cities, the little group of salvationists, the immediate sense of seeing what is described. And there is emphasis throughout on Clyde's vision, his 'seeking eyes', a point of attraction to all who meet him, the eyes that the Reverend Macmillan cannot get out of his mind at the end when Clyde sinks limply into that terrible chair.

Now Dreiser's life-span was almost exactly the same as that of D.W. Griffith, the moving spirit of early American film; and the American naturalistic novelists (Norris, David Graham Phillips, Dreiser himself) provided many of the literary bases of the American silent film. *An American Tragedy* was published in 1925, when the silent film was at the peak of its achievement and its popularity; and Dreiser, whose contacts with Hollywood over the years were many, was at this time fascinated by film, the people's art; was living, for much of the writing of the novel, in and around Hollywood; and was living with the woman he later made his second wife, who was working in the film industry.

It is therefore not surprising to find many references to film in the novel. As Clyde casts about for an escape from the pregnant Roberta, 'he drifted – thinking most idly at times of some possible fake or mock marriage such as he had seen in some melodramatic movie' (2:6). (It is distinctly possible here that Dreiser may have been thinking of the central scene in Griffith's 'melodramatic movie' *Way Down East*, the most popular of his pictures, which had appeared on the screens of America in 1920.) As Roberta projects in her mind the very marriage Clyde is trying to avoid, she envisages 'a flowered grey taffeta after-noon dress, such as she had once seen in a movie, in which should Clyde keep his word, she could be married' (2:16). And looking over the crowded courtroom at his trial, Clyde whispers to his lawyers, 'quite a full house, eh?' (2:226). While this metaphor might suggest only the legitimate theatre, Orville Mason, rising to open the prosecution, is described in terms which move the *mise en scène* more directly into the cinema: 'This was his opportunity. Were not the eyes of all the citizens of the United States upon him? He believed so. It was as if someone had suddenly exclaimed: "Lights! Camera!"' (2:231). Indeed, isn't there even a reference to film in the murder weapon Clyde uses? Chester Gillette hit Grace Brown, in the event which inspired *An American Tragedy*, with a tennis racquet. Clyde hits Roberta, albeit uninten-tionally, with a camera.

The principal effect of these filmic references and analogies is both to enforce the naturalistic point and remind the reader yet again that these characters are locked into a world of dreams and illusions, and also to underline the fact that they are all speaking parts written for them by other people, other forces outside themselves. When Clyde

walks to his execution, his voice emerges as though spoken by somebody else, 'another being walking alongside of him' (2:405). He is the
role as well as the actor; his part has been assigned by his director.
The yellow, unimposing door that the small company enters at the
end of the first chapter and which they enter again at the end of the
novel, without Esta's Russel, who seems to be on the way to becoming
another Clyde, predicts and looks back on the door that opens for
Clyde as he enters the death chamber. His uneasiness at being a part
of the opening group, his two protectors shouldering closer and closer
to him while he shrinks down within himself mentally on the way to
his trial (with the cameras clicking and whirring in the background)
– these are dress rehearsals for the 'shuffle' as they push him toward
the execution chamber at the end. But the sense, more widely, has
been there from the beginning of the novel that here is a group of
actors – Clyde, his parents, Roberta and hers, Sondra, even Mason,
Belknap, and Jephson – playing roles written for them by forces located
in their genes, in their psyches, in their upbringings, and above all in
their society, *American* society, itself. It is appropriate, therefore, that
the metaphors used are not those of the theatre, such as Dreiser used
in *Sister Carrie*, but those of the distinctively *American* art of the cinema.

But the Americanness of Clyde's tragedy asserts itself in other ways
as well. Dreiser for years studied (and clipped from newspapers) accounts of actual cases in which young men, rising in the world, aspiring
to young women above them in social status, murdered girls who would
hold them back in their original class. This effect of upward mobility
Dreiser saw as essentially American. Writing in 1935, he put it like this:

> It was in 1892, at which time I began as a newspaperman, that I began
> to observe a certain type of crime in the United States. It seemed to
> spring from the fact that almost every young person was possessed of an
> ingrowing ambition to be somebody financially and socially. In short, the
> general mood of America was directed toward escape from any form of
> poverty ... In the main, as I can show by my records, it was the murder
> of a young lady by an ambitious young man ... What produced this par-
> ticular type of crime about which I am talking was the fact that it was
> not always possible to drop the first girl. What usually stood in the way
> was pregnancy, plus the genuine affection of the girl herself for her lover,
> plus also her determination to hold him.[7]

After the publication of *An American Tragedy*, Dreiser noted the number of letters he received from people who said 'Clyde Griffiths might have been me'; and certainly there is a large amount of Dreiser himself in Clyde – the deprived background, the stern religious upbringing, the yearning for social advancement and sexual conquest, the dominating mother of mixed motives, the father for whom, though for reasons other than Clyde's, he felt contempt. This American tragedy takes the nineteenth-century Horatio Alger myth[8] which was still the basis of much contemporary fiction (not to say the blueprint for many a successful career) and turns it on its head. And the lesson it teaches is just as exemplary as Alger's *Making His Way* or Herrick's *The Memoirs of an American Citizen*, and the hero is just as much an authorial surrogate. The difference between *An American Tragedy* and the school of Horatio Alger lies in the degree of criticism to which the society itself is subjected, the extent to which it is actually blamed for the tragedy.

But if there is much of Dreiser in Clyde Griffiths, there is a good deal of another young man as well – Chester Gillette;[9] and *An American Tragedy* is based fairly closely on the famous murder and trial that had taken place in upstate New York some fifteen years before. Rejecting other versions of this 'certain type of crime in the United States,' where the murderer had been a medical student, or a clergyman, Dreiser chose the nomadic Chester Gillette, the son of Salvation Army parents, and supplied him with his, Dreiser's own, seduced and abandoned elder sister. He then gave him a two-fold defence that Gillette's lawyers never considered, of 'mental and moral cowardice' and 'change of heart.' He also reduced Gillette, in transforming him into Clyde, to a lower social status. Chester's parents had travelled as far as Hawaii; and he himself was a fairly sophisticated Westerner who left the mission background of his parents to seek the favour of his uncle, who owned a skirt factory in Cortland; he had already passed through a series of minor service jobs. But he had never known true poverty, was given a supervisory position in the factory, of which his cousin was superintendent, and used his authority to seduce one of the factory girls, the daughter of poor country farming people, whose name was Grace – 'Billy' – Brown. Gillette had a taste of high society in both Cortland and around Lake Skaneateles, and laid siege to a local debutante, who was quite amenable to his courtship, and who did in fact give evidence, though for the prosecution, at his trial. Billy, now pregnant, pursued him; he took her on a lake tour – they travelled as man and wife, and one of his false names was Carl Graham, keeping his initials – hit her over the head with a tennis racquet, and swam away as she drowned, leaving a second straw hat floating in the lake to establish his own drowning. There were in the background of his trial a number of small-town political squabbles (the district attorney was running for country judge on the Republican ticket, and the defence counsel were Democrats); he was convicted, his mother tried without success to over-turn the verdict, and he was executed in 1908, two years after the crime.

What Dreiser made out of these relatively unaltered facts, trans-forming Chester Gillette's life and character, and his own, into that of Clyde Griffiths, was this his sixth novel, and his most successful, artistically as well as commercially. It sold twenty-five thousand copies in its first six months, was banned (only) in Boston, and was hailed by two reigning naturalists on the other side of the water, H.G. Wells and Arnold Bennett, as one of the greatest novels of the century.[10] That judgment has been confirmed, if somewhat shaded, over sixty years.

The immediate effect of its great popularity, joined with what I have insisted upon as its visual qualities, was to ensure a film version. But there would be delays: the basic theme seemed too raw for the mass medium, and there were long wrangles between Dreiser and his pub-lishers over their shares in the proceeds of the sale of the film rights. D.W. Griffith, Erich Von Stroheim, even Ernst Lubitsch, the master of sophisticated film comedy, have recorded plans to turn the novel into film.[11] But it was not until 1930 that Paramount brought Sergei Eisenstein, no less, to Hollywood to make a version.[12] This version, of which Dreiser whole-heartedly approved, for it placed the blame for Clyde's tragedy firmly on the shoulders of the capitalist society, was rejected by the studio for that same reason. The next version was actually realized, directed by the very pictorial Josef von Sternberg in 1931. This version Dreiser whole-heartedly deplored, and sued the stu-dio for misrepresenting his novel. He lost his case. Twenty years later there was a third version, much admired and much honoured, *A Place in the Sun*, directed by George Stevens, with two of the most glittering stars of the day, Montgomery Clift and Elizabeth Taylor.

Let us then take the cue for the structure of our present inquiry from Eisenstein, who wrote in 1933 – two years after his dismissal by Paramount – that he had prepared a script according to 'the formula of a sociological treatise,' when all the studio wanted was 'a strong, simple detective story,' or 'a love affair between a boy and a girl.'[13] To varying extents, *An American Tragedy* belongs to all three genres

Eisenstein mentions – sociological treatise, detective story, love affair – and each of the three film versions emphasizes one generic aspect. But leaving the films aside, let us read the novel in each of these three ways.

Predominantly, it is true, it is a sociological treatise; hence Dreiser's approval of Eisenstein's script. In writing his inverted Horatio Alger story, Dreiser is deeply critical of the society which produced and destroyed Clyde. It is also, however, true that some of Clyde's failures come from within, from his own chemic compulsions and just plain temperamental weaknesses. His defence at the trial is that of mental and moral cowardice; and his attempts to plan Roberta's murder and then cover up his role in it are all extremely inept ('What a dunce you are! – what a poor plotter' (2:150), as Mason tells him in the courtroom). Clyde's sexual urges might appear to be a major internal factor in his downfall, but they are really a part of his romantic yearning, thrust upon him by a hostile society. Thus women, from Hortense and her yen for a fur coat, to Rita and Roberta to Sondra herself, are an essential part of Clyde's paradisiac dreams. A work with which *An American Tragedy* has many affinities is *Great Expectations*, which with a more conscious irony of title makes the same link between sexual and social ascent, and yet perceives the dream as just as tainted, the hero just as self-deceived. With Dickens' greater skill, the girl and the fortune are both shown as springing from the same source, the convict; the final difference between the two novels lies in Pip's escape from the dream, and his consequent reformation; his 'murder' (of Mrs Joe) is done for him by another. And to see the sexually charged nature of much social aspiration one need stray no further than the box watched nightly by so many, whether 'goin' down with Pepsi,' or turning Fortune's wheel (a debased invocation of naturalistic determinism!) with Vanna.

The three deterministic strands, of social, sexual, and hereditary determinism, are finely interwoven in the opening pages of the novel. Clyde is clearly 'outa place' (1:7) in this group of evangelical zealots, as of course is Esta, whose dereliction, in sexual terms, will shortly predict his own; he is admiring of his mother, yet ashamed of both her and especially his father, the ineffectual. The family presents anomalies 'of psychic and social reflex and motivation such as would tax the skill of not only the psychologist but the chemist and physicist as well, to unravel,' as Dreiser says. Clyde, 'a thing apart,' is marked by 'a certain emotionalism and exotic sense of romance' (1:10), and in the next few years as they are surveyed in the second chapter, 'the sex lure or appeal had begun to manifest itself and he was already intensely interested and troubled by the beauty of the opposite sex' (1:15) – this at the very same time 'the fact that his family was the unhappy thing it was ... was now tending more and more to induce a kind of mental depression or melancholia which promised not so well for his future': sexual and psychological determinism, the latter associated particularly with the family, go hand in hand.

Yet the dominant note in these opening pages, for all the attention given to that family background, is of Clyde's yearning for a life beyond the confines of this one, and that yearning calls attention to the way his life is already being predetermined by *social* forces. The tall walls of the city, the canyon-like ways, their path 'just an alley between two tall structures,' predict the narrow path of his life. His parents' poverty prevents them from giving him a car of his own, as other parents do; and the main vision in Clyde's mind – his first dream – is also one that predicts the course, and the destruction, of his life: 'The handsome automobiles that sped by, the loitering pedestrians moving off to what interests and comforts he could only surmise; the gay pairs of young people, laughing and jesting and the "kids" staring, all troubled him with a sense of something different, better, more beautiful than his, or rather their life' (1:6).

There are two characters in the novel who are primary registers or indices of Clyde's progress and downfall: Gilbert Griffiths, his cousin, and Orville Mason, his prosecutor or persecutor. Both are in some sense his alter egos,[14] and both are used by Dreiser for commentary on the social forces at work in the novel. Dreiser goes out of his way to underline the physical similarity between Gilbert and Clyde, which fuels Gilbert's jealousy of his cousin, and his fear of being supplanted, since it is perhaps that similarity which has persuaded Samuel Griffiths to employ Clyde in the collar factory in the first place. The likeness also prompts Sondra to take up Clyde when they meet in town, at the beginning of what Dreiser calls 'a chain of events,' 'destined,' which leads, immediately following as it does Clyde's seduction of Roberta, to the catastrophe. She takes him up – having momentarily mistaken him *for* Gilbert – because Gilbert has wounded her pride by his indifference to her. She initiates the fatal relationship with Clyde to get back at his double. And the chain of events associated with Gilbert's likeness to Clyde ends at last with Gilbert's persuasion of his father to drop the family's support for Clyde at the end of the trial.

Of primary importance, too, is the role Gilbert plays in warning Clyde against the very course of action which ultimately brings him to the execution chamber. It is Gilbert who lays down to Clyde the rule that those who hold responsible positions in the factory must have nothing to do with the female employees. Drawn by his sexual urges to the factory girls like Hortense, Rita, and now Roberta, and by his aspirations of wealth and romance to such as Sondra, Clyde is destroyed by the class system and by the vested interests of the social order.

When Clyde first sees Gilbert, he sees 'a youth who looked, if anything, smaller and a little older and certainly much colder and shrewder than himself – such a youth, in short, as Clyde would have liked to imagine himself to be ... deep down in himself he felt that this young man, an heir and nothing more to this great industry, was taking to himself airs and superiorities which, but for the father's skill before him, would not have been possible' (1:186). As he muses when approaching dinner with his wealthy relatives: 'Think of being such a youth, having so much power at one's command!' (1:223). Dreiser's implication is clear that were there no class system based upon money and the inheritance of it, the roles of Clyde and Gilbert might be interchangeable: all that locks Clyde out of wealth and leisure is the chance fate that has bestowed these gifts on Gilbert. That Gilbert is the Eastern cousin while Clyde is the Western one, aside from its probably ironic allusion to Aesop, does not carry the point that Fitzgerald was making the same year (1925) in *The Great Gatsby*, that a strength and continuity belong to the Westerners like Nick and Gatsby himself, and only a decadence attaches to Daisy and Tom, the destructive Easterners. Rather, Dreiser presents the ironical obverse, that even the Western, characteristically American values are being subverted by Eastern metropolitan values – the novel ends in San Francisco, with the cycle of determinism perhaps about to begin again. And that the Western Griffiths show absolutely none of the enterprise or independence associated with the West, which is here given to Samuel, shows a further subversion of the American way, another facet of the *Americanness* of the tragedy.

Orville Mason, on the other hand, the district attorney, is Clyde's double in a different sense, another poor boy with romantic yearnings who, unlike Clyde, lacks the good looks which seduce women and open social doors: 'in his late youth [he] had been so unfortunate as to have an otherwise pleasant and even arresting face marred by a broken nose, which gave to him a most unprepossessing, almost sinister, look. Yet he was far from sinister. Rather, romantic and emotional. His boyhood had been one of poverty and neglect, causing him in his later and somewhat more successful years to look on those with whom life had dealt more kindly as too favorably treated' (2:91–2). His disfigurement 'had eventually resulted in what the Freudians are accustomed to describe as a psychic sex scar.' Mason hounds Clyde to the electric chair, pursuing him like 'an angry wasp or hornet' (2:147), ignoring Clyde's similarly poor background in favour of delivering to justice the seducer and killer of the equally impoverished Roberta, with whom and her family Mason feels the greater affinity. His jealousy of Clyde's sexual conquest leads him to prosecute him with more than professional enthusiasm.

If this suggests that Mason is Clyde's double or mirror image, there is a further dimension, and a further reason for Mason's prosecution of the case. He wants a quick conviction to further his political ambitions, and this too blinds him to Clyde's humble origins. Clyde's adoption by the Finchley set 'suggested all the means as well as the impulse to quiet such a scandal as this. Wealth. Luxury. Important names and connections to protect no doubt ... [M]ight it not be possible that long before he could hope to convict him, he himself would automatically be disposed of as a prosecutor and without being nominated for and elected to the judgeship he so craved and needed' (2:145).

Mason too is a part of the social order, another representative of the society that destroys Clyde Griffiths. He is a Republican politician running for county judge, which transcends considerations of justice or even his prosecution of the case against Clyde: Clyde's lawyers, Belknap and Jephson, are Democrats, and a large part of their being chosen to represent him is to prevent Mason from making too much political capital out of the case: 'Fate seemed too obviously to be favouring the Republican machine in the person of and crime committed by Clyde' (2:182). Clyde thus becomes a pawn in a political battle, his guilt or innocence less important than the outcome of the next local election. The judge too, a Democrat, but one appointed by the previous administration, perhaps rules against Belknap and Jephson on political lines of self-preservation, and even after the trial, the newly installed governor must decide Clyde's fate primarily on political grounds. Belknap's youthful peccadillo, exactly the same as Clyde's, did not end as Clyde's does, but in marriage to *his* Sondra, for he belongs to a class who can buy off *his* Roberta. These are the members of the legal and social order who now, in the trial, combine to destroy Clyde Griffiths. Even the jury represents that order: the one juryman who holds out, 'pretending that he had doubts,' is 'politically opposed to Mason and taken with the personality of Jephson' (2:329), and is brought round to a guilty verdict by threat of a public exposure which would endanger his drug business.

Such, then, is the case for seeing *An American Tragedy* as Eisenstein most emphatically saw it, as a sociological treatise in which society is ultimately indicted for its destructive power. 'The essential tragedy of life,' as Dreiser had written,[15] is that man is 'a waif and an interloper in Nature' (for which we may also read *society* and other environmental factors), which seeks only 'to work through him,' so that he has 'no power to make his own way.' As a matter of course, we may note in passing, Eisenstein's film treatment deepens Dreiser's more or less Marxist view of American society, and this was why Paramount rejected it; for them it really did represent what Eisenstein ironically called 'a monstrous challenge to American society.'[16] No less truly, this was why Dreiser whole-heartedly approved of it.

One of the most memorable scenes in Eisenstein's script comes at the end of reel twelve, when we hear and see a series of telephone bells ringing in succession, as the political influence necessary to keep Sondra's name out of the trial moves upwards through the echelons of power. 'The last light is turned on in the house grandest of all, and from this house can be heard the wanted promise.'[17] Though Eisenstein eliminated everything from the novel that did not go towards Clyde's victimization by a bourgeois society, in doing so he remained faithful to Dreiser, adding nothing that was not already implicitly there.

Eisenstein's statement that the studio wanted a detective story or a love affair, rather than what he gave them, is certainly hyperbole, though *An American Tragedy* has elements of both. However, though it is a story dealing with crime, it hardly belongs to the genre of detective fiction. That genre, which reached its apogee of popularity at the very time Dreiser was writing his novel, has always at its centre a percipient and analytic detective, with whom the reader is asked to identify, and who unmasks the hitherto unidentified criminal one step before the reader at the end and who in doing so restores the social order upset by the original crime: Dupin, Holmes, Father Brown, Hercule Poirot; all but the first were alive and well at the time Dreiser was writing. But Orville Mason (despite, perhaps, his invocation of one of the famous early fictional detectives, Randolph Mason, and perhaps even his anticipation of Perry Mason) does not belong in that family, any more than *An American Tragedy*, with its revelation of the criminal from the beginning, belongs in that genre; as F.O. Matthiessen has noted, 'As Clyde plots murder in spite of himself, Dreiser goes to the opposite extreme from the writer of a detective story.'[18] Certainly what is restored at the end of *An American Tragedy* looks much more like the continuation of chaos. Indeed, Clyde's ineptness makes him almost a parody of the criminal of detective fiction who matches wits with the percipient detective – he plans nothing effectively, he leaves a train of clues behind him which will convict and execute him with or without a 'change of heart' or a 'palsy of the will'; he lies in the face of evidence proving him a liar. It is true that one reads *An American Tragedy* with something of the compulsiveness that many readers bring to detective fiction, with what John Berryman has called 'the febrile, self-indulgent eagerness Dreiser is apt to induce,'[19] but the essential sense of a world built upon logical principles, and therefore amenable to the detective's analysis, is missing, has, indeed, been replaced by a highly illogical and unpredictable one.

There are certainly some elements of the police procedural genre in *An American Tragedy*, as Mason, Kraut, Sissel, and Swenk gather evidence for the prosecution, and Belknap and Jephson try to forestall their efforts; one official even fabricates evidence, attaching some of Roberta's hair to the camera which Mason has dredged from the lake. But primarily the novel is the psychological study of a murderer, a crime novel rather than a detective story, as Julian Symons defines that form, in terms which apply uncannily well to *An American Tragedy*: character is the basis of the story, setting is frequently an integral part of the crime itself, and the social attitude is 'often radical in the sense of questioning some aspect of law, justice, or the way society is run.'[20]

The classic crime novel is no doubt Dostoevski's *Crime and Punishment*, a work which transcends mere social discontentment to attain a level of *tragedy* which most critics have denied to Dreiser's novel because of Clyde's triviality and the mental and moral cowardice which prevent him from accepting the full moral responsibility for his crime. But Dreiser once told an interviewer that Raskolnikov was his favourite character in fiction – this was about the time he was finishing his own novel – and he urged the inclusion of *Crime and Punishment* in the Modern Library, which was put out by his own publishers. Raskolnikov and Clyde Griffiths are, however, worlds apart, the Russian an intellectual post-Nietzschean man who kills a woman he hardly knows, not for the money, but for the rather abstract good of society. Four years after he made Dreiser's novel into a film (and brought on Dreiser's suit for distortion of his work), Josef von Sternberg put *Crime and Punishment* on the screen. The difference is there to see: despite Dreiser's protest, the essentials of his novel have been captured in the picture, but no picture could capture the complexities of Dostoevski's novel.[21]

Another feature of the detective, or even crime, novel is its paucity of social detail; except where the social purpose transcends, as sometimes occurs in the crime novel, only such details as are necessary for the solution or understanding of the crime are provided. This paucity of detail is certainly not a feature of *An American Tragedy*! Dreiser is writing a case history in the naturalistic mode, a tremendous amassing of facts and even figures which more than amply illustrate the reasons for Clyde Griffiths' rise and fall. Roberta's and Sondra's backgrounds are detailed, as are Mason's, Belknap's, even such minor figures as Sheriff Heit and Catchuman. We know how much a shirt costs as well as the price of an abortion or the pills to secure a miscarriage. And we are taken laboriously through the testimony of the 127 witnesses who appear at Clyde's trial.

As to the third characterization by Eisenstein of the novel, a love affair between a boy and girl, it would hardly be worth consideration were it not for the romantic strain in the novel, as in American naturalism generally. And it is, predominantly, the interpretation given to the novel in the most successful of the film versions. But it is absurd to suggest that Clyde's love affair with either girl transcends the social aspects, or even the criminal elements in *An American Tragedy*. It is adjunct to both – his attempt to abandon the girl of one class for the girl of another leads him to commit the crime for which the class system combines to destroy him. Sondra, and even Roberta, like Hortense and Rita before her, are all in the novel to suggest Clyde's increasingly romantic dreams of Paradise, his Aladdinish pursuit of the beautiful princess. They are the reasons for his crime, and the reasons for his destruction.

So that the final view of *An American Tragedy* as an example of crime in literature is that it follows the standard pattern of the crime novel, an amorphous but fairly formulaic genre, governed by the presuppositions of naturalism. A contemporary analogy might be found not in the novels of the most famous current practitioner of the genre, Patricia Highsmith, whose interest is in the Maileresque exploration of, and perverse sympathy with, the psychotic criminal mind, but in the novels of John Bingham, who, from *My Name is Michael Sibley* (1953) on, has been seeing the forces of legally constituted order as being often as reprehensible as the criminal, a view which may derive from Dickens via Dostoevski. Is Clyde's *crime* worthy of his *punishment?* A lawyer-reader of *An American Tragedy* may find the leading interest in the trial, which indeed takes up a third of the novel. (A literary colleague of mine once admitted to having skipped this section!) Without justifying such a reading, and noting that Dreiser went out of his way to take advice in grasping the legal questions involved, one may reasonably point out that the trial pits Clyde's defence of mental and moral cowardice, and therefore diminished or even non-existent responsibility, against the determination of the eager bloodhounds of the legal establishment. In doing so, it merely confirms the struggle enacted throughout the novel. Clyde has no defence because his society leaves him with none. His society made him, and it is finally free – freedom being something reserved to the state rather than the individual – to break him. And Dreiser, while he buttressed his argument with both supporting legal evidence and what he read into the Gillette case, was leading, and loading, the case against that society.

Notes

Barrie Hayne received his PHD from Harvard University in 1964. His broad interest is in American culture, including film and detective stories. His publications include an article on the film versions of *An American Tragedy* in the *Canadian Review of American Studies* and various essays in *Twentieth-Century Crime and Mystery Writers*. He is currently engaged in research on the film-maker D.W. Griffith.

1 The best accounts of *American* literary naturalism, which is the main concern here, may be found in Charles C. Walcutt *American Literary Naturalism: A Divided Stream* (Minneapolis: University of Minnesota 1956), and Donald Pizer *Realism and Naturalism in Nineteenth-Century American Literature* (Carbondale: Southern Illinois University Press 1966). For the practitioner's view, see Frank Norris *The Responsibilities of the Novelist* (London: Grant Richards 1903), and Emile Zola *The Naturalist Novel* ed Maxwell Geismar (Montreal: Harvest House 1964).

2 William Dean Howells' familiar, and much derided, reference to 'the smiling aspects of life, which are the more American,' is contained in his *Criticism and Fiction* (Boston: Harper and Brothers 1891).

3 Walcutt 3

4 Norris 220; see as well 215: 'Zola has been dubbed a Realist, but he is, on the contrary, the very head of the Romanticists.' Hawthorne's definitions of Romance are to be found throughout his writings; the most familiar phrases occur in the preface to *The House of the Seven Gables* (1851): 'When a writer calls his work a Romance, it need hardly be observed that he wishes to claim a certain latitude, both as to its fashion and material, which he would not have felt himself entitled to assume had he professed to be writing a Novel. The latter form of composition is presumed to aim at a very minute fidelity, not merely to the possible, but to the probable and ordinary course of man's experience. The former – while, as a work of art, it must rigidly subscribe itself to laws, and while it sins unpardonably so far as it may swerve aside from the truth of the human heart – has fairly a right to present that truth under circumstances, to a great extent, of the writer's own choosing or creation.'

5 Frank Norris 'Zola as a Romantic Writer' in *Novels and Essays* ed D. Pizer (New York: Library of America (1986) 1108

6 Theodore Dreiser *An American Tragedy* (New York: Liveright 1925) 2 volumes, 1:51. All subsequent references to the novel are to this edition, and are included in the text of this article.

7 See Ellen Moers *Two Dreisers* (New York: Viking 1969), especially 192–205. This, along with Matthiessen's, is the best critical biography of Dreiser.

8 Alger wrote well over a hundred self-improving fictions in the second half of the nineteenth century. Though his vogue, which sold some two hundred million copies, was spent by the time Dreiser was writing *An American Tragedy*, he has received some attention, largely patronizing and nostalgic, in recent years. Perhaps the new vogue begins with *Struggling Upward and Other Works* ed Russel Crouse (New York: Bonanza Books 1950).

9 Two examinations of the facts surrounding the Gillette case have been published in the last few years: Joseph W. Brownell and Patricia A. Wawrzaszek *Adirondack Tragedy: The Gillette Murder Case of 1906* (Interlaken, NY: Heart of the Lakes Publishing 1986), and Craig Brandon *Murder in the Adirondacks: An American Tragedy Revisited* (Utica: North Country Books 1986).

10 F.O. Matthiessen *Dreiser* (New York: William Sloane Associates 1951) 94, 127, 210

11 For an account of the film versions, projected or executed, see my article 'Sociological Treatise, Detective Story, Love Affair: The Film Versions of *An American Tragedy*' *Canadian Review of American Studies* 8:2 (Fall 1977) 131–53.

12 Eisenstein's 'treatment,' which is in fact a rather full scenario, without dialogue, is printed in Ivor Montagu *With Eisenstein in Hollywood: A Chapter of Autobiography* (New York: International Publishers 1969). For Eisenstein's own account, see *Close Up* 10:2 (June 1933), and as reprinted (in different translation) in *Film Form: Essays in Film Theory* ed Jay Leyda (New York: Harcourt, Brace 1949).

13 *Close Up* 110

14 For a discussion of the theme of the double in *An American Tragedy* as it relates to Gilbert Griffiths, see Lauriat Lane, Jr 'The Double in *An American Tragedy*' *Modern Fiction Studies* 12 (Summer 1966) 213–20.

15 Matthiessen 204–5

16 *Close Up* 110. Dreiser wrote to Eisenstein on 3 January 1938 urging him to produce his scenario; see *Letters of Theodore Dreiser* ed Robert Elias (Philadelphia: University of Pennsylvania Press 1959).

17 'Scenario' *With Eisenstein in Hollywood* 312–13

18 *Dreiser* 203

19 John Berryman 'Dreiser's Imagination' in *The Stature of Theodore Dreiser* ed Alfred Kazin and Charles Shapiro (Bloomington: University of Indiana Press 1955) 150

20 Julian Symons *Bloody Murder: From the Detective Story to the Crime Novel: A History* (London: Faber and Faber 1972) chapter 14, 'Crime Novel and Police Novel' 163

21 See both von Sternberg's own account in *Fun in a Chinese Laundry: An Autobiography* (New York: Macmillan 1965) and Andrew Sarris *The Films of Josef von Sternberg* (New York: Museum of Modern Art 1966).

CAESAR R. BLAKE

On Richard Wright's *Native Son*

Richard Wright's *Native Son* is a novel of 1940. It is a novel by an American Negro, about a specifically realized view of the perennially and profoundly vexed problem of the Negro in American history and life. The novel was an instantaneous popular success with blacks and whites alike: it was a best-seller and a selection of the Book of the Month Club. There had been a tradition of Afro-American fiction for many decades, burgeoning in the Harlem Renaissance of the 1920s and 1930s, but it was fiction read largely by other Afro-Americans. Wright's *Native Son* in 1940 radically shifted this parochial engagement of writer and audience to a wide, excited – indeed, very agitated – social and literary engagement for the general American public. The book was much discussed, heatedly argued about, the source of pride and vexation among blacks and whites. It was adapted for the stage by Orson Welles, and in time translated into European languages, extending its range of influence far beyond its author's expectation, if not his hope.

In the nearly fifty years since its publication, something of its original force as a literary and social document has diminished or been superseded, but one can still read it and feel its indisputable power, whether one interprets the book as historical literature or as uncommonly effective propaganda, or even as the occasion for sad reflections and ruminations. Powerful as it is, there was always some unease about the novel. Its uneven literary quality bothered some of its first readers; its 'message,' and its social analysis, deeply troubled many others; some blacks, frequently complacent middle-class ones, even thought it embarrassing (at the least, they were thought to be philistine by embattled social and political activists); and no less a critic and artist than Robert

Penn Warren worried that its readers were not sufficiently alarmed by what he called Wright's para-Marxist neo-naturalism.

The unease has continued over the subsequent years and some of the persistent arguments about *Native Son* may be generalized as a few broadly formulated questions: Does the novel focus and represent fictionally a clear perception of the social and historical reality of the problem of the black in American society? If the novel is, in any mimetic sense 'true,' what must we make of Wright's analysis of the problem and his implied or proclaimed remedy? What, in all of its implications, is the meaning or the validity of Bigger Thomas as symbol, emblem, hero/villain, victim, or victimizer? And what are we to make of the tangled relation the novel posits among law, morality, justice, and the exigencies of social fact and social reality?

Some compelling figures in twentieth-century thought and criticism have addressed these questions, or variations of them. Among them, Irving Howe argues that Wright's 'black wrath' and his insistence that 'history can be a punishment'[1] are the principal sources of Wright's powerful indictment of American society, but that 'between Wright's feelings as a Negro and his beliefs as a Communist there is hardly a genuine fusion, and it is through this gap that a good part of the novel's unreality pours in.'[2] We may assume that the 'unreality' here adumbrated (and later in Howe's essay explored) has to do generally with the connections Wright made between problems of ideology, law, justice, and the kind and quality of personal moral responsibility.

Alfred Kazin is frequently quoted for a harsh objection to *Native Son*: Wright's impulse in the novel is evident in 'his own indignation and the sickness of the age [which] make him dependent on violence and shock, to astonish the reader by torrential scenes of cruelty, hunger, rape, murder, and flight and then enlighten him by crude Stalinist homilies.'[3] Howe and Kazin are two of the most gifted and influential men in twentieth-century American intellectual and cultural life, and they speak with exceptional sophistication and authority. They are also white, and virtual icons of informed, careful, liberal advocacy in the American cultural enterprise.

James Baldwin and Ralph Ellison are, of course, not white. They are black, and in addition exceptionally accomplished writers of great intellectual force and passion. Coming in the generation after Wright, they also tended to distrust that other kind of categorization by white liberals like Howe which they claimed left the Negro still an abstraction, a cipher, a statistic in a liberal view of American social destiny.

Baldwin's and Ellison's objections to *Native Son* came a decade and more after 1940, and no one would suggest, I think, that theirs were philistine, middle-class, or otherwise defensive views. Baldwin's celebrated attack on *Native Son* – and on Wright himself in 'Alas, Poor Richard' – is essentially an attack on the book as a 'protest' novel which Baldwin at one point (he has cast his net to include another protest novel, Mrs Stowe's *Uncle Tom's Cabin*) characterizes as 'the formula created by the necessity to find a lie more palatable than the truth.'[4] Baldwin remarks that 'the failure of the protest novel lies in its rejection of life, the human being, the denial of his beauty, dread, power, in its insistence that it is his categorization alone which is real and which cannot be transcended.'[5] And further, of Bigger as Wright's vessel of truth and illustration, Baldwin says, 'Bigger's tragedy is not that he is cold or black or hungry, not even that he is American, black; but that he has accepted a theology that denies him life, that he admits the possibility of his being sub-human and feels constrained, therefore, to battle for his humanity according to those brutal criteria bequeathed him at his birth.'[6]

Baldwin and Ellison, the latter on a more loftily intellectual and aesthetic note in his public argument with Irving Howe,[7] both distrusted the categories of the left (whether from Howe or from the fictional lawyer Max) and the categories of what, with some hesitation, may be called the privileged establishment (that is to say, those *other* whites). Baldwin and Ellison eschewed the programmatic – in Wright and elsewhere – and insisted that the only game of importance to be played was on the field of the black's sense of his own humanity, however imperilled, and his sense of self, however constrained. No Bigger Thomas as Wright conceived him could sustain that austere demand and such a morally challenging scrutiny.

What are we to make of this racial divide between Howe on the one hand (who hailed *Native Son* as an American cultural landmark, while saying 'that *Native Son* has grave faults anyone can see')[8] and Baldwin and Ellison on the other, who harshly criticized the book? Baldwin, speaking of Bigger, perhaps inadvertently commented on the book's critical reception: 'It is the socially conscious whites who receive him – the Negroes being capable of no such objectivity – and we have, by way of illustration, that lamentable scene in which Jan, Mary's lover, forgives him for her murder; and, carrying the explicit burden of the novel, Max's long speech to the jury.'[9]

With the exception of David Bradley's reaction, discussed below, the impulse to respond to *Native Son*, Richard Wright, and his time in American history, personally and on the polemical level, seems to have cooled, and there are no ongoing personal confrontations to rival the intensity of that between Howe, Baldwin, and Ellison. Instead, the critical response, as is always the case, refines itself to greater and greater scrutiny of what in fact is the novel and what it may be said to mean in the end.

And what can we make of this controversy that may be in some way helpful to the interests of this collection? Two general considerations seem to me promising. One concerns Dostoevski's *Crime and Punishment*; the other, what is called the naturalistic tradition in the history of the novel. The advantage of these interests involves both the frequency with which both are invoked by disputants in arguments about the nature of *Native Son* and what the novel may be said to reveal about its author's attitudes towards crime.

The translation of the title of Dostoevski's great novel of 1866 into English comes to us as *Crime and Punishment*. The translation into German comes as *Die Schuld und die Sühne*, or *Guilt and Redemption*. To meditate on the difference between 'crime' and 'guilt' on the one hand, and 'punishment' and 'redemption' on the other, is to contemplate an extraordinary conceptual difference that touches upon law, morality, philosophy, psychology, religion, and that capacious term which sometimes can embrace them all: justice. In Dostoevski's novel there is the crime of murder; eventually there is legal conviction and punishment; the crime begets a stultifying guilt in Raskolnikov the hero; the guilt and his legal punishment work toward his spiritual redemption through the agency of his own complex, sometimes quasi-mystical religious sentiments, and the love of his almost saintly girl-friend Sonya. The whole is achieved with a masterly probing and analysis of the psychology of guilt, the meaning of moral law, and the essential force of the moral will in a criminal whose immediate motivation to murder arose from his poverty, his family's misery, and his rage against the forces of his oppression.

In his recent study of *Crime and Punishment* and *Native Son*, Tony Magistrale asserts that 'Wright's personal experiences would have sufficed to enable the construction of a story about Bigger Thomas without knowledge of *Crime and Punishment*, but *Native Son* would have been a far less complex and engaging book had its author never been aware of Dostoevski.'[10] Magistrale credits 'Dostoevski's model of the criminal mind – the motivations and consequences of antisocial behaviour – and the antithetical struggle towards moral advancement and spiritual growth'[11] as the most important influence on Wright and *Native Son*. Magistrale also goes on to detail the plot and theme similarities between the two works, which include imagery and settings of physical confinement, the main character's thoughts of a charismatic and powerful leader for his people (Bigger's leader of the black people and Raskolnikov's 'extraordinary man'), and revealing dream sequences. But the endings that the criminal justice system (the punishment for the crime) dictates are radically different. Magistrale observes that 'in *Native Son* Bigger Thomas is not provided the chance for a new life in Siberia, and American society, as represented by a Chicago courtroom, once again forfeits the opportunity to liberate itself.'[12]

The obvious temptation to say *Native Son* is a redaction of Dostoevski's great novel transposed to Chicago and fitted to a young black man is clear. There is probably an even stronger urge to question the validity of any ultimate analogy, even historically accommodated, between the two novels. Part of the urge may be necessitated by Wright's presumed 'naturalism,' even when we leave aside any invidious comparisons of capacities, visions, or sensibilities in the two authors.

The tradition of naturalism aspired to apply something of what, in the nineteenth century, was regarded as scientific objectivity to human life either in its individual or social reality. Following the inclinations of scientific determinism in seeing human life as basically analogous to all animal life, the tradition concentrated its interest on the socially and economically disadvantaged, not only because of their significant numbers, but also because of their greater exposure to the elemental realities of life. It eschewed, because they were uncertain, moral and theological preoccupations. It regarded the determinants of human destiny or fate as heredity and environment against which a powerless individual human will could only struggle in futility, though it sometimes, in some hands, acknowledged the utility of art, especially literature, in effecting the improvement of the social, political, and economic environment for the consequent improvement of human life. Its chief and most redoubtable exemplar in the novel was Emile Zola in France. In the United States, the chief inheritor of this tradition was the novelist Theodore Dreiser, writing at the turn of the century and influential in the emergence of what came to be known as the proletarian novel, the novel of social realism, or – to come home again – the protest novel.

Richard Wright's *Native Son* situates itself for many who write about it as a black American's version of Dostoevski's subject filtered through the ideological screen of a naturalist *cum* Marxist inspired by Dreiser. In 1940, Clifton Fadiman called *Native Son* the black *An American Tragedy*: '*Native Son* does for the Negro what Theodore Dreiser in *An American Tragedy* did a decade and a half ago for the bewildered, inarticulate American white.'[13] The resemblance was also noted by Irving Howe in 'Black Boys and Native Sons.' Howe remarked that Wright was influenced by the Dreiser who knew that 'there are situations so oppressive that only violence can provide their victims with the hope of dignity.' 'Yet,' Howe continues, 'the comparison is finally of limited value, and for the disconcerting reason that Dreiser had a white skin and Wright a black one.'[14] Howe's comment raises an important issue. Dreiser dealt with class alone as the basis of determinism, while Wright examined race (and, necessarily, class) and its relation to crime.

In his lengthy and doctrinaire speech, Boris Max argues that Bigger's 'very existence is a crime against the state!' (367). Earlier, Bigger thinks, in response to his friends' fear of him: 'Had he not taken fully upon himself the crime of being black?' (275). Indeed, Kathleen Gallagher argued in a recent paper, 'that in a racist society blacks become criminals by virtue of their very existence is a predominant theme of Richard Wright's fiction' and that 'in the eyes of the dominant society, they are guilty and not to be proved innocent.'[15] This, surely, is an intensity and irrevocability of determinism not found in Dreiser's novel. If *An American Tragedy* can be seen as an inverted Horatio Alger story, it is because the possibility of the Horatio Alger ending exists in Dreiser; there seems to be no such possibility in *Native Son*, since Bigger is a criminal, in his world, literally from birth. Baldwin remarked:

> It [*Native Son*] is, in a certain American tradition, the story of an unremarkable youth in battle with the force of circumstance; that force of circumstance which plays and which has played so important a part in the national fables of success or failure. In this case the force of circumstance is not poverty merely but color, a circumstance which cannot be overcome, against which the protagonist battles for his life and loses.[16]

Wright felt this societal determinism keenly and personally. Robert Butler argues: 'Wright's selection of naturalism as a literary mode was not an ideologically self-conscious choice as it was for novelists such as Dos Passos and Steinbeck, who grew up in worlds quite remote from the more brutal determinants of the naturalistic universe. Rather, it was the recognition that his own life was closely mirrored in the naturalistic fiction which he read so avidly.'[17] In 'How Bigger Was Born,' Wright affirms that the environment into which he, as the naturalistic author, placed Bigger ('like a scientist in a laboratory, [who would] use my imagination and invent test-tube situations ...' [xxi]) was that in which he himself was raised, and describes its racism in terms of the criminal-justice system and its view of blacks as habitual and perpetual criminals: 'Any Negro who has lived in the North or the South knows that times without number he has heard of some Negro boy being picked up on the streets and carted off to jail and charged with "rape." ... Life had made the plot over and over again, to the extent that I knew it by heart' (xxviii).

One part of that world which forms a major and controversial part of *Native Son* relating to crime is the violence in the novel. While critics like Baldwin objected to violence that was 'gratuitous and compulsive,'[18] Robert Butler, in 'The Function of Violence in Richard Wright's *Native Son*,' argues that it serves a thematic purpose: '*Native Son* dramatizes a bleak environment in which people touch each other only in violence, almost never in love or friendship.'[19] Thus, Butler argues, the tension created by Bigger's divided nature is expressed in the violence (and the resulting criminality) of the novel's first two parts. Bigger's nature is divided, Butler asserts, between the harsh determinism of the Chicago slums and the optimism and potential represented by Mary Dalton's world. The unrelenting violence of books I and II are displaced by the self-awareness Bigger achieves in book III: 'Bigger is no longer divided into two mutually exclusive selves. As a result of this momentary wholeness, he can tentatively reach out to the world in love rather than violence.'[20]

The naturalist orientation of *Native Son* is thus universally recognized. Similarly, its correspondence to Wright's Marxist beliefs seems clear. But whether one agrees with Robert Penn Warren that Wright's novel is 'para-Marxist neo-naturalism' depends on how one interprets critical events in the fiction.

Should we consider that the opening scene of the novel is the paradigm, the controlling image, of the entire, complex working-out of the neo-naturalist orientation? It is the rat scene, where Bigger Thomas and his family, in their squalid South Side Chicago apartment, confront a huge black rat. With the mother and sister screaming in fear and terror, Bigger and his brother try to kill the screeching rat with a skillet. The rat is defensive, caught in his own terror, and showing his yellow fangs, tries to find an escape hole in the wall. Bigger tries to hit the rat, misses, goes after him again and gets a ripped trouser leg as the rat strikes at him. The women, standing on the bed, yell, 'Kill 'im!' Bigger hurls the skillet, strikes and stuns the rat, and then to be sure he 'got him' pounds and crushes the rat's head with his shoe, cursing hysterically, 'You sonofa*bitch*!'[21] The episode with the rat presages not only Bigger's relationship with Mary and Bessie, but also white society's relationship with all that Bigger represents. Robert Butler observes that 'society does to him precisely what he did to Mary and Bessie – it kills him, partly out of fear and partly out of hatred.'[22]

From here on, in the novel – given a naturalist orientation – there is a great concatenation of rats (black and white), skillets (black and white), screams of 'Kill 'im!' (black and white), and hysterical cursings (black and white). Horror succeeds horror, there is murder, there is flight, motives get mixed up (Bigger wants to 'help' Mary and Mrs Dalton, but kills Mary in the process); Mr Dalton is a self-satisfied benefactor of Negro causes but owns the very accommodation in which the Thomas family confronts the interloping rat. Jan wants to help Bigger, but understands little enough of him and his situation to discomfit him by insisting that he eat with him and Mary. In all of this, Wright defines fictionally the 'real reality' of racial oppression and moral confusion of American capitalist culture as he sees them. The determinism and determinants are palpable.

And in the end, because there is law, Bigger is tried for murder, defended by Max on crypto-Marxist lines which seek to transmute the rat from threat and danger to victim; the frying-pan from weapon of defence or offence to instrument of justice; the double murderer to victim of murderous dehumanization and exploitation. And all of this within the permissible constraints of Illinois law, but with a larger, deeply felt pleading for the presumed concomitant of law: justice. Bigger has known his crime and will know his punishment; he does not clearly understand any available means to redemption, nor perhaps the fundamental nature of his guilt. At the very end, Bigger says, 'I didn't want to kill!' 'But what I killed for, I *am*! It must've been pretty deep in me to make me kill! I must have felt it awful hard to murder ...'[23]

This final climactic scene in which Bigger achieves awareness, like the earlier scene in which Bigger realized Jan's basic humanity, is played out between two men. Often forgotten in critical responses to the novel are the exclusively female objects of male criminal behaviour. Alan France argues that the subtext to the authorized racial dialectic which motivates Bigger's crimes is a suppressed sexual dialectic: 'the struggle to appropriate (and thus dehumanize) women by reducing them to objects of male status conflict.'[24] The confrontation between Jan and Bigger after Bigger has confessed thus becomes the confrontation between the man whose property (and thus his status) has been appropriated and the man who has appropriated that property (and status) through crime. Is there any doubt that Bigger conceives of his crime as conferring status?

To see the way in which racism and sexism co-operate in the novel to objectify and dehumanize black women, we need look no further than the appalling display of Bessie's battered body at Bigger's trial. Yet, France is careful to point out that his reading of *Native Son* should not detract from the legitimate, authorized theme of racial struggle. Rather, it should help us understand more clearly 'the interrelationship among patriarchal repression, racism, and capitalist culture'[25] (we might also add criminal prosecution). Having reclaimed Bigger's humanity and individuality from the programmatic approach of the protest novel, then, it seems that modern critics are now finding ways in which a novel condemning oppression can itself authorize or perpetuate abuse.

Yet something of its basic picture of a too appalling reality in American society is still there at the heart of the novel. That Wright's analysis, his reading of that truth, may have been grossly flawed, and that his prescriptive theme may have been misguided should not altogether disqualify the novel to us as a very provocative insistence on once again examining the meaning of law, of morality, of justice, of the modifying contingencies of social fact and social reality. That the whole enterprise hinges on the appalling weight and density of Bigger Thomas as a character leads one from question to question about the ultimate 'truth' of the novel.

Recently, a young Afro-American writer of considerable interest published in the *New York Times Magazine* an article titled 'On Rereading *Native Son*.'[26] David Bradley first tried to read the novel in 1971 when he was an undergraduate. Conscious of his own blackness, his aspirations to write, and the 'canonical' status of *Native Son* in Afro-American literature, he felt, we are told, terribly disappointed. More than that, he realized he *hated* it, and most of all, hated Bigger Thomas with a passion. To him the novel was not only badly written in parts, but it offered him a '"meaningful and prophetic symbol" of the black masses'[27] which appalled him, and whom he could only loathe and wish dead – legally or otherwise.

Again, in 1973, Bradley tried *Native Son* when he was a graduate student in England. Apparently he understood the novel better, but did not like it any better. Something of its assumptions, much of the presented image of black American life and spirit infuriated him. But he also understood how, as he says, the novel could be called – especially by white critics – a classic. He remembered Irving Howe's pronouncement that 'the day *Native Son* appeared, American culture was changed forever.'[28] But Bradley was depressed that so crude and misleading a social document, so flawed in conception and truth-telling, augured ill for him as a black American and as an aspiring black writer.

Finally, on still another reading, Bradley felt a profound sorrow for Richard Wright himself. Given the facts of Wright's life experiences, the circumstances of his moment in American social and political history, Wright *had* to write what he did, and his image of black American life in its large, corporate sense, was not, after all, so inaccurate. Bradley is eloquent: 'Not that there was great validity in Wright's use of Bigger Thomas as a type ... *Native Son*, I realized, shows the vision one black man held of his people, his country, and, ultimately, himself. And I thought, Dear God, how horrible for a man to have to write this. And, Please, God, let no one ever have to write this again.'[29] Because Bigger Thomas' story (however lamentable *he* was) 'was no more melodramatic, crude or claustrophobic than the times themselves.'[30] There was, after all, the Robert Nixon case in Chicago (bearing the form, if not the specific content of Bigger's).

In 'How Bigger Was Born,' Wright mentions that 'when I was halfway through the first draft of *Native Son* a case paralleling Bigger's flared forth in the newspapers of Chicago' (xxviii). This was the trial of Robert Nixon and Earl Hicks for the murder of a woman who was beaten to death with a brick. Nixon was sentenced to death after a one-week trial and only one hour of jury deliberation. The newspaper accounts of Bigger and his trial, as sensationalistic and exaggerated as they seem today, were drawn quite closely from the Chicago *Tribune*, as Wright points out. Keneth Kinnamon observed that 'though no evidence of rape was adduced, the *Tribune* from the beginning called the murder a sex crime and exploited fully this apparently quite false accusation.'[31] Like Bigger, Nixon was accused of a number of other, unsolved crimes by the Chicago and Los Angeles police. The material for Bigger's fears of false accusation, and their realization, were thus close at hand for Wright, quite apart from his own experiences described in 'How Bigger Was Born.' As well, there *were* still the national tremors over the famous Scottsboro case. There *were* lynchings. The list multiplies. And there *were*, deep down, the absolutely elemental impulses to survive, with or without something called dignity. And a writer, himself so conditioned that to impeach his environment drew forth a sense of self and of his world that can only now be seen as deep sorrow.

Bradley concludes his essay on this note: 'I find that Wright, after all these years, has failed in an ironic way. He wanted *Native Son* to be a book "no one would weep over." With me, he once succeeded. He no longer does. *Native Son* is an ineffably sad expression of what once were the realities of this nation. We have not come as far as we ought. But I hope we have come far enough by now to read *Native Son* and weep.'[32] I trust we ourselves need not weep over this novel. We might better contemplate its passionate, if flawed, effort to define, in the face of appalling realities, some ordered relation among our inescapable involvements in the vagaries of crime, law, guilt, punishment, redemption – for the human individual and for a coherent community – in the overarching order of justice.

Notes

Caesar R. Blake received his PHD from the University of Michigan in 1958. His publications include *Dorothy Richardson* and *The Recognition of Emily Dickinson*, and he is one of the editors of *The Norton Reader* and *The Norton Anthology of Poetry*. He has been a consultant to the 'Consortium on Higher Education in Predominantly Black Colleges and Universities.'

1 Irving Howe 'Black Boys and Native Sons' *Dissent* 10 (1963) 355
2 Ibid 357
3 Alfred Kazin *On Native Grounds* (New York: Reynal & Hitchcock 1942) 387
4 James Baldwin 'Everybody's Protest Novel' in *Notes of a Native Son* (New York: Bantam 1964) 11

5 Ibid 17
6 Ibid
7 Ralph Ellison's views are partly set out in 'Richard Wright's Blues.' In response to Howe's strictures on Baldwin and himself, Ellison wrote a rejoinder; Howe retorted: Ellison then answered again, very fully, and the two essays are reprinted in his *Shadow and Act* (New York: Random House 1964) under the general title 'The World and the Jug.'
8 Howe 'Black Boys' 357
9 James Baldwin 'Many Thousands Gone' in *Notes of a Native Son* (New York: Bantam 1964) 32
10 Tony Magistrale 'From St. Petersburg to Chicago: Wright's *Crime and Punishment*' *Comparative Literature Studies* 23 (1986) 59
11 Ibid
12 Ibid 67-8
13 Clifton Fadiman *The New Yorker* 2 March 1940, 52-3
14 Howe 'Black Boys' 356
15 Kathleen Gallagher 'Bigger's Great Leap to the Figurative' *College Language Association Journal* 27 (1984) 293
16 Baldwin 'Many Thousands Gone' 24
17 Robert James Butler 'Wright's *Native Son* and Two Novels by Zola: A Comparative Study' *Black American Literature Forum* 18 (1984) 100
18 James Baldwin 'Alas Poor Richard' in *Nobody Knows My Name* (New York: Dell 1963) 151
19 Robert James Butler 'The Function of Violence in Richard Wright's *Native Son*' *Black American Literature Forum* 20 (1986) 15
20 Ibid 20
21 Richard Wright *Native Son* (New York: Harper & Row 1940) 9-10
22 Butler 'The Function of Violence' 19
23 *Native Son* 391-2
24 Alan W. France 'Misogyny and Appropriation in Wright's *Native Son*' *Modern Fiction Studies* 34 (1988) 414
25 Ibid 422
26 David Bradley 'On Rereading "Native Son,"' *New York Times Magazine* 7 December 1986, 68
27 Bradley ibid, quoting 'How Bigger Was Born' 70
28 Howe 'Black Boys' 354
29 Bradley 'On Rereading "Native Son"' 78-9
30 Ibid 78

31 Keneth Kinnamon '*Native Son*: The Personal, Social, and Political
    Background' in *Critical Essays on Richard Wright* ed Yoshinobu Hakutani
    (Boston: G.K. Hall 1982) 122
32 Bradley 'On Rereading "Native Son"' 79

DENNIS DUFFY

Wiebe's Real Riel? *The Scorched-Wood People* and Its Audience

Imaginative versions of Louis Riel and his crime preoccupy Canadian culture. Literature, drama, opera have all featured him. Social scientists have studied him as political leader, visionary, rebel lunatic, and criminal. To these, add Rudy Wiebe's novel, *The Scorched-Wood People* (1977), the subject of this paper. It deals with Riel's two rebellions from the inside. Using an omniscient Métis narrator (a historical figure in fact dead by the time much of the novel takes place), this postmodernist narrative plays with literal truth in an effort to capture another version of it. Playing off the character of the mystical Riel against that of the earthy Dumont, the text raises questions that still simmer in its readers' memory. Can a society employing liberal, rationalist methods of social control accommodate groups who reject those norms? Just how much of the Other can we tolerate? If we yearn to create heroes out of aliens, what price do we pay in consistency of belief?

Considered in the light of fiction's standard list of virtues, Wiebe's book appears more pleasing and compelling than its predecessors. Its message seems complex, its formal balance and symmetry apparent, its portrayal of Riel's inner world convincing. If representational, mimetic strengths were all that made literature interesting, if the appearance of verisimilitude proved to be literature's greatest attraction, Wiebe's fiction then surpasses every novel before it. Any conventional reading of the texts I cite below will bring this to light. Two additional factors made it important for me to extend the discussion beyond this kind of analysis: (1) an essay's appearance in a series on crime and literature requires more of it than a listing of its subject's belles-lettristic graces; (2) a demonstration of *The Scorched-Wood People*'s high mimetic qualities still falls short of conveying exactly why the book merits close attention *here*.

True, Wiebe's presentation may strike us as convincing. After all, it agrees with what we know about visionaries, political leaders, and rebels. Produced by one of us for us, the text then reflects us. Does that mean that it therefore reflects Riel as a historical figure? By no means! Even if we reside contentedly in the familiar, the almost-classical Canadian critical conviction that fidelity to observed Canadian fact merits canonical placement in our literature,[1] our satisfaction with the text rests upon conviction rather than demonstration.

My discussion therefore emphasizes the specifically composed, made-up, stylized aspects of the novel. I proceed from this to an examination of the relevance of other artistic treatments of Riel. I finally attempt to match the response elicited from Wiebe's readers with those demanded of anyone contemplating the nature of Riel and his crime.

Wiebe's most notable critic, W.J. Keith, has termed his fiction 'epic.'[2] I prefer to see the writer's work as metafictional rather than epic. If we go back to the very beginning, we will discover that calendrical time yields in the novel to visions of infinite, cyclical duration. This sense of meta-time propels us toward Wiebe's recreation of the foundations of Riel's world-view. Outlining this entails presenting a little bit of background.

Begin at the beginning, with the history of the ancient Hebrews. A remnant of them landed long ago on the east coast of North America. Slaves of the Egyptian merchants who controlled the ship, the Jews outnumbered their masters, whom they easily evaded after the landing. The Egyptians journeyed southward on the American continent to found, in time, the Aztec and Incan empires. The Jews, largely uneducated, 'newly emerged from oppression,' were fated to lead a simple life. Their wanderings brought them in touch with the plains tribes of the north, with whom they merged. Later, when North America's pre-history had concluded, this Jewish-Amerind mixture would be further enriched by the blood of trappers and voyageurs from New France. The Métis, the French-speaking half-breeds, the bois-brulées, the scorched-wood people who had settled at the confluence of the Red and Assiniboine Rivers had thus descended from the Israelites. They therefore shared in the historic and religious mission of the Jews. Rather than merely existing as a nomadic remnant outside of history, the Métis occupied the stage in the timeless pageant of sacred history. The God of the Hebrews stood within history; He had parted the Red Sea in answer to His people's needs. He had granted them victory when they proved faithful to His commands and punished them when they had strayed. He had accomplished all these great things before. He would do so again for those who truly believed.

A cosmic timepiece ticked away and marked His interventions. The conventional chronology of Old Testament history placed the reforms of Ezra in 457 BC. This Babylonian Jew's purification of an ancient religion began the period of preparation for the birth of the Messiah that would occur 457 years later. This Old World phase of the Christian era, embodied in the Roman papacy, would continue for 1876 years. Adding 457 to 1876 produces 2333, the length of the Old World religious cycle.

Then a new age begins with the transfer of the papacy from Rome to Montreal in 1876 AD. This opens the period of French-Canadian preparation for a new revelation. As happened earlier, the process will require 457 years and end in 2333 AD. A new papacy will then shift westward to St Vital in Manitoba. This period of 1876 years will conclude with the Second Coming in 4209 AD. When added to the preparation time of 457 years, the figure 1876 produces 2333. Figures don't lie. Thus the New world period of revelation matches in length that of the Old World. At the junction of the two time periods, at the centre of significant history, rests the year 1876 AD, the year in which Louis Riel composed this chronology. It had originated during his vision of 8 December 1875 at the Roman Catholic cathedral in Washington, DC.[3] 1876 saw also the death of General Custer and the centennial of the USA, events dwarfed in their importance by Riel's cosmic calendar.

The same Lord who created design and symmetry in nature could be assumed to possess similar intentions in structuring temporality. The midpoint of history, 1876, looks backward to the refounding of Judaism and forward to the era of its successors, each side balanced by a papal era.

When the novel opens with an image of the four-years-times-four time period that so resonated within Cree culture, we know that we are watching a non-scientific clock.[4] Beyond this recede the aeons denoted by the Riel calendar. Time begins in the novel in the mythic and cyclical way of pre-modern numerologies: 4 x 4. Arching beyond this in the actual writings of Riel, barely glimpsed in the novel itself, stand those two 1876s crucial to Louis 'David' Riel, prophet of the new world. Such a construct may not be scientific, yet it most certainly is would-be scientific. It aspires to the precision of science even while positing the symmetry of myth. That atmosphere of a hesitantly grasped modernity, of an attempt to cull from modernity only those elements that will reinforce the traditional world-views held by Riel's culture(s) pervades Wiebe's novel. Here is a text awash in duality.

The most common instance of a dualism underlying events appears through the juxtapositions of everyday reality with the visionary. Sometimes this surfaces in the conflict between faith in things unseen as against belief in things seen, a scriptural dichotomy (Heb 11:1) repeatedly echoed in the novel. Riel and Dumont appear as complementary leaders ('the planning and ceremony of Riel, the emotion of Gabriel' [33]), as the juxtapositioning of their similar-sounding names would suggest. Wiebe bends historical fact by putting the two men in close contact from 1869 on rather than letting this wait until later, in order to keep that dualism before his reader from the beginning. Two popular ballads are cited in the novel, one celebrating a Métis victory, the other proleptically alluding to Riel's defeat (39–41, 93). The Métis slide into extremes of behaviour, we are told, torn as they are between two cultures (112–13). The novel is dualistic even in its typography, setting Riel's visionary experiences (often lifted directly from the man's own writings) in italic, distinguishing them from the rest of the text.

This last technique reinforces the postmodern feel of the text. The typographic play forces two orders of experience together in a value-free way, carefully advancing neither. Considering such examples of postmodern Canadian fiction as Jack Hodgins' *The Invention of the World* (1977), Robert Kroetsch's *What the Crow Said* (1978), and Timothy Findley's *Famous Last Words* (1981) shows how incongruous positionings of the ordinary alongside the fantastic mark this kind of work. There we find narrators offering accounts of experiences closed to them. We see talking animals and mythic genealogies humming alongside our world of supermarkets and tourist sites. Riel's visionary moments are presented in 'deadpan' style, to be invested by the reader with whatever credibility he extends to anything else in the fiction. When the Duke of Wellington harrumphed that a man who could believe *that* could believe anything, he was anticipating the responses demanded of a postmodern literary public.

Mentioning Wiebe's use of historical texts in depicting Riel's visions shifts the discussion toward the nature of narrative as this novel employs it. This in turn separates into two features: first, the impossibility of the actual narrator; second, the extra-narrative nature of the story itself. I will explain what I mean by the second after treating the first.

This chronicle of Riel and his people from 1869–85 (in view of the incorporation of historical material, chronicle may be a term more appropriate than novel) is related by a historical figure who was dead by 1876. Wiebe uses the Métis bard Pierre Falcon, one surmises, in order to suggest the folkloric quality of his narrative. Far from an objective observer, Falcon compounds this flaw by failing to stay alive. Why? One assumes that Wiebe wants to impress again upon his audience the point once made about his earlier *Temptations of Big Bear* (1973). In an account of the novel's origins he emphasizes the gaps in the historical record and his right to provide his own version of disputed events.[5] Here that slipperiness is built into the narrator himself, who represents only the idea of a tribal voice celebrating its heroes from beyond the grave. Falcon's historical role as a folk poet gives us a glimpse into the assumptions behind this novel. It seems to be attempting something beyond the usual scope of narrative. Here is where form and content merge. Consider the content of the story-within-the-story: scripture. That is, the novel recounts the history of Riel and the Métis. But through Riel's influence they came to see their story as a replication of the story of the ancient Hebrews. Once again, Wiebe's narration takes no objective distance from this, so that again and again a character quite deliberately places his experience within a scriptural framework. The fact that Wiebe's creations see themselves as the New Israel places them in a light similar to that of Hawthorne's characters in *The Scarlet Letter*. After all, the historical record attests that both peoples did in fact so believe.

To that 'inner' scriptural preoccupation, a Riel eliciting Biblical analogies to contemporary events, for example, add the Biblical analogies implicit in the style of the novel itself. That is, the text abounds in Biblical echoes and sonorous uses of language, and the reader discovers parallels between the events of the story and those of scripture to which the narrative does not call overt attention. All this results finally in a series of Russian dolls, of which I will offer one example. Historically, Louis Riel renamed himself David because he viewed himself as priest, prophet, and king in the way that tradition now views the Biblical ruler and psalmist. In the novel, Riel alludes to this. The reader then applies this to the relationship between Riel and Sir John A. Macdonald, where that figure emerges as a blind, bad-tempered, and proud

Saul rebuffing the man who would be his friend. So far, so good. Let us now extend this chain of relevance and recall that the novel's title tells us that Wiebe is trying to write the story of a despised, outcast *people* who saw their remote experience as central to the human project. In other words, Wiebe has himself undertaken a project analogous to that advanced by the Hebrew Bible and its Christian successor. This is a pattern extending beyond, for example, Margaret Laurence's use of Biblical parallels to grant resonance to the experiences of her heroine Hagar Shipley in *The Stone Angel* (1964). Wiebe's pattern, on the contrary, seeks to replicate – and here the narrative turns in upon itself – the scriptural project. Wiebe is stating in effect that a new Bible can be written about things here, in Canada, in a time past when the fate of the world centred upon the doings of our own peoples. Readers may not wish to walk all the way with an author on a journey of that scope, but no reader can deny that he is in the presence of extraordinary narrative indeed. Some primal act recalling the foundations of narrative in our culture is occurring here.

My readers must bear with me now as I move from the adoption, really incorporation, of scripture as a mark of the novel's attempt to return to the foundations of narrative. Let me conclude this part of my argument by taking the final step in foundation-making, and illustrate the novel's preoccupation with the use of language itself.

Any text as immersed in scripture as this already bears a 'built-in' drift toward a self-consciousness about language and its uses. The Christian Bible does refer to Godhead as the Word, and Christians are, after all, people of the Book. The novel's historical setting refines this even further, in that the Métis were largely not a literate people. Part of Riel's power lay in his own literacy, stemming from his clerical education, but his chief influence lay in preaching. The novel reflects this, as again and again it is the spoken word whose power is stressed, with the gospel proclaimed rather than read. Thus it is the Word-as-Voice that the people yearn for. Repeatedly, they praise Riel for putting their thoughts into words, for articulating what had been left unsaid (13, 31, 54, 80, 264, 318, 340). Wiebe has dealt with this phenomenon before, in his story 'Where Is the Voice Coming From?' (1974), and voicing and naming are activities central to much of Wiebe's fiction. Small wonder that they play a major role in *The Scorched-Wood People*.

Riel may organize the propaganda of the word, but Gabriel (beheld in a dream as a 'giant fist' [343]) delivers the propaganda of the deed.

Yet Gabriel's deference to his visionary leader helps bring about their defeat. Even so, his respect for Riel remains undimmed at the end of the novel. What is the implication of this? Even when mastery of the word is not accompanied by mastery of the deed, the latter remains properly subordinated to the former. Riel was in fact enough of a word-player to set his tribal council (he had renamed them the 'Exovedate') the task of renaming the days of the week. This, in a time of war! That Riel comes to be Wiebe's Riel, and in Wiebe's fiction the subordinate characters remain content to follow so unworldly and super-wordy a person. His preoccupation with language and with visionary experience makes this novel the latest in a long line of artist-as-hero fictions.

Therefore, to engage in another Russian doll exercise, we end up with a pattern like this. On the outside stands scripture, the great whale swallowing this one. Then comes scripture's valuation of the Word. Then comes an oral culture's reverence for scripture as the spoken word, the lessons read aloud central to Christian services. Then comes Riel's prowess at reducing the abstractions so necessary to literate societies into the concrete expressions of nationhood that his people yearn for. The historical Riel and Wiebe's Riel alike utter the stunningly concrete (one must go to the psalms to find similar reification of spiritual realities) justification of a people's need for territory: 'God cannot create a tribe without locating it. Even birds have a place; we have to walk upon the ground' (324). In such activities Riel's power is made manifest. But within that doll stands the smaller, the reflection that this power may not always prevail in the world of concrete actuality. Very well, proclaims the tiniest doll, the hierarchy remains, despite its practical results. Thus this text's ultimate faith resides in the power of things unseen, though these are not the mystical entities St Paul invoked. The things unseen are spoken words, drifting about in the air like flocks of birds, until they nest among the hearts of men.

The question I started with remains. Given that *The Scorched-Wood People* remains a text that is self-reflexive, scriptural in aim and steeped in the conviction that language seems our ultimate reality, what has all that to do with the exploration of literature's strategies for discovering meaning in crime? In fact, it is only after pointing out all the ways in which Wiebe's novel fulfils those now-standard requirements for postmodernist fiction that I can begin to deal with the focus of this series of essays.

Scripture assures us that even if the Lord cannot be found either in the wind, the earthquake, or the fire, He yet appears in the still, small voice (1 Kings 19:11–12). Antigone, that emblem of resistance to civil authority, was she not also a still, small voice? And Creon, her oppressor laden with all the burdens of leadership following a civil war, attempting nothing more than showing that the threat to civil peace had been extinguished and stability restored, how could he have been expected to have listened to that voice? 'The Naming of Albert Johnson' is a Wiebe story of 1974 that deals with language's power to shape and mould a person's being and to set him on a course of action ending in his destruction. Wiebe's magnum opus, *Temptations of Big Bear*, deals with two cultures whose mutual incomprehension will result in the destruction of the technologically inferior one. We all know where our sympathies lie, with the inferior, the defeated, the heroic, and the primitive. Yet at its best, the novel forces us to turn our attention to matters wider than smug moralism grasps, a response that I have outlined elsewhere.[6]

The Scorched-Wood People enables us better to understand crime than to establish blame for it. This is a refreshing change in our imaginative literature, for the sad fact is that anyone in search of the imaginative recreation of time past, the empathic understanding of the Other, and the bold assembling of facts into gripping narrative will be better off with the histories rather than the novels and plays. Except for Wiebe's novel, I find nothing in the imaginative literature sharing the quality of such non-fictional treatments of Riel as George Woodcock's *Gabriel Dumont and the Northwest Rebellion* (1975), Joseph Kinsey Howard's *Strange Empire* (1952), and Thomas Flanagan's *Louis 'David' Riel: 'Prophet of the New World'* (1979). For example, pulp and popular fiction and cinema fail to come up with the interestingly wacky asides that make memorable even poor treatments of their subject. Edmund Collins' *Annette, The Metis Spy: A Heroine of the N.W. Rebellion* (1886), Anne Mercier and Violet Watts's *The Red House By the Rockies; A Tale of Riel's Rebellion* (1896), and John Mackie's *The Rising of the Red Man; A Romance of the Louis Riel Rebellion* (1904) follow the boy-meets-girl formulae of pulp fiction and use Riel as a distant or ranting backdrop. This tradition finds a visual equivalent in Cecil B. de Mille's 1940 film epic *North West Mounted Police* in which Canada is saved from rule by vicious half-breeds through the efforts of Gary Cooper and a Gatling gun. The promotion of the American gun-fighter as the solution to the problems posed by Riel continues in Giles A. Lutz's novel, *The Magnificent Failure* (1967).

We may object that these are the product of pop writers, English or Americans in search of events to squeeze into the cookie-cutter formulae their generic work required. Yet serious Canadians do little better here. R.D. Symons' *Still the Wind Blows: A Historical Novel of the Canadian Northwest 1860–1916* (1971) is charmingly illustrated by the author and filled with love for its subject. Yet its hackneyed plot and banal writing style force a reader to ignore the compassion it shows for all the actors in the drama it treats. James McNamee's *them damn Canadians hanged Louis Riel!* (1971) makes its point by drawing a set of 'Western'-originated stereotypes as narrow and absurd as anything perpetrated by 'Easterners'.

Things grow a little brighter with poetry and drama. Dorothy Livesay's drama, 'Prophet of the New World' (1945; later revised for *Collected Poems* 1972) makes an artist manqué of its subject, even as Don Gutteridge's *Riel: A Poem for Voices* (1968) dematerializes him finally into some sort of Prairie spirit. Both these 'voice' poems (radio plays) fail to account for the fact that the man's impact upon history did not come solely from his utterances. John Coulter's three Riel plays seek to return the figure to history rather than leaving him in a poetic limbo. Thus *The Trial of Louis Riel* (1968) stands as courtroom drama condensed from actual trial records. *Riel* (1962) presents a series of tableaux in the Brechtian mode, concentrating upon the public issues raised by Riel's actions. *The Crime of Louis Riel* (1976) sees Riel as an anti-colonial rebel, precursor of nationalist and tribal anti-imperial heroes the world over. As far as this aspect of Riel is concerned, Coulter's plays lead to a renewed appreciation of Riel's historical importance. Yet this portrait lacks the complexity of Wiebe's treatment. For Riel and his followers did not see him as just another nationalist leader, a seeker of the political kingdom in the manner of a Jefferson Davis trying to establish a separatist state somewhere to the South. He was instead a religious visionary trying to set up the kingdom of God on earth. In life and death alike he seems close to the radical Protestants who founded the messianic Mennonite faith that Rudy Wiebe was himself born into.

Pause here. John Coulter's view of Riel may disagree with mine and Rudy Wiebe's. The fact remains that we are looking at imaginative constructs, and so whatever actuality Wiebe's figure possesses may not be inherently greater than any accruing to other versions of Riel. That is not my argument. I believe instead that recognizing the complexity of Wiebe's portrayal takes a first step toward grasping the importance of his treatment of Riel's crime. Only one other imaginative work comes near to achieving the complexity of Wiebe's. To whatever limited degree one can separate an operatic libretto from its musical accompaniment, an examination of Mavor Moore's script for Harry Somers' *Louis Riel: An Opera in Three Acts* (1967) unearths a visionary subject. Moore calls for a series of brief, episodic scenes where depth of character yields to breadth of action. While Riel the visionary is highlighted near the end of act 1, with the eerie music heightening our sense of this, that aspect of him never really returns for the rest of the opera. The concentration on the political dénouement and the harsh, percussive score add to our sense of the submersion of the visionary. Is this the libretto's point?

Granted that Wiebe's pictures of Riel at prayer seem as integral to his portrait as the depiction of Riel on trial, granted that the concentration on issues involving religion and language place the novel's political events within a rich realm of implication, what has this to do with Riel's crime?

The historical records show that Riel was hanged for a crime that he could not feel that he had committed.[7] On the other hand, the jury who convicted him could have acted in no other way, once Riel had spurned the loophole of an insanity plea. To put this in more objective terms, a non-modern, religious, oral culture collided with a modern, secular, written culture and was shattered by the force of the encounter. The clay pot will break when it bumps the iron one; no amount of understanding will change their natures; destruction of one is inevitable once collision occurs. Such a view ignores the fact that humanity makes its own nature and history, and that historical struggles cannot be reduced to such simplicity. But there is a tiny shard of truth, or at least relevance to my argument in this line of reasoning. Allow me to pursue it.

Wiebe's Riel takes it for granted that his visions produce his politics. Far from being a modern social scientist seeking to unravel from each other the threads of personal ambition, ideological impulse, cultural paradigms, and historical determination that produce any decision, Wiebe's Riel is a whole person who does not grade orders of reality on the basis of their degree of materiality. That is, the visionary to him is an order of reality superior to the mundane. He distinguishes between the two on the basis of what he perceives to be their moral worth, rather than through determining which is more palpable and therefore subject to scientific analysis and quantification. In this, he differs from the society of his enemies, our society. Our society can only view this attitude as delusory. When it leads one to the commission of political crime, we can pardon it only when the criminal appears hopelessly in the grip of those delusions. That avenue of retreat Riel shunned. Therefore we acted accordingly and condemned his actions. Where is the moral?

The moral is not to find a moral, but to use Wiebe's novel to draw us closer to an understanding of the issues that Riel's crime raises. We use the text best once we grasp its implicit message: the incompatibility of differing cultural discourses.

The concept of legality that a social system like ours rests upon could have handled satisfactorily only a uni-vocal Riel. Had he been only a visionary, we would have allowed him all the latitude he needed in proclaiming his doctrines. Until, of course, he sought to implement them. Had Riel been only a freedom-fighter, we could have handled him also. Some would have called us unjust, but everyone would have agreed about the framework of assumptions behind our treatment. Successful revolutionaries ('bandits' translated into 'freedom fighters') eliminate their erstwhile superiors under codes of justice similar to those they overthrew. Specific definitions of criminal behaviour may change (company shares become controlled substances; profit-taking becomes theft), but criminality remains definable in terms of secular experience. Political criminals appealing to God and History can entertain us in courtroom drama. But how can one accommodate unearthly visions within the range of our discourse on the nature of a criminal act? And when these visions culminate in armed insurrection, how can we grant them the latitude that we do to acts of civil disobedience? Our position remains clear: vision that results in action will be judged on the basis of action alone. We will not presume to evaluate the quality of a vision. We will instead punish any untoward actions resulting from it.

A work of this scope and power forces its audience to reach for the mysterious wholeness of a historical situation rather than rest content with a packageable fragment of it. Wiebe's is not a neutral text. Macdonald and other Canadians, for example, come on as an obtuse, self-centred and cynical group. This invitation to hiss the villain diminishes the novel's power. This fact plus a host of atmospherics leave us with little doubt about Riel and the process that hanged him. Since these days of post-colonial enlightenment require a politically correct response on our part, we can emerge from the novel with Riel fitted smoothly into our pat orthodoxy.

Against this bias of content, I would place the neutrality of form. Contemplating this can provoke us into considering our own views and pondering the nature of the crime in a clearer fashion. If metafiction can do no more than confirm us in our smug, superior distance from the past, then why bother reading such demanding texts? In fact, whatever the content of such enterprises, they serve to hammer home to us the arbitrary nature of human activity, especially the activity of using language. In such works, crime emerges from a welter of circumstances, and not just from the moralistic stand-bys of greed and pride. Desperation, sloth, fumbling, aspiration, nobility, and endurance, both our highest and lowest characteristics, come into play. We can none of us gain an acquittal from the charge of perpetrating language.

Preparing this paper sent me to the literature on Riel's crime and trial. That literature in turn sent me back to Wiebe because I found no balm in Gilead. Instead a reader accumulates instances of inappropriate description and self-serving rhetoric, the slogans of the victor and the would-be victor, often encased in the jargon of a pseudo-science.[8] My own language, that of the scientifically trained liberal academic, in fact inches no closer than these others to expressing the nature of Riel's crime. Nor can I smugly accuse those who condemned Riel of a greater crime, without falling myself into the trap of easy judgment from afar.

A flabby sentimentality about underdogs could make us acquit Riel at the sacrifice of any integrity we may possess as moderns. Are we willing to live under an ayatollah? Are we prepared to accept the consequences of allowing armed resistance to the state we support? Can our vaunted peaceable kingdom continue if our state relinquishes its monopoly on violence? Granted that we would enjoy Riel as some John the Baptist come back to tell us all (on the talk-show circuit), do we not deface his image by making it into the subject of a postage stamp?

The novel instead offers us a new scripture that questions itself, that turns in upon its own modes and motives. Our response should be commensurate, challenging ourselves in deciding whether our escape clause (our liberal beliefs alone admit the possibility of those beliefs being in error and ensure the discussion of those errors) worked in Riel's case. Our own modes of knowing and their authenticity then come into question and we have passed beyond criticism into self-reflection. Can art provoke any greater response from us? Can we demand anything more of it?

Notes

Dennis Duffy received his PHD from the University of Toronto in 1964. His publications include *Marshall McLuhan*; *Gardens, Covenants, Exiles: Images of Loyalism in the Literature of Upper Canada / Ontario*; and *Sounding the Iceberg: An Essay on Canadian Historical Novels*.

This paper is a substantial revision of one first delivered in 1985. The author acknowledges his debt to an anonymous publisher's reader whose criticism of the original suggested the germ of the idea behind this revision.

1 Robert Lecker 'The Canonization of Canadian Literature: An Inquiry into Value' *Critical Inquiry* 16:3 (Spring 1990) 656–70
2 W.J. Keith *Epic Fiction: The Art of Rudy Wiebe* (Edmonton: University of Alberta Press 1981)
3 *The Diaries of Louis Riel* ed Thomas Flanagan (Edmonton: Hurtig 1976) 166; Thomas Flanagan *Louis 'David' Riel: 'Prophet of the New World'* (Toronto: University of Toronto Press 1979) 88–9
4 Rudy Wiebe *The Scorched-Wood People* (Toronto: New Canadian Library 1977). References to this are found in parentheses in the body of the essay.
5 Rudy Wiebe 'On the Trail of Big Bear' in W.J.Keith ed *A Voice in the Land; Essays By and About Rudy Wiebe* (Edmonton: NeWest Press 1981) 132–41
6 *Sounding the Iceberg: An Essay on Canadian Historical Novels* (Toronto: ECW Press 1986) 73–5
7 My sense of the record comes from the two books mentioned in note 3, and also: Bob Beal and Rod Macleod *Prairie Fire: The 1885 North-West Rebellion* (Edmonton: Hurtig 1984); Joseph Kinsey Howard *Strange Empire* (Toronto: George J. McLeod 1952); Desmond Morton *The Last War Drum: The North West Campaign of 1885* (Toronto: Hakkert 1972); George F.G. Stanley *The Birth of Western Canada, a History of the Riel*

Rebellions (London: Longmans 1936) and *Louis Riel* (Toronto: McGraw-Hill Ryerson 1963); George Woodcock *Gabriel Dumont: The Metis Chief and His Lost World* (Edmonton: Hurtig 1975).

For Riel's trial, see Thomas Flanagan *Riel and The Rebellion: 1885 Reconsidered* (Saskatoon: Western Producer Prairie Books 1983) 116–34; Kenneth McNaught 'Political Trials and the Canadian Political Tradition' in M.L. Friedland ed *Courts and Trials: A Multidisciplinary Approach* (Toronto: University of Toronto Press 1975) 137–61; Desmond Morton ed *The Queen v Louis Riel* (Toronto: University of Toronto Press 1974); Lewis H. Thomas 'A Judicial Murder – The Trial of Louis Riel' in Howard Palmer ed *The Settlement of the West* (Calgary: University of Calgary Press 1977) 37–59; R.E. Turner 'The Life and Death of Louis Riel: A Study in Forensic Psychiatry. Part III – Medico-Legal Issues' *Canadian Psychiatric Association Journal* 10 (1965) 259–64

8 Forensic psychiatry's inability to come to grips with the fact of extraordinary people emerges during its description of Riel through such terms as 'omnipotent idealized parental introjects' and 'psychosis with predominant manic and paranoid features.' See E.R. Markson 'The Life and Death of Louis Riel: A Study in Forensic Psychiatry. Part I – A Psychoanalytic Commentary' *Canadian Psychiatric Association Journal* 10 (1965) 250, 249.

ANN SADDLEMYER

Crime in Literature: Canadian Drama

Action ... Suspense ... Immediacy ... Persuasion ... Conflict ... Revelation ... Climax ... Resolution. These are the qualities of theatre, of story-telling, and, coincidentally, of the lawcourts. It is not surprising, then, that playwrights have been drawn to depict crime and the criminal on trial from the time of the excellent suspense drama *Oedipus Rex*; and Canadian dramatists are no exception. Take, for example, *The Penguin Book of Modern Canadian Drama*: seven of the twelve plays have to do with crime, either domestic or political; one (*Fortune and Men's Eyes*) is actually set in a jail, another (*Handcuffs*) attempts to exonerate and reclaim the folk criminal, while a third (*Riel*) includes a courtroom scene.[1] Trial scenes are, of course, as old as the theatre – Oedipus, after all, sits in judgment on himself; medieval mystery cycles always include lots of Herod scenes and end with the Last Judgment; at least a quarter of Shakespeare's plays contain judgment scenes, that in *The Merchant of Venice* being perhaps most familiar; some might say that Bernard Shaw's *Saint Joan* is one vast trial; J.M. Synge's *The Playboy of the Western World*, whose hero is adulated for a murder he did not commit, caused almost a week's rioting in Dublin when first produced; Galsworthy's *Justice* actually provoked prison reform in Britain; while Lawrence and Lee's *Inherit the Wind* not only raised serious questions (still with us in Ontario) about the teaching of evolution but in Henry Drummond, the Clarence Darrow character, as surely provided the model for Perry Mason and even Jessica Fletcher. John Coulter's *Riel*, first produced in 1950, was so popular that he wrote *The Trial of Louis Riel*, which is produced every summer in the old Regina court-house (the very building in which Riel was condemned to be hanged as a traitor) with an eager audience of tourists serving as jury. Reverse the procedure, and the lawcourts themselves can be seen as theatres, evidence and situations being replayed before an audience of judge and jury, plays within plays when one includes the public gallery observing both actors and audience breathlessly awaiting the outcome. The cliché 'courtroom drama' is in fact theatrically apt.

But even when the court is not visible on stage, drama involves the process of judgment, assigning responsibility for action, distinguishing truth from fiction, sifting the pertinent from the irrelevant, and, before a discriminating audience, re-creating what happened and why. No matter that the facts presented may themselves be a fiction – they are enacted before us as reality, drawn by the author from some inner truth, and as audience we willingly suspend our disbelief (in Coleridge's famous phrase)[2] in order to participate in that ritual, ever alert to the confession that will reveal motive and deed.

The two Canadian plays this paper will deal with, George Ryga's *Indian* and Sharon Pollock's *Blood Relations*, compound that process by inviting us to sit in judgment on different levels at once, merging past with present, creating a new suspense out of the confessional, using that very ambiguity to force the audience to accept some responsibility in turn for the deeds enacted before them. *Indian* is a one-act play originally written for television. There are only three characters: farmer Watson, who has hired three Indians to put in fence posts; one of the Indians, who is recovering from a drunken spree held by him and his two cohorts the night before with advance pay cajoled by complaints of hunger; and – after the exasperated Watson has left, threatening to lock up Indian's nephew until the job is completed – an Agent from the Department of Indian Affairs, who learns more than he wants or can handle about the life of his charges when forced by Indian (his only name in the play) to listen to how and why he had to murder his brother. The action of *Blood Relations* also rests on three characters: Lizzie Borden of the famous axe-murder case, her inquisitive actress friend from Boston who, after repeatedly asking for the 'truth' about the murder of the Bordens, is challenged by an impatient Lizzie to re-enact that fateful day ten years earlier, and – in the final few minutes of the play – Lizzie's older sister Emma. The other characters who appear in *Blood Relations*, Lizzie's Irish friend Doctor Patrick, her father and hated stepmother, her stepmother's grasping brother, and the maid Bridget, although present on stage, are all summoned out of the dark by the two actresses' imaginations.

Thus there is an acknowledged crime at the centre of both plays, but confession reveals more than the admission of guilt; violent action is but the foreplay to an internal trial that involves us not merely as spectators, but as conspirators in fact. This reversal continues throughout each play: imprisonment causes violent action; but that imprisonment is of the spirit, and society is judged guilty of a crime far more heinous in the eyes of the playwright than the violence narrated on stage. In fact neither murder takes place on stage; in *Indian* we are told of it, in *Blood Relations* it is assumed. Murder is, in both, presented as a necessary and reasonable act, a release. The murderers themselves feel they have nothing to lose, had no rights to begin with, and attempt to gain them through their crimes; in Miss Lizzie's words, 'not all life is precious.'³ Both plays tease out an undercurrent of pain and feeling rather than dwell on factual truths; both protagonists mock the institutions which have made them helpless, frustrated, angry, and defiant. The process of judgment is forced to turn in upon itself, to examine the very roots of justice and equality, without ever allowing us to retreat into indifference or evasion. Both plays move from the general to the particular, from what we have always accepted as publicly 'known,' to specific individual condemnation. Both plays start, not with the quest for identity, but rather with an earlier search for what is lacking to create an identity in the first place. Both attempt to go beyond the simple 'whodunit' of the present to a re-examination of the past in an effort to determine the original crime. And in so doing fact becomes less important than fiction, style and form as persuasive as content.

This process of manipulation of fact, theory, and audience is evident in the shorter of the two plays, George Ryga's *Indian*. Best known perhaps for his other 'Indian play,' *The Ecstasy of Rita Joe* (1967), which weaves various trial scenes throughout the life story of a young Indian girl caught up in the dangerous world of the city and eventually killed there, Ryga was a playwright who identified fiercely and emotionally with his causes, the more so, perhaps, because as the child of Ukrainian parents in northern Alberta he himself had enjoyed few advantages, his formal schooling interrupted by various labouring jobs among the people whose cause he passionately and publicly espoused throughout his life and whose situations he depicted in his plays and fiction. Theatre, in fact, for Ryga must be 'a substantial ingredient in our daily lives,' an educational force taking 'a vanguard position in expression of national ideals and international humanism,' its role 'to give light, color and nobility to the quality of our lives.'⁴ Playwrights must be allowed to 'attempt to reflect the reality of our own lives, myths and worth.' At present, theatre is instead reflecting what he saw as the most significant Canadian failing: 'Our inability to cope with *any* problem ... faced with the choice of either destroying our Indian people or giving them an opportunity for life, we could do neither.'5 And how can theatre overcome this inertia? By finding a form which will reflect us and our life-condition, by interpreting 'the language, symbolisms and experiences' which are uniquely our own. By creating 'a different theatre, rooted in an inescapable reality and of a dimension which would not be harnessed into a nice Sunday afternoon.'6 By devising, in fact, a new mythology, a modern folk art which will express 'the authentic fears, preoccupations and exaltation of the people.' 'The key to self-reliance is self-understanding ... the issue in national survival is development of a popular, genuine people's culture ... whether it be literature, theatre, music or film.'7 The key statement in *Indian* is directed not only at the Agent within the play: 'Now you know what is like to be me.'8

Art for Ryga must provide a revelation, and the artist 'must care for those of whom he speaks, and of the audiences to whom he addresses his art. There can be no sham or treachery, or we have failed our obligations.'9 In practice this means getting rid of the stereotypes and clichés, putting in their stead a sense of the individual with his or her hurts and rages and sense of frustration within a context which is urgently identifiable for the audience. It means forcing the audience members to respond as individuals, unable to duck out of responsibility, while at the same time refusing to let them wallow in that equally evasive response, the breast-beating *mea culpa* of the educated white liberal prepared to condemn faceless and nameless society and go home satisfied with a good job well done. The test for the artist, in Ryga's terms, then, is to achieve the effect of melodrama – which is based on recognition of good and evil – without the trappings of easy sentiment and the thrilling *frisson* of unbelievable (therefore harmless) danger.

Yet *Indian* courts that very risk of melodrama: the play begins with stereotypes, characters made all the more vivid for the no-man's land in which they are set and for which we, the white settlers, must take some responsibility – a fence post, some telephone wires, a few tufts of scraggy growth in the distance, high fierce white light, the harsh sound of low wind. This is, on the one hand, a deliberately Canadian, almost regional setting; on the other, 'non-country,' universal. We are quickly introduced to three characters – a drunken, shiftless Indian (his burnt-out campsite in the distance), wearing, ironically, the costume familiar to all from western movies: '*Tight-fitting jeans, dirty dark shirt brightened by outlandish western designs over pockets ... cowboy boots which are cracked and aged. A wide-brimmed black western hat*'(153). However, this heroic costume is not traditionally the Indian's; even his identity is borrowed. Farmer Watson, the only character to have a name in this play, brutal and thoughtless though he may be, does have a point, we must concede, in this tale of the employer versus the unemployable: 'I got that story yesterday,' he grunts, when Indian tries to con even more advance pay out of him by pleading hunger (156). *We* don't believe Watson when he threatens to shoot Indian's nephew Alphonse; we cannot believe that Indian does either. His words are only the necessary exaggeration required to stir the lazy, the dishonest, the shiftless into work. Still, we are uncomfortable; these are not the polite images we are accustomed to in civilized Canadian society; this is a mockery of the deprived minority.

It is almost a relief when Watson becomes so ugly that we can deny kinship. For a well-fed, domineering property-owner to abuse the underprivileged and the have-not is against our principles, even if the Indian shows no shame at his trickery and the hangover is his own fault. And when jokes about 'Indian whisky' and old baloney slide sideways to reveal the winter of 1956 with its tough catmeat, we cease to identify with Watson at all, almost longing for Indian, as he '*teeters between two worlds*' (158), to attack. But instead his incipient violence is transferred to the fence posts, pounded '*mechanically with an incredible rhythm of defeat,*' and Watson hastily leaves the stage (159). We the audience are, though alert, once again outside.

But not for long. Agent – another faceless, nameless person – arrives with his fancy cigarettes, privileged government car, permanent job, and access to good whisky, white man's institutions, hospitals, and justice. If we are to identify with anyone it is, reluctantly, with this product of our world and our creation, 'the comfortable civil servant.' He is, after all, only doing his duty, even if, like Watson, he looks upon Indian as a thing of laughter and annoyance, to be controlled through threats of withdrawal and withholding of privileges. But paternalism can only work from a distance. Indian challenges him (and us) with defiance, insult, mockery, immediacy: 'It makes you scare you should know too much about me!' (161). Turning the tables, he threatens Agent with the same institutions: 'I report you for beating Indian an' you lose job' ... 'How you gonna explain that, bossman?' (163). This is not the plain honest-to-God violence Watson might have deserved. Like Agent, we are forced into asking, 'What do you want with me?' (163).

With Indian's reply, 'I want to tell you somethin'' (164), the play takes on a new dimension. What was apparently realistic action becomes indirect narration as we wind back through Indian's pasts – beyond last night's rowdy drunken spree to the tale of his brother and another 'bossman,' cruelly reflected in the ugliness we rejected in Watson. The indictment is swift and certain – what right has one man to force another down a well, into the hell of quicksand, and refuse him help? We revolt against the inhumanity – but can only echo Agent: 'I wasn't there! I couldn't help him! ... I don't want to hear about him!' (167). The point is driven home to Agent (and to us) with the story of the wounded moose: 'Moose not run away from you – you run away from moose!' (168). The implications of two ways of life – those who hunt for pleasure, literal 'blood sports,' and those who depend upon hunting for food – could not be lost on citizens of tourist-seeking Canada. By now it is too late to 'take our problems where they belong' (166) and look the other way. Humiliated, shoved around, insulted, Agent can only respond by clutching once again to his support institutions: 'You belong in jail!' Indian's reply puts us too in our place: 'We been in jail a long time now, sementos ...' (169). The attack begins again, this time entirely on a verbal level, with no further physical violence; none is necessary as we are drawn once more back into the past, into Indian's tent by the quiet side of the lake, to watch his brother die.

With this knowledge forced upon us, it is too late to 'get back to your job and leave me alone' (164). We are implicated: Agent's hospitals are our hospitals, his justice ours, 'the laws of this country' are made by our representatives. But what of Indian's justice? 'One brother kill another brother – why?' (173). By the end of the play Ryga has bound that painful question with yet another: can law and white man's justice apply to those for whom it apparently does not exist? 'I nobody. I not even live in this world ... I never been anybody. *I not just dead ... I never live at all*' (173). The final accusation encompasses both Agent and the audience. If such things can happen, then we are truly *sementos* – soulless, without the encompassing vision of a whole universe, without compassion. Again the implications extend beyond the play to contrast the Indian concept of a natural world that cannot be *owned*, that encompasses animal, vegetable, mineral, and spirit, with the white man's divisive territoriality.

Ryga's *Indian* is a powerful indictment, in the words of the play's first producer Daryl Duke, of 'the peculiar damnation our kind of world has condemned the Indian to.'[10] 'All Indians same – nobody' (173). There is physical violence and murder at the centre of this brief play, but its greatest accusation is of a crime that does not take place within the action at all, but is rather its context. And Ryga refuses to let us deny that context even while, with Agent, we protest that 'Ours is a civilized country' (171). Being 'just a simple joe doing my job' (166) becomes an even more painful cliché than the shiftless Indian with which we began, and namelessness becomes more real than the anonymous characters framing the play. Just how powerful is the effect of the charges can be judged by the work's critical reception. Now almost compulsory reading in any Canadian literature course, on the occasion of its first production in 1962 as part of the CBC *Quest* television series, questions were raised in the Alberta legislature and one Conservative MP demanded that the program be cancelled altogether for showing this 'most corrupt and immoral' drama.[11]

George Ryga wrote *Indian* out of the anger of his own social conscience, as one who has lived and worked beside the people he portrays in his plays. During an interview in 1982 he admitted, 'It's the only play I can look back on over all these years that I would not write any differently. I was working in a form, in a content – with language and the mythological implications – that was very close to me. And in historical terms this was an actuality.'[12] His next play, *The Ecstasy of Rita Joe*, was informed by the same anger and compassion, but here anger breaks through traditional form altogether to encompass music, brilliant lighting effects, dance, and a flowing multi-level stage design which sweeps down to the end of the audience and back upstage to incorporate many times and many settings. Again, the last line of the play, over Rita Joe's dead and abused body, is spoken directly to the audience, and again a simple detail carries the full force of pity and helplessness: 'When Rita Joe first come to the city – she told me ... the cement made her feet hurt.'[13] The play has been adapted to ballet form, commissioned by the Manitoba Indian Brotherhood. When first published, it carried a foreword by Chief Dan George of British Columbia, who played Rita Joe's father in the play and the ballet.

Ryga's emphasis on the creation of a new mythology is significant. In addition to personal indignation can be seen the playwright's attempt to carve out his own position and seek his own roots by having to disentangle the roots, language, and vision of those who were here before him and still linger on. For Ryga's two plays are part of a long tradition of theatre dealing with Indian subjects, the result of the Canadian dramatist's exploration of place, voice, and self in a land we perhaps feel is still not entirely ours. And if those plays are not always about crime, they are certainly obsessed with guilt.

One of the earliest with Indian as hero is *Ponteach, or The Savages of America*, written in 1766 by Major Robert Rogers who was later charged with treason in Montreal for pursuing his beliefs that Chief Ponteach should have his own nation, separate from British authority. The play shows all the weaknesses of an eighteenth-century closet drama written by a military man with a cause: the cast of characters ranges from historical figures to comedy-of-manners parodies, noble savages, and melodramatic sub-plot, heroic defender, and awful pseudo-Shakespearean blank verse. But there is a dignity to *Ponteach* also, borne of the sincerity of Roger's cause, which envelopes the whole. The last line, reminiscent of Webster's *The Duchess of Malfi*, has a noble ring: 'Ponteach I am, and Ponteach I shall be still.' Two hundred years later Robertson Davies wrote a play about Rogers and his literary endeavour, called *Ponteach and the Green Man*; its central scene was a trial.[14]

After Rogers, early American theatre continued with a rash of Indian plays, about forty recorded between 1830 and 1850 alone. The first of many plays to feature Pocahontas appeared as early as 1808; Tecumseh took centre stage later in the century; and by the late 1890s Indians themselves were getting into the act. Pauline Johnson, complete with head-dress and moccasins, toured North America and Europe with recitals of her own poetry; even before Buffalo Bill's famous 'Wild West Show' (including, for one season, Chief Sitting Bull himself), a troupe called 'Macdonald's Trained Indians' had toured the Canadian west. When John Coulter wrote the first of his three Riel plays in 1950, then, the Indian was an established figure of stature on the stage. There are also early records of productions by Indians of plays, usually of a religious nature, written by Jesuit missionaries. One of these multi-cultural events occurred in 1900, when, in an ironical twist, seventy-five Ojibwa Indians performed in *Mana-Bozho*, a translation of Longfellow's *Song of Hiawatha*. But by the mid-twentieth century Indians were establishing their own theatre companies and offering their own views of prairie heroes and traditional creation myths. The 1970s and 1980s continue this fascination with the noble savage: at least three plays are based on Sitting Bull, as many more on Gabriel Dumont, and there are many written expressly for young audiences based on Indian and Eskimo myths. With the advent of Indian playwrights such as Maria Campbell and Tomson Highway in recent years, the subject has taken yet another turn towards self-evaluation and reassessment.

Many of these plays, whether produced by Indians or whites, sensitively explore the contemporary struggles of the younger generation fighting the contrary pulls of two cultures, as does Gwen Ringwood's short play *Lament for Harmonica* (1959), which actually includes an on-stage murder. (Ringwood was Ryga's teacher when he won his first scholarship to attend the playwriting course at the Banff School of Fine Arts.) Thus another cultural struggle can also be observed in the Canadian stage history of the Indian, again intimately related to what Ryga has called our need for a mythology and our attempt to find indigenous heroes belonging to our own space. (As James Reaney, author of *Wacousta*, put it, 'You hear the heartbeat and try to give it head, guts, and limbs.')[15] In attending to that heartbeat, the Canadian dramatic treatment of the Indian has come to differ from the American, perhaps representing differing attempts to come to terms with history – or, as Ryga would have it, remaking that history into a more manageable mythology.

One brief comparison must suffice: *Walsh* by Sharon Pollock deals with precisely the same time span and individuals as *Indians* by American playwright Arthur Kopit.[16] Kopit uses as his basic structure the wild west show and within it studies Chief Sitting Bull as victim of Buffalo Bill, the metamorphosis of genuine frontier into Wild West under the Big Top, and then the recreation of the Indian himself in the white man's image. Kopit's Indian is a scapegoat in a battle of which he was unaware; the playwright deals with us and our guilt only, not with the Indian and his place. Interviewed after the first production (which was further transplanted to London and baffled the audience), Kopit stated, 'I'm not concerned in the play with the terrible plight of the Indian now – they were finished from the moment the first white man arrived. What I want is to show a series of confrontations between the two alien systems.'[17]

Pollock on the other hand struggles with the plight of the Indian as individual, and through coming to terms with that, attempts to identify the plight of every Canadian seeking roots in a blood-stained soil. She writes from the Canadian side of the border also – her scenes with Sitting Bull take place between the acts, as it were, of the historical events Kopit selects, when Sitting Bull fled to Canada with his people after Custer's death and sat out a long, weary, weakening exile. Where the American political solution was to kill, the Canadian was to starve to death. The process takes longer, allows room for further discussion, above all is quieter. But because the guilt is less obvious, the recognition is all the more pervasive and disturbing. Walsh is the captain in charge of the fort where Sitting Bull seeks help. He is a man of quiet honour; like Buffalo Bill Cody, he becomes a friend and like Cody he was trusted by Sitting Bull. But unlike the Cody of Kopit's play, Walsh is not directly, actively responsible for the Indians' plight. In a prologue and at the end of the play he is shown a broken man, broken not by Cody's personal greed and selfish yet well-meaning goal to create his beloved nation while doing what it wanted, but by an impersonal and equally well-meaning desire to be a good soldier to queen and country while respecting and honoring his Indian friends. Pollock's ending, silent, intense without the brassy assurance of Kopit's vaudeville techniques, reflects a coming to terms with 'the Indian question' in our past. The plays represent two points of view, both incomplete, both edged with the knowledge of frustration and incompleteness. Life and history are not as simple as the cowboys and Indians, the good guys and bad guys. Guilt cannot be scrubbed away by admission alone; acknowledgment must be made of the paradox of two different world views, perhaps of two different – but opposing – justices, and the acknowledgment that it must never happen again. *Walsh* was revived on the occasion of the 1988 Calgary Olympics; a review of first night rests uneasily next to a court judgment rejecting an Indian group's claim that a spirit mask is too privately religious in nature to be on public exhibition and a report concerning the Lubicon land claim.[18] Pollock, whose program notes for this revival consisted entirely of historical and contemporary quotations drawing parallels with the conflict in her play, would appreciate the irony.

Ryga moved on to explore other social issues, other heroes of place, the making of mythology itself, and the celebration of 'the marvellous realization that no matter where we are, we can be better.' But he never let go of the conviction that 'Our present definition of history is faulty. We're playing with lies.'[19] 'Until we recognize our past, we cannot change our future,' agrees Sharon Pollock.[20] Like him, she sees the historical situation as a metaphor for the present and began her playwriting career (after a brief span as an actress) by insisting we reexamine our history: 'to know where we are going, we must know where we have been and what we have come from.'[21] Like Ryga also, Pollock believes that 'theatre should hit people emotionally.'[22] And she also winds us in through the age-old process of story-telling.

After a series of plays, including *Walsh*, indicting us for social crimes and atrocities which she claims Canadian historians have expurgated from our histories, Pollock too turned to an examination of other processes of mythmaking and began to ask questions about other victims of patriarchy. '*Of course* it says something about women today,' Pollock protested after innumerable male reviewers denied or downplayed the feminist message embodied in *Blood Relations*.[23] In many ways the play epitomizes the strengths and originality of theatre about women imprisoned in a man-ordered universe; but at the same time as does Ryga's *Indian*, it speaks beyond this framework to explore even more far-reaching concerns of time and spirit. 'All of us are capable of murder given the right situation,' Pollock continues in the same interview. But *did* Lizzie Borden ... or didn't she? The question remains ambiguous to the very end of the play – it is the Actress who raises the axe; it is the Actress who triumphantly accuses Lizzie. Meanwhile Miss Lizzie stands apart, always watching, content to 'paint the background' (572) but never admitting guilt. She was, after all, acquitted.

Pollock deliberately plays with this ambiguity throughout the action, making it the fulcrum on which both action and message turn. In fact, there are games within games performed in time within time, observed by the audience who watches Miss Lizzie observe the actions she has set in motion: psycho-dramatic narrative, but for whose benefit? Lizzie retains her secret to the end; the Actress feels her way fumblingly through Lizzie's story only to be reminded at the end that this is her interpretation only. This is the ritual of theatre itself – watching games being enacted for our single delectation. (An early production of the play, at the Tarragon Theatre in Toronto, emphasized the role of audience as participating spectator by having the Actress, as she looks at the hatchet, turning to stare at the audience with Lizzie's last words, 'I didn't. You did' [635]. This stage direction is omitted from the second edition of the play.) Pollock's social message is clear: the Lizzie Bordens of this world, hemmed in and caged by Victorian institutions which deny them the right to be personalities, to work, play, and live as individuals, are maimed as surely as Lizzie's birds were, blinded if not decapitated, deprived of dreams and fulfilment. 'You got no rights,' her stepmother reminds her (601), and Lizzie in despair cries out after Dr Patrick (himself, as an Irish Catholic, an outsider in Fall River),

'Do you suppose there's a formula, a magic formula for being "a woman"? I was born ... defective.' She corrects herself, 'Not defective. Just ... born' (592–3). She accuses her family of the game others want her to play: 'I'm supposed to be a mirror. I'm supposed to reflect what you want to see' (597). 'It's not ... *fair* that I have to' (602).

But social message alone could lock the play back into 1902, reflecting the 'dream thesis' (as Pollock revealingly calls the re-enactment of 1892) when the Bordens were killed. Today's audience could easily escape, as Pollock accuses the male reviewers of doing, by smugly echoing Ryga's Agent: 'It has nothing to do with me ... I wasn't there.' And so she winds us further in, first through the game with Miss Lizzie's Actress/Lover, 'painting the background.' Next, through the Actress' game, calling up four imaginary people who in turn evoke a fifth. What is real? What is unreal? Even the relationship between Miss Lizzie and the Actress is ambiguous: during the first production in Edmonton in 1980, Miss Lizzie suggests the game of pretend in order to keep the Actress' interest in her, which she loses once the game is played through and the question is answered. The second production at the National Arts Centre in Ottawa introduced a different interpretation which Pollock found more interesting, with Miss Lizzie angrily suggesting the game because she is fed up of being questioned. Like Ryga's Indian she challenges the Actress (and the audience): 'Now you know what is like to be me.'

The Actress/Miss Lizzie relationship, itself a duality, is duplicated by the relationship between Lizzie and her sister Emma, the third 'real' character on stage. 'You remind me of my sister,' Lizzie comments to her lover in the opening scene (570); by the final scene, we see that Lizzie has treated the Actress as her puppet in the same way she accuses Emma of behaving towards her: 'My head your hand, yes, your hand working my mouth, me saying all the things you felt like saying, me doing all the things you felt like doing, me spewing forth, me hitting out ...' (634–5). Emma too is implicated in the murders; she too 'did' it. The net of responsibility is cast further still, more dangerously close to us, in the words of the Defence (called forth by Lizzie and the Actress): 'If this gentlewoman is capable of such an act ... look to your daughters ... your wife' (593). If we are convinced by the drama played out before us, then we too are capable of such an act. (Interestingly, Ann Jones in her fine study *Women Who Kill* convincingly argues that the social hypocrisy which led Lizzie to murder was in turn responsible for the further moral hypocrisy that led to her acquittal.)[24]

But still we the audience could deny responsibility. Taking another person's life cannot be equated with Mr Borden's drowning puppies that are 'different' on the farm; within civilized society, people don't calmly do such things. But Lizzie's calm reasonableness is the underlying force of argument in the play. Only really herself in the present time of 1902 with her Lover, to whom she can tell 'the most personal things, ... thoughts, ... dreams, ... but never that' (569), the 1892 Lizzie in the recreated scenes with Dr Patrick almost gives herself away, flexing her brains and tongue, indulging in her wit and fancy, pretending it is possible to have some freedom to soar. Full trust, full flight prove to be illusory, but just as the Actress teases Lizzie into painting the background with more details of the foreground, so Dr Patrick encourages her to believe in herself as a valued person. Only then is she led to push him to the edge of confession: 'Which would you save?' she challenges him in another 'game,' daring him to choose between two patients where only one could be saved, one 'a bad person,' the other 'trying to be good' (624). 'Not all life is precious, is it?' (626). Dr Patrick can only paint in the background, but Miss Lizzie, like the Actress, is given enough details to take the next step in the drama. *Her* life is precious. Unlike her mother, the doctor assures her, she cannot die. 'I want to die, but something inside won't let me.' And so she must will to live. 'I can do anything' (614). In order to save her own life (answering her own challenge to Dr Patrick), she must kill.

Miss Lizzie's reasoning threads through the play, tying the scenes together in both time periods, pulling the past into our present time as the games delicately balance on either side of the equation 'We have to do something'/'There's nothing we can do' (612). The intensity of Lizzie's thought processes is reflected in the wide-eyed staring that pervades the play from the opening scene when the Actress comments, 'You know ... you do this thing ... you stare at me ... You look directly at my eyes. I think ... you think ... that if I'm lying ... it will come up, like lemons on a slot machine' (567). The Actress then observes Miss Lizzie as she leads her into the scene and the part she must play; Miss Lizzie in turn observes the action that unfolds before her. She stares at each character in turn; she dreams that the mask she wears on the carousel (society's larger cage?) hides her own eyelessness; she comments, 'when a person dies, retained on her eye is the image of the last thing she saw. Isn't that interesting?' (627). Perhaps by the second edition of the play Pollock had realized that it was no longer necessary at the curtain for the Actress to look at the audience. The process of observing, of 'seeing' and therefore comprehending, of equating 'eye-lessness' with 'I-lessness' (no first person at all), had already taken place.

In addition to its visual aspects, *Blood Relations* is also a complex work on a literary level, beginning, of course, with the title. For the act of relating is to narrate; however, in order to prevent history (the once-told story) from restricting and falsifying in turn, Miss Lizzie refuses to commit herself to the telling. Instead, she instructs the Actress in the art of re-creation, leaving open the multiple possibilities of more than one truth. But relating in the passive sense is also to be committed to family relationships – and others. Miss Lizzie and the Actress are bound together by the closest of female friendships as lesbian lovers; they discuss the almost symbiotic nature of their relationship in the first scene, when Lizzie admits that 'sometimes you think like me ... do you feel that?' and the Actress replies, 'Sometimes' (571). Sister Emma is not only Lizzie's puppeteer, as Lizzie accuses, but in turn her puppet, for the question of Lizzie's guilt binds them irrevocably together as much as the property they inherited. In the play within the play, all relationships are unfulfilled or uncommitted: Andrew Borden cannot choose between his daughter's demands and his wife's wishes, and fails both; his brother-in-law Harry is alternately triumphantly in power or sneaking out the back to chop wood (the axe also weaves its way through the play); Emma fails Lizzie by running away; Dr Patrick refuses to commit himself either to Lizzie or her philosophical challenge; servant Bridget, whom the real Lizzie re-enacts as the Actress realizes her lover's role, is in more ways than one a creature of Lizzie's imagination. It is not until ten years after the murders, with the retrial before us echoing the earlier Defence, that Lizzie can relive – and thus complete – her own past. With the Actress' weekend visits from Boston, Lizzie also finally exorcises the need she so often played out in her game with Dr Patrick, of 'running away to Boston' (588). She may not, after all, have retrieved the farm, that childhood dream, already signed over to her mother's brother, but she is in control of her space at last.

Blood Relations is a disturbing play; like *Indian*, it is meant to be. Through it, the audience is forced to comprehend what it must be to want to kill: spectators through that comprehension become 'blood relations'; the play yet another 'blood sport.' The passage the Actress is rehearsing at the opening of the play is from act 3 of *The Winter's Tale* in which Hermione, unjustly accused wife, explains her dilemma to her inflexible, judgmental husband. Like Lizzie Borden, Hermione is damned if she protests her innocence (the Actress would 'be disappointed'), and damned if she confesses falsely (the Actress would 'be horrified' [572]). Shakespeare's lines continue, 'You, my lord, best know – / who least will seem to do so' and conclude,

> which is more
> Than history can pattern, though devised
> And played to take spectators. (3.2.32–7)

In the children's song which serves as yet another framework to the play (and in many other light-hearted refrains such as that in the Broadway musical *New Faces of 1952*: 'You can't chop your poppa up in Massachusetts / Then get dressed up and go for a walk'),[25] history has indeed patterned. In the play Pollock has created, Lizzie Borden's story is once again devised 'to take spectators.' The question has been translated: 'did she or didn't she?' has become 'would you or wouldn't you?' And, like George Ryga, Sharon Pollock asks which is the greatest crime: imprisonment of the soul, or life at any price?

'Part of the reason a person writes is to try to see some design, to create order out of chaos, to try to understand things about myself as well as the world around me,' explains Pollock in words that George Ryga might easily have echoed.[26] For both playwrights, theatre is more than a place of entertainment – although it must first of all be that; it is also a place for understanding, and through comprehension, an instrument for change. But 'obviously real change only occurs when the broad base is altered. The collection of individuals in a society is that base. They must change if anything meaningful is to happen.'[27] Only then can justice be the same for all.

Notes

Ann Saddlemyer received her PHD from the University of London in 1961 and has acted in numerous plays. Her many publications on Irish and Canadian drama include *The Collected Letters of John Millington Synge*, which received the British Academy's Rose Mary Crawshay Award for criticism, and *Early Stages: Essays on the Theatre in Ontario, 1800–1914*. She is preparing the authorized biography of Georgie (Mrs William Butler) Yeats and, for

Oxford University Press, the World's Classics edition of the works of J.M. Synge.

1 *The Penguin Book of Modern Canadian Drama* ed Richard Plant (Toronto: Penguin 1984) includes John Coulter's *Riel* (1950), George Ryga's *Indian* (1962), John Herbert's *Fortune and Men's Eyes* (1963), William Fruet's *Wedding in White* (1970), David E. Freeman's *Creeps* (1971), David French's *Of the Fields, Lately* (1973), James Reaney's *Handcuffs* (1975), Sharon Pollock's *Blood Relations* (1980), Margaret Hollingsworth's *Ever Loving* (1980), Allan Stratton's *Rexy!* (1981), Gwen Pharis Ringwood's *Garage Sale* (1981), George F. Walker's *The Art of War* (1982). All quotations from *Indian* and *Blood Relations* are from this edition.
2 Samuel Taylor Coleridge *Biographia Literaria* ch 14
3 Sharon Pollock *Blood Relations*, *The Penguin Book of Modern Canadian Drama* 626
4 George Ryga 'Theatre in Canada: A Viewpoint on its Development and Future' *Canadian Theatre Review* 1 (Winter 1974) 28–32
5 George Ryga 'The Need for a Mythology' *Canadian Theatre Review* 16 (Fall 1977) 4
6 George Ryga 'Contemporary Theatre and Its Language' *Canadian Theatre Review* 14 (Spring 1977) 8
7 Ryga 'The Need for a Mythology' 5
8 George Ryga *Indian* 167
9 Ryga 'Contemporary Theatre' 9
10 *Maclean's* 1 December 1962, 30
11 Christopher Innes *Politics and the Playwright: George Ryga* (Toronto: Simon and Pierre 1985) 28
12 'Political Mythologies. An Interview with George Ryga' by David Watson ed Christopher Innes *Canadian Drama* 8, 2 (1982) 160–7
13 George Ryga *The Ecstasy of Rita Joe and Other Plays* ed Brian Parker (Toronto: new press 1971) 130
14 Davies' play, commissioned by the Graduate Centre for Study of Drama and produced at MacMillan Theatre, University of Toronto, in collaboration with the Faculty of Music 26 October to 5 November 1977, has never been published; Rogers' *Ponteach, or The Savages of America* (1766) was reprinted in *Representative Plays by American Dramatists* vol 1 ed Montrose Moses (New York: Dutton 1918).
15 'James Reaney' in *Stage Voices* ed Geraldine Anthony (Toronto and Garden City: Doubleday 1978) 174

16 Sharon Pollock *Walsh* (Vancouver: Talonbooks 1974) 2nd printing; Arthur Kopit *Indians* (New York: Hill and Wang 1969)

17 Arthur Kopit quoted in an interview with Irving Wardle *Times Saturday Review* 29 June 1968

18 Stephen Godfrey 'Debate Soars Above Earthbound Historical Drama' *The Globe and Mail* 29 January 1988, D11

19 Ryga quoted by David Watson *Canadian Drama* 168

20 Sharon Pollock quoted by Bob Allen 'Play Reveals Shame of Komagata Maru' *Vancouver Province* 16 January 1976, 31

21 Sharon Pollock, program note to first production of *The Komagata Maru Incident*

22 Sharon Pollock, note to the *The Komagata Maru Incident* (Toronto: Playwright's Co–op 1978) [v]

23 'Sharon Pollock' in Robert Wallace and Cynthia Zimmerman *The Work: Conversations with English-Canadian Playwrights* (Toronto: Coach House Press 1982) 123

24 Ann Jones *Women Who Kill* (New York: Holt, Rinehart and Winston 1980) 209–37

25 'Lizzie Borden' words and music by Michael Brown

26 Sharon Pollock quoted by Margo Dunn in *Makara* (August 1977) 4

27 Sharon Pollock quoted by Bob Allen 'Play Reveals Shame of Komagata Maru' 35

JOSEF ŠKVORECKÝ

Detective Stories: Some Notes on *Fingerprints*

When it comes to detective stories, I am a true tory of the darkest hue. I hope that this attitude is understandable, and that it can be tolerated by my more liberal fellow-lovers of imaginative murder. Who was it who said that anybody who was not a revolutionary at twenty, and a conservative at sixty must be a fool?

As a young man I was a kind of revolutionary – as far as detective fiction is concerned. I wrote my first detective novel, *Murder for Luck (Vražda pro štěstí)* in 1960, at a time when such literary artefacts were still viewed with suspicion by the literary establishment in Czechoslovakia. After all, it was just a few years back when they had not been viewed with suspicion only. They were quite seriously characterized as decadent, cosmopolitan, bourgeois, unhealthy, and unsuitable for the socialist reader. The east German practitioner and theoretician of the genre, Hans Pfeiffer, in his book *The Mummy in the Glass Coffin (Die Mumie im Glassarg* 1960), predicted with selfless enthusiasm the almost immediate demise of the literature that provided him with bread and butter because, due to socialist human relationships, soon nobody would have either reason or inclination to deprive a comrade of his life. After all, detective stories dealt primarily in death, and the Stalinist variety of Marxism-Leninism dealt in life. That, I suppose, is Marxist dialectics: all truly deadly regimes (including Hitler's) are great extollers of life and peace, and to write about corpses is taboo. True Leninists *make* corpses, but they don't *write* about them. If a writer does write about them, they must be *heroic* corpses, not the bodies of wealthy old gentlemen found stabbed to death in libraries who deserved what they got anyway. Their fate cannot interest the socialist reader because they are invariably of the exploiting class.

My debut as crime writer was, moreover, complicated not only by the general critical aversion towards fiction about murders but also by my personal situation. I had been banned from publishing in 1959, and by 1960 the ban was not yet lifted. I could not very well offer a manuscript that dealt in death, a work belonging to what was referred to as a 'debased genre.' The term was a borrowing from Viktor Shklovsky, not a favourite with the Bolshevik regime either, but then that regime was always ready to borrow even from its adversaries, as long as such borrowing suited its purpose. The most widely used party slogan in Czechoslovakia, attacking political émigrés, which goes 'If you leave me, [ie, if you leave your native land] I shall not perish. If you leave me, it's you who will perish,' is a verse from a poem by Viktor Dyk,[1] a very great poet but also a leading ultra-conservative anti-Communist of the twenties.

In 1960 I fell in love with detective fiction. Until then I had more or less ignored the genre and did not think highly of it. I was a dead-serious young novelist, an admirer of Faulkner, Hemingway, Dickens, and Evelyn Waugh. I had studied at the university right after the war when Western books were scarce and the profs, had someone told them that pop literature was a legitimate field of academic study, would think such person either a madman or a provocateur. I had only a fragmentary knowledge of the masters of the genre; I knew nothing about Faulkner's excursions into Edgar Allan Poe's provenance, and I had never read Dickens' *The Mystery of Edwin Drood* (1870). That novel was presented to us by our English professor as a marginal and, moreover, unfinished work.

But in 1960 I fell very seriously ill with infectious hepatitis contracted during minor surgery, and lived for almost four months on the threshold of death, in the contagious diseases ward of the Motol hospital in Prague. There was a hospital library but it contained only the works of Marx, Engels, and Lenin – no longer Stalin at that time – some Czech and Russian classics, and a wealth of socialist-realist 'builders' novels which, as popular lore had it, when you perused them, put you to sleep because you were physically tired from all the hard work in them. When a man is faced with a very real possibility of departing the valley of tears, Dostoevski is rarely of great interest to him. Friends, naturally, could send me books to the hospital, but since I was in a ward full of dangerous germs, these books were not allowed to leave the premises. Therefore, my friends sent me books they felt they could live without: old, badly mangled paperback editions of detective novels. In the four months I spent at Motol I must have read close to two hundred of them, and acquired a respect for the trash. The bloody tales took my mind off unpleasant thoughts; they literally helped me to survive those one hundred and twenty days in a room with fifteen other sufferers, with neither television nor radio, and with a library that could not offer much else than a course in Marxism.

I returned home and had to keep to my bed for another four months or so. During that time of return to life I wrote my first detective novel. A dear old friend of mine, Jan Zábrana, an excellent translator and an unpublished poet – unpublished not because he was bad but because his parents, members of the banned Socialist Party, were in the camps – lent me his name, and the novel, which we plotted together, with great enthusiasm, turned into an enormous success. Between 1960 and 1967 I wrote two more enormously long detective novels, featuring the same detective and his female Watson who, of course, was the real solver of the inept sleuth's problems for which he invariably received all the praise. Even though by the mid-sixties I could again publish under my own name – and I did: the Lieutenant Borůvka stories – we decided to keep the series consistent. The novels, therefore, continued to appear under my friend's name. Altogether we planned five novels. They were to cover – in their twisted way – the most critical periods of Czechoslovakia's modern history. The first was set in the depression years; the second, *Guaranteed Murder* (*Vražda se zárukou* 1964), after Munich and before the Nazi occupation in 1939; the third, *Murder by Proxy* (*Vražda v zastoupení* 1967), in the times of Nazi rule. The fourth was to capture the post-war years before the Communist coup of 1948, the fifth and final one, Stalinism after the coup. Then, we vaguely thought, we would divulge the secret. But the steel chariots of the Soviets came first.

I left the country in 1969, my friend decided to stay. We never finished the historical saga. Then, in 1983, since an establishment publishing house needed a potential bestseller, it republished the wartime story, *Murder by Proxy*. Our secret was, apparently, well-guarded, and the censors had not solved the acrostic which we had inserted right into the text of the novel: if you read the first letters of the first sentences in consecutive chapters you get the Latin message, 'Škvorecký et Zábrana fecerunt ioculum' – Škvorecký and Zábrana made this joke. Although, naturally, all my books were, until recently, banned in Czechoslovakia – copies were removed from public libraries and my name was deleted from studies of contemporary Czech literature

– I was probably the only Czech political exile whose work was actually published in Prague. A copy of the novel is in the Thomas Fisher Rare Book Library at the University of Toronto, where anyone can verify that I am telling the truth, even if he or she does not read Czech.

In 1988, *Murder by Proxy* was even made into a film for Czechoslovak television. The reviews were mostly negative, stressing that whereas the novel was full of life and peopled by amusing characters, the film concentrated on the political (anti-Nazi) aspect of the book and was therefore only a shadow of the entertaining literary opus. I speak freely about all this because my friend Jan Zábrana, at the age of merely fifty-three, most regrettably died a number of years ago, and is therefore beyond the reach of the cops.

I apologize for this lengthy introduction to what is supposed to be a discussion of *Fingerprints*,[2] a contemporary Canadian anthology of crime stories. I merely wanted to justify my extremely conservative approach to the genre. As you see, my way to the detective story was not an easy one, which may explain why I am such a reactionary.

There is another reason for my toryism: the title of the anthology. *Fingerprints* is a reference to the method of identification of criminals which, until the advent of the most recent and advanced methods, had been the principal way to identify culprits. (By the way: the method had been first suggested by my compatriot, the great nineteenth-century physiologist Jan Evangelista Purkyně, about half a century before – who was it? A British army doctor? – persuaded Scotland Yard to replace Bertillon's complicated system with dactyloscopy.) A title like *Fingerprints* creates an expectation that one is going to be treated to stories about crimes, the perpetrators of which are unknown, and which are solved by strictly logical means by detectives, either professional, police or private, or amateur. That, I believe, is the definition of the detective story in the only proper,[3] and therefore classical sense. There may be one acceptable exception, though I am not sure – the so called 'inverted' story invented by R. Austin Freeman. There the perpetrator is revealed at the very beginning, and the reader's task is to notice the little errors the criminal committed in the course of the execution of his crime: the errors that, later on, will be uncovered by the detective and eventually hang the murderer. When some years ago American TV released the *Colombo* serial, very, very few watchers knew that the trick was a very, very old one, developed by one of the very early writers in the genre. I know, because I repeatedly asked my students. Without any exception they had never heard about R. Austin Freeman, or about a book entitled *The Singing Bone* (1912).

For that matter – and this may come as a surprise to the reader, as it did to me – very few of them had heard about an essay called 'The Philosophy of Composition' (1846).[4] Many of those students were Americans, boys and girls I taught at Amherst College, Massachusetts, all of them with many years of high-school English, and even college English behind them. It was a mind-boggling experience, for I like to imagine that the detective story, at the dawn of its history, was born out of poetry. Not in the sense in which G.K. Chesterton saw the genre – as expressing the poetry of the modern big city[5] – but in the sense that the man who founded the genre was a major American poet who defined some of the basic things about composing a detective story in an essay concerned with composing poetry. I consciously say 'a major American poet' even though I know that Edgar Allan Poe's status as a poet is rather low among American literary scholars. I say it because a man whom Baudelaire loved and adored could not have been a minor poet. And if excellent books always survive bad translations, why could excellent books not survive badly written originals?

Poe pointed out basic things about the construction of a detective story in an essay that purports to describe how his poem 'The Raven' was composed. No matter that the essay was written five years after the publication of 'The Murders in Rue Morgue.' The idea must have lingered in Poe's mind long before the writing of 'The Raven' in 1845 and of 'The Philosophy of Composition' which begins with the famous line: 'Charles Dickens, in a note now lying before me, alluding to an examination I once made of the mechanism of "Barnaby Rudge," says – "By the way, are you aware that Godwin wrote his 'Caleb Williams' backwards?"'[6]

For that is the first rule for writing detective stories. It is probably valid for writing any kind of short story; at least in the sense that the ending of the story, which should include its climax, is the most important part of the thing. But it is true that good and even great short stories have been written intuitively, without working out an outline first, perhaps because this rule is an integral part of a good fiction writer's subconscious equipment. Good detective stories, however, can hardly be written without proper premeditation. It is, after all, a rational, or as Poe would have it, a ratiocinative genre, and the climax, the dénouement, the final effect must be sought, established, and constructed before the fact. For a writer of detective stories this rule – write backwards – is absolute.

The second rule is also contained in 'The Philosophy of Composition.' Poe explains how he commenced the construction of 'The Raven' by composing the last stanza first, and then continued to work backwards. Then he says: 'Had I been able, in the subsequent composition, to construct more vigorous stanzas, I should, without scruple, have purposely enfeebled them, so as not to interfere with the climacteric effect.'[7]

While the first rule is hardly ever neglected – although occasionally it was, as in the case of Raymond Chandler, with results disastrous to the logic, though not necessarily to the aesthetics, of the tale – the second rule, unfortunately, is violated all the time. You will recall, for instance, Agatha Christie's *4.50 from Paddington* (in the US, *What Mrs. McGillicuddy Saw* [1957]), with its truly marvellous opening effect. Mrs McGillicuddy, sitting in a train which is just leaving the station, witnesses a murder that is being committed in a compartment of a train moving on parallel rails. She calls the conductor, but before the man arrives one train slows down, and the locale of the crime inevitably drifts away, and Mrs McGillicuddy is unable to persuade the male-chauvinist conductor that the evil deed was not just a figment of a bluestocking's frightened imagination. A splendid opening – but it should have been reserved for the climax; an opening effect that should have been the final effect. Even such a master schemer as Christie was unable to beat the introductory effect later on in the novel which deteriorates into a rather commonplace and boring series of interrogations, resulting in a bitter disappointment for the reader.

A whole sub-genre is really based on what in effect is a violation of Poe's second rule: the so-called 'locked-room mystery.' The master founder himself did not avoid a sin against his own law. If there is an adult reader who is impressed and thrilled by the revelation that the murders in Rue Morgue were committed by an orang-outan, I have yet to find him. The best known practitioner of the sub-genre, John Dickson Carr, rationally explains this phenomenon which I like to call, with Karel Čapek 'the terrible disappointment of the ending.'[8] In Dr Fell's lecture on the 'locked-room mystery' in *The Three Coffins*, the corpulent detective says: 'You see, the effect [of the opening] is so magical that we somehow expect the cause [and therefore the conclusion] to be magical also. When we see that it isn't wizardry, we call it tomfoolery.'[9] And indeed, the image of the body in a room locked on the inside, from which the murderer could not have escaped, and yet he did, is a 'stanza so vigorous' that no imagination can invent a solution that would be yet more vigorous. To my knowledge, only one writer ever pulled off the trick successfully: Melville Davisson Post in 'The Doomdorf Mystery' (1914). But, then, the murderer in the story is the Good Lord Himself.

The final effect, the strongest point reserved for the end, would seem by now to be the ABC of short-story composition. Modern literary theoreticians, more sophisticated than poor Poe, have come to identical conclusions, and backed them by more scholarly arguments. 'By its very essence,' writes one of the fathers of Soviet formalism B.M. Ejxenbaum in *O. Henry and the Theory of the Short Story* (*O. Genry i teoria novelly* 1925), 'the short story, just as the anecdote, amasses its whole weight towards the ending.' And with typical Soviet peace imagery he adds: 'Like a bomb dropped from an airplane, it must speed downwards so as to strike with its warhead full-force on the target.'[10] Which, by the way, is identical with Chandler's ideal of a one-line solution that sheds light on the mystery in one strong flash.

And yet ... If I wonder how it is that American students of literature have never read a text so classical, and so valid even today, as 'The Philosophy of Composition,' what should I think of one of the most successful practitioners of the crime story, the late Stanley Ellin who, apparently, was also innocent of such knowledge. Doing, unawares, to his celebrated story 'The Specialty of the House' (1948) something similar to what Poe did to 'The Raven,' he rediscovered Poe's discovery or, as the Czech saying goes, he discovered America:

> It took me ten long years of apprenticeship at my trade to learn that the closing lines of a mystery story are more important than the opening lines, which is why I was a haggard thirty when writing became my vocation, and not a fresh and bouncing twenty ... So it was that I finally won my first bout with the editors by treating a story idea from back to front. The idea concerned a restaurant where the customers themselves, when properly fattened like Hansel and Gretel by the solicitous restaurateur, were literally fed to each other, although without knowing it. The story treatment, I decided, would not make any great effort to conceal this shocking fact from the reader; the climax would simply be a sentence or two which would assure him that his macabre supposition about what was going on in that restaurant was gruesomely correct.
>
> I got off to a dozen futile starts on the story, and then at last it dawned

on me that I was in trouble because I didn't know exactly what my final climactic and revelatory lines were going to be. The solution, I decided, was to write those final lines before anything else, and it took a couple of weeks before I even understood exactly what they had to set forth. It was the picture of a customer, a key character in the story, being happily led into that fatal kitchen by my restaurateur, and, without specifically stating it, I had to make it plain that this customer was a lamb for the slaughter. The lines I decided on read:

> The restaurateur held his kitchen door invitingly wide with one hand, while the other rested, almost tenderly, on his customer's meaty shoulder.

> It was that word 'meaty' which took the longest time to hit on and which, I knew intuitively, locked up the story. From that instant, the restaurant owner, his doomed patron, the restaurant itself, and the whole structure of the story started to take on form by themselves; an outline of episodes leading to the finale seemed to spring magically to mind. It took much revision to get everything trimmed down to its essence, but now that I knew exactly what I wanted to say, the revisions, like the story's episodes, almost imposed themselves on the material.[11]

Isn't this a sorry example of the short historical memory of so many North Americans? Certainly, this type of forgetfulness cannot have the tragic results that potentially threaten the future of Western democracy in the case of other historical short memories, but in an American writer it is to be regretted.

But then, poor Poe has traditionally been slighted by his compatriots and appreciated by Europeans. 'The Purloined Letter?' A clever little idea, I can hear many an American literary scholar comment sneeringly.[12] Just an intellectual whimsy, like all Poe's detective stories. Real police would never be fooled by the Minister's trick. But would they not? The late Milan Šimečka, a Slovak dissident historian, tells in an article printed in a Czech journal published in the West how, while expecting a police search, he remembered 'The Purloined Letter' and decided that he had nothing to lose by following the story's advice. He put the manuscript of his highly treasonable book about the post-Soviet invasion developments in Czechoslovakia on his writing desk. The police came, searched the premises and left Šimečka's apartment in shambles – but the manuscript remained, untouched and unnoticed, on the author's desk. Later on it was smuggled out of the country and came out in the West.

I have always believed that Poe was a genius.

With Poe, the rational composition of a poem led to the emergence of a brand-new literary genre. The detective story was born out of poetry. Poe's mental process while composing 'The Raven,' as professors of literature suggest, may not have followed all the steps described in 'The Philosophy of Composition' but I do not see any reason to doubt that the essay tells the essential truth.

The structure of the short story, identical with the structure of the anecdote, of the joke where the last triumphant line is always reserved for the underdog, the Jew, the Irishman, the Newfie, led, in the nineteenth century, to the coming of age of a special type of story where the inherent amassing of weight towards the ending was blown out of proportion, and eventually became almost an end in itself: the story with the surprise ending, the tale with a twist in the tail. Ambrose Bierce was the master in the macabre sub-category which contains even such indisputable giants of serious literature as Faulkner – just remember 'A Rose for Emily.' O. Henry was the champion of the humorous and sentimental sub-category. As years went by, detective-fiction writers revolted against the tradition originated by Poe, and continued by Conan Doyle and the British crossword-puzzle school of the thirties. They felt classical detection had become increasingly mechanical, actionless, indeed lifeless, detached from the realities of the world, and they turned away from it in two basic directions. The first, the celebrated hard-boiled school, underplayed the strictly logical process of detection and stressed action and style. S.S. Van Dine's credo held that 'a "literary" style, replete with descriptive passages, metaphors, and word pictures ... [diverts] the reader's mind from the mere record of facts (which is what he is concerned with) [in a detective story], ... focusing it on irrelevant aesthetic appeals.'[13] Van Dine, a once successful American writer in the classical traditional, appeared to Raymond Chandler as the creator of 'the most asinine character in detective fiction' Philo Vance.[14] His belief that a detective story should contain 'no literary dallying with side-issues, no subtly worked-out character analyses, no "atmospheric" preoccupations,'[15] stands in sharp contrast to Chandler's conviction that what the readers are really after in a detective novel is not the solution of the puzzle but emotions, evoked chiefly by style, ie, by the aesthetic element of the story.

The second development led to a contamination of the detective story proper with the T.I.T. story, the Twist in the Tail tale, and caused a terminological confusion which eventually created a vagueness. We now promiscuously use terms like 'detective story,' 'thriller,' 'mystery story,' and 'crime story.' And so we have an anthology entitled *Fingerprints*.

So, let me first of all repeat my definitions.

The detective story is a story about the solving of a crime, usually a murder, the perpetrator of which is unknown to the detective and to the reader. The solution is effected by strictly logical means. It poses every crime's three basic questions – Who? How? Why? – and answers them by the results of the detective's investigations.

The crime story is a tale about the committing of a crime. It leaves the reader in no doubt as to who did it, how he did it, and why.

The mystery story is simply a general category, of which the detective story is merely one form. As John G. Cawelti defines it, it is a story about 'the investigation and discovery of hidden secrets':[16] the treasure on the island, the identity of Oedipus' mother, the whereabouts of a fugitive child.

Bearing these definitions and developments in mind, let us have a look at some of the stories in *Fingerprints* to illustrate the points I have been making. The stories I will examine fall into two main classes: those that take the form of detective stories in the classical sense I have described, and those that combine the twist-in-the-tail tale with some elements of the detective or crime story, to varying degrees of coherence and success. Strictly speaking, from the orthodox point of view, this collection with its suggestive title contains only about three detective stories proper: Howard Engel's 'My Vacation in the Numbers Racket,' John Ballem's 'Death on Horseback,' and my own 'Strange Archaeology.' When I say proper I don't mean perfect. The only comment I shall make about my own story, since I don't believe that, in literature, it is appropriate to self-analyse, is that it certainly sins against the rules of orthodoxy as codified in the Father Ronald Arbuthnott Knox decalogue,[17] simply because I knew no better. There is probably an inadmissible degree of coincidence in the story, paired with intuition which clearly violates Knox's commandment number 6: 'No accident must ever help the detective, nor must he ever have an unaccountable intuition which proves to be right.'[18] The sin of Lieutenant Borůvka is that he connects his accidental encounter with the Professor's wife, who is wearing a beautiful necklace, with the undescribed jewelry mentioned in the file of the murdered girl Květuše in a way that cannot be accounted for except by intuition.

The problem with Howard Engel's story as I see it – and there is always the danger that most of my reservations about the stories in *Fingerprints* are the consequence of my ineptitude – is that its narrative mode, first-person singular in the great North American tradition of folksy or quasi-folksy raconteurism, draws attention to the form and to inessential particles, and away from the problem and its solution. What S.S. Van Dine had in mind when he exhorted against 'literary dallying' were probably Dorothy Sayers' efforts to revivify the Collins-Dickens tradition which had been overshadowed by the Conan Doyle school, and to create a new novel of manners: fictions which – while adhering to Knoxian orthodoxy – would flesh out the skeleton-like tale with what, in the light of that orthodoxy, certainly were digressions. And such literary dallying – Harriet Vane's protracted love affair with her charming lord, lessons on campanology, extended passages of feminist social criticism, etc. – were certainly inessential in view of the problem at hand. But when Dorothy Sayers is read today – at least when her best structured novels, such as *Strong Poison* (1930) are read – the reader hardly perceives her Dickensian ramblings as elements which 'hold up the action, and introduce issues irrelevant to the main purpose, which is to state a problem, analyze it, and bring it to a successful conclusion.'[19] The problem of *Strong Poison* – namely how did the murderer poison his victim while surviving himself, although he partook in the poisoned meal? – is always firmly stated, and the detective returns to it with sufficient frequency so that the digressive episodes do not seem to detract from the reader's interest in the mystery. I would even say that an effect sets in that is the very opposite of Van Dine's fears: these episodes, written with charm and feeling, and not at all so badly as Edmund Wilson thought,[20] rather refresh the book and whet the reader's appetite for the solution. They are simply extensions of a necessity which Van Dine himself grudgingly acknowledged: 'To be sure, there must be a sufficient descriptiveness and character delineation to give the novel verisimilitude.'[21] They are handled well by the hand of a cultivated and refined writer behind whose 'light' products lurked solid learning, considerable knowledge, and a poetic sense nurtured by devotion to high literature.

And yet Van Dine was not entirely mistaken when he warned against 'literary dallying.' The danger, however, was elsewhere. Not in loose episodes, in metaphors, in evocative descriptions, and character analysis, but in the seductiveness of style, in the brilliance of the narrative voice, in the hypnotic power of virtuoso raconteurism which inavoidably lures attention from the content to the form, from the whole to the detail. A good example of this danger are the best novels by Rex Stout. The problems in them are stated, to be sure, but analysis and successful conclusions pale in the dazzling light of Archie Goodwin's narrative effects, in his bon mots, witty observations, etc – simply in the flow of his remarkable speech with its roots in the long American tradition that goes from pre-Mark Twain humorists, through *Huckleberry Finn*, through Ring Lardner to Faulkner on the highest level, and to Damon Runyon or Anita Loos on the – let's say – pop level, or to detective fiction writers such as Peter Cheney or Chester Himes. Hypnotized by the fireworks of language, the reader, indeed, loses interest in the problem at hand and in its solution. He is literally lost in the charms of the presentation.

And that is the gist of the problem: the charms of the presentation must be sufficiently charming to become rewarding. If they are not, they merely detract from the purpose of the story which is to state the problem, analyse it, and solve it – and the reader becomes impatient. If the problem in such a narrative is not stated with sufficient clarity but only vaguely suggested in the roundabout way of the talkative narrator's circling around it, and if the solution depends on subtle hints that require considerable mental energy to be noticed and interpreted correctly, the result may be a feeling of dissatisfaction, even of irritation. I am not sure whether this is not the case of Howard Engel's story. To be sure, it has its charms: the well-sustained tone of the narrator's voice, the amusing ex-murderer who acquired a more than impressive literary education while doing time, the folksy macabrosa the little tale is peppered with, the feeling of the lurking horror of a mobster's life. But, unless I am obtuse beyond the norm, the story ends, rather than begins with a mystery.

The other detective story proper in *Fingerprints*, John Ballem's 'Death on Horseback,' has the advantage of an unusual setting, makes good use of a few atmospheric touches, and in fact seems to me the most perfect of the three detective stories proper in the volume; in terms of technical requirements, not necessarily in terms of aesthetics. It works with a solid set of red herrings and an equally solid number of tangible clues, some of which are interpreted first falsely and then, after the 'detective,' a horse-racing professional Hal Innes, notices the main intangible clue in the story, they are reinterpreted correctly. That is as it should be. The only flaw with that is that whereas the intangible clue is at first introduced with subtlety and in an equivocal manner, when it appears for the second time – and that's the crucial appearance

– it is, I feel, too blatant, too crude, and too obvious. After the frightened horse drags its dead rider into the ranch, the detective encounters the manager, Mike Dawes: 'It was the bitterness in Mike Dawes' voice that snapped Hal out of his daze. The stable manager was saying, "You get to tell her parents. You were her latest boyfriend."' The correct understanding of this passage hinges on the word 'bitterness,' and on Dawes referring to the detective's intimate relationship with the killed girl. Since, however, the reader does not know about the crush Dawes had on Vicky Bennett, the 'bitterness' may be interpreted as a perfectly honest feeling which accompanies the death of the Poesque 'beautiful young woman,' and the reference to her sexual entanglement with the jockey is a simple statement of a generally known fact. But late in the story, after Hal has managed to interpret all the tangible clues wrongly, and to pin the murder on the classically innocent suspect with the suspiciously ethnic name of Stan Starchuk, the intangible clue re-emerges with the subtlety of Victorian melodrama: Hall notices a 'venomous look from Mike Dawes' which the murderer tries to camouflage too late, so that the impression of 'the hatred burning from [Mike's] eyes' is inculcated into the detective's mind with such a force that it leads him safely to the solution of the case. From then on the 'Who?' changes into 'How?' and the case becomes that of an 'unbreakable alibi' which proves to be extremely breakable. The method of the murder belongs more to the British puzzle school than to a story with a realistic flavour such as Ballem's. It is extremely risky and depends on so many incalculable circumstances that no murderer in his right mind – unless he is an entertainer in a J.D. Carr type of locked-room mystery – would venture it. Although the murder is one of passion it is premeditated, but with a carelessness that makes the reader wonder.

The flaw of a highly risky and insecure method of providing an alibi mars the next story in *Fingerprints* that displays some features of the detective story proper: Ellen Godfrey's 'Common or Garden Murder.' The killer is well-known: the timetable on which his alibi depends, itself depends on actions by characters the exact timings of which depend in turn on incalculable factors and on unexplained and rather eccentric behaviour. The victim, Mr Kieran, arrives at the place where he is used to holding a nocturnal vigil at 'exactly' eleven PM. He holds the vigil for 'precisely' half an hour, so that at eleven-thirty the murderer can be sure to encounter him in the dark alley that leads from the place of meditation to the highway. Mr Kieran moves hither and thither with such an accuracy and regularity that the good people living in the neighbourhood could set their watches by his movements, as the good people of Königsberg did watching the daily routine of Immanuel Kant's outings. But this is not all: synchronized with Kieran's movements must be the movements of the story's narrator Angela who has to leave the party so that she would be home at eleven PM, before the porno movies begin on the TV. She, however, must arrive at *precisely* eleven PM, neither one minute sooner nor one minute later, since Kieran is *always absolutely* precise. And all this accuracy is part of the murderer's premeditation. One has to work very hard to suspend one's disbelief.

All this is not to say that Ms Godfrey's story has no charms – there are nice touches of sarcasm, irony, and self-irony, and the author has a gift, by no means negligible, of acute indirect characterization – but the reader has no trouble seeing that the writer's heart is much more in the sensitive rendering of a divorced mother's ordeal than in the crime-puzzle.

The next group of stories shows the variety in the T.I.T. story, from relative orthodoxy to serious plot problems which detract from the simple charm of the T.I.T. tale. The T.I.T. of Elaine Slater's 'Hard Luck Joey' is the revelation that the contract killer hired by Joey to murder Joey's nagging wife is his mistress' husband, who somehow found out about their affair and has an ugly surprise in store for Joey. We don't know how he found out, but we can assume that he did, since his wife Carol is killed by him as she tries to reach her lover's house, presumably to warn him about what happened. Wouldn't she phone rather than run to his house? But perhaps her contract-killer husband was running after her in hot pursuit. In that case how is it that the neighbours who observed the shooting missed the shooter? Or was the contract man, in compliance with his contract, waiting for Joey's wife behind the bushes, and his unfaithful spouse, by a lucky coincidence, chose precisely this moment to run 'frightened out of her skin' in the direction of her sweetheart's closely watched house? Not terribly important questions, perhaps, to ask about a simple T.I.T. story, but left unanswered, they may spoil the enjoyment of the cruel joke.

A nearly perfect T.I.T. story is, I think, Tim Wynne-Jones' 'St. Anthony's Man.' It features an original character in the beggar-bum with his printed calling cards, is well-plotted, and has an exceptionally cruel surprise ending: the likable bum Munk, in love with the cold-blooded murderess Harriet, is apparently headed for a frame-up.

This story, in connection with Sandra Woodruff's 'A Natural Death,' brings to mind another Wynne, Anthony, the author of the classic 'The Cyprian Bees' (1924). 'St. Anthony's Man' is an absolutely amoral piece of black humour, down to the concept of a patron saint protecting the murderess and delivering into her hands an innocent victim to provide her with an alibi. Ms Woodruff's tale, on the other hand, is highly moral, even moralistic. The scheming and perhaps not so cold-blooded would-be murderess Emily Forbes is punished by death for her evil intentions. What is especially appealing about the tale is that Emily is trying to establish, in the Lord's court, a sort of moral alibi for herself. Unlike the methodical Harriet of Mr Wynne-Jones' story, Emily, in fact, only flirts with the idea of murdering her daughter-in-law Rose. The death of that pitiful young woman is to be the result of only a probability, not of a certainty. Emily apparently thinks that to plan a probable death is not as grave a sin as to plan a certain death. But in the eyes of the good and just Lord, such a murder is aggravated by cowardice (as Northrop Frye noted in his comments on the Sermon on the Mount). And so Emily dies by the hand of her intended victim – clearly a case of the Lord using a proxy. Rose, the would-be victim, is really innocent of murder: all she wanted was to have a good sting placed on the chubby forearm of her distasteful mother-in-law. She knew only that her in-law was afraid of wasps; she did not know that the lady was suffering from anaphylaxis, a mortal reaction to wasp poison, just as in 'The Cyprian Bees' where the perpetrator was aware of his victim's peculiar condition. Rose it not, and the trouble is that we are not either. If Emily's death is not Lord's punishment, it is a lucky coincidence. Which I hope it is not.

I must confess I was puzzled by Margaret Millar's 'McGowney's Miracle' and I don't think the story belongs among the masterpieces of its distinguished author. To assess it properly would, I think, require a lawyer rather than a dabbler in fictional mysteries. As I understand it, McGowney, in the end, murdered his wife whom he had 'resurrected' a short time ago, in order to inherit her money. But having been certified as dead by an 'honest' doctor, and then having secretly risen from the dead and married her mortician – didn't she create a pretty mind-boggling legal problem? Wouldn't her greedy children be able to contest her will with success? Could the mortician claim his inheritance at all? And how could the mortician's profession of love be 'the first time in Mrs. Keating's life she had been told she was loved' if she was a mother of two daughters? Was her first husband such an improbable ruffian that he never once told her a few endearing words? Would a girl marry such a monster if he did not at least pretend an emotional attachment? And did, in fact, McGowney murder his res- urrected wife?

We have no such doubts at the end of Anna Sandor and Bill Gough's little melodrama 'An Evening at the Opera.' What is wrong with this story are its improbabilities. Within the realistic framework of the story, people behave as they could only in a fantasy completely detached from this Canadian world. In classic detective stories, feebleness of mind is traditionally the trade mark of the police. But could any po- liceman in present-day Canada hold his job if he succumbed so easily to the faulty arguments of a murderer as Inspector John Newman did? Alex Laszlo is caught with the murder weapon in his hand, having been seen by a number of witnesses. He has just stabbed a man to death who was sitting in the neighbouring seat in a theatre. Yet this is how he successfully argues himself out of the clutches of the police: 'How could I know I would end up next to my supposed victim?' he asks Inspector Newman, and this useful (to the author) idiot declares: 'That's what I can't figure' (250). It never occurs to him that Laszlo might have found himself in the seat by accident. For if it was not an accident would he choose that precarious situation to murder someone whom he had intended to kill for years? The suspicious fact that both the victim and the suspected murderer are of the same ethnic origin, and most probably shared a common past is easily dismissed by the inane officer because of Laszlo's syllogism: 'You're a Newfoundlander. The constable [Newman's assistant] is a Newfoundlander. That doesn't mean you're going to kill him' (248). The topper in a series of such 'convincing' arguments comes when Laszlo asks his final, apparently very convincing rhetorical question: 'Do you think that I'd kill a per- fect stranger?' At this point the 'Inspector decided that just this once Alex Laszlo was telling the truth' (251). This, without any further in- terrogation after he had established the fact that both Laszlo and the murdered man were Hungarians. Isn't he really a character from a Newfie joke?

Permit me to conclude on a personal and, admittedly, moralistic note. Of the sixteen stories in *Fingerprints*, more than one-half are tales imbued with cynicism. People murder without the slightest of moral scruples, and the authors do not allow themselves even the faintest indication of moral condemnation. Admittedly, these are not serious works of literature, but they are not the fruits of genuine black humour either. Black humour stems from utter moral indignation, not from an intent to shock for the purpose of entertainment. Its essence is best caught by the celebrated migratory line from Negro blues: 'If you see me laughing, I'm laughing to keep from crying.' One feels that 'crying,' the unvoiced voice of disgusted condemnation of the evil world, in the most grotesque of black humour stories. This is certainly not the case with *Fingerprints'* tales of mayhem. Sure, I repeat, they are merely more or less clever entertainment. And yet ...

Many years ago, Harrison R. Steeves, writing in *Harper's* magazine, offered these thoughtful lines: 'I should like to see the detective story renew its youth and flourish ... But I painfully suspect that it has been acquiring years as men acquire them, that what it has gained during its prime in spread, in cleverness, in diversification, in actual (though not consistent) power to stimulate the mind, has been gained as men's experience and aptitudes are gained, at the price of hardened arteries and cellular disintegration and exhaustion of physical resources. The signs of decadence seem unmistakable – excessive ingenuity, dissonant cleverness, an infectious flippancy and indifference to moral scruple; above all, a failure of humane interest.'[22]

I wonder if these ancient words have lost much of their validity.

Notes

Josef Škvorecký received his PHD from Charles University in Czechoslovakia in 1951 and emigrated to Canada in 1969. While in Czechoslovakia, he prepared Czech editions of numerous English-language detective stories. His many novels translated into English include *The End of Lieutenant Boruvka*; *The Return of Lieutenant Boruvka*; and *The Engineer of Human Souls*, which won the 1984 Governor-General's Award for fiction.

1 Viktor Dyk 'Země mluví' in *Okno – Poslední rok* (Praha: Fr Borový 1938) 77–9

2 *Fingerprints* ed Beverley Beetham-Endersby (Toronto: Irwin 1984)

3 For other viewpoints, see, as a small sample, *Essays on Detective Fiction* ed Bernard Benstock (London: Macmillan 1983), John G. Cawelti *Adventure, Mystery, and Romance: Formula Stories as Art and Popular Culture* (Chicago: University of Chicago Press 1976), Julian Symons *Bloody Murder: From the Detective Story to the Crime Novel* (Harmonds-

worth: Penguin 1975), Alma Elizabeth Murch *The Development of the Detective Novel* (London: P. Owen 1958), and *The Art of the Mystery Story* ed Howard Haycraft (New York: Carroll & Graf 1946).

4 Edgar Allen Poe 'The Philosophy of Composition' in *Complete Works* ed J.A. Harrison 14 (New York: AMS Press 1965) 193–208. (Hereinafter 'Poe.')

5 See G.K. Chesterton, 'A Defence of Detective Stories' (1902) in *The Art of the Mystery Story* 3–6.

6 Poe 193

7 Poe 203

8 Karel Čapek 'Holmesiana čili o detektivkách' in *Marsyas čili na okraj literatury* (Praha: Fr Borový 1948) 208

9 John Dickson Carr 'The Locked Room Lecture' from *The Three Coffins* (1935) in *The Art of the Mystery Story* 276

10 B.M. Ejxenbaum *O. Henry and the Theory of the Short Story* (Ann Arbor: Michigan Slavic Contributions 1968) 4

11 Stanley Ellin 'Planning a Mystery' in *The Writer's Handbook* ed A.S. Burack (Boston: The Writer, Inc. 1974) 192–6

12 Continental critics have afforded 'The Purloined Letter' more attention. See for example *The Purloined Poe: Lacan, Derrida & Psychoanalytic Reading* ed John P. Muller and William J. Richardson (Baltimore: Johns Hopkins University Press 1988).

13 S.S. Van Dine (Willard Huntington Wright) 'The Great Detective Stories' (1927) in *The Art of the Mystery Story* 39

14 Raymond Chandler 'The Simple Art of Murder' (1944) in *The Art of the Mystery Story* 230

15 S.S. Van Dine (Willard Huntington Wright) 'Twenty Rules for Writing Detective Stories' (1928) in *The Art of the Mystery Story* 192

16 Cawelti *Adventure, Mystery, and Romance* 42

17 Ronald Arbuthnott Knox 'A Detective Story Decalogue' (1928) in *The Art of the Mystery Story* 194–6

18 Knox 'Decalogue' 195

19 Van Dine 'Twenty Rules' 192

20 Edmond Wilson 'Who Cares Who Killed Roger Ackroyd?' (1945) in *The Art of the Mystery Story* 391–2

21 Van Dine 'Twenty Rules' 192

22 Harrison R. Steeves 'A Sober Word on the Detective Story' (1941) in *The Art of the Mystery Story* 526